Jamaican volunteers in the First World War

D0861324

Published in our
centenary year
～ **2004** ～
MANCHESTER
UNIVERSITY
PRESS

Jamaican volunteers in the First World War

Race, masculinity
and the development of national consciousness

RICHARD SMITH

Manchester University Press

Manchester and New York

distributed exclusively in the USA by Palgrave

The right of Richard Smith to be identified as the editor of this work has been asserted by her in accordance with the Copyright, Designs and Patents Act 1988.

Published by Manchester University Press
Oxford Road, Manchester M13 9NR, UK
and Room 400, 175 Fifth Avenue, New York, NY 10010, USA
www.manchesteruniversitypress.co.uk

Distributed exclusively in the USA by
Palgrave, 175 Fifth Avenue, New York NY 10010, USA

Distributed exclusively in Canada by
UBC Press, University of British Columbia, 2029 West Mall,
Vancouver, BC, Canada V6T 1Z2

British Library Cataloguing-in-Publication Data
A catalogue record for this book is available from the British Library

Library of Congress Cataloging-in-Publication Data
A catalog record for this book is available from the Library of Congress

ISBN: 0 7190 6986 6 paperback

ISBN 13: 978 0 7190 6986 4

First published 2004 by Manchester University Press

First digital, on-demand edition produced by Lightning Source 2010

Contents

Figures

Acknowledgements

Throughout the seven years I have been studying the experience of Jamaicans in the First World War, my partner, Jeanette Cordery, has given me all the love and encouragement I could possibly ask for. Jeanette has added her own insight and expertise more than she knows. I dedicate this book to her and our two children, Eva and Leo.

The enthusiasm and generous support of Bill Schwarz has been crucial in ensuring that my research made the difficult transition from thesis to book. I would also particularly like to thank the following friends and colleagues who have provided inspiration and freely contributed their vast collective knowledge: Brian Dyde, Catherine Hall, Winston James, David Killingray, David Omissi, Julian Putkowski, Clem Seecharan, Jean Stubbs.

Abbreviations

AAG   Assistant Adjutant General
AC   Army Council
ADMS   Assistant Director of Medical Services
AG   Adjutant General
AIF   Australian Imperial Force
ANZAC   Australian and New Zealand Army Corps
AO   Army Order
ASC   Army Service Corps
BWIR   British West Indies Regiment
C-in-C   Commander-in-Chief
Cmdt   Commandant
CO   Colonial Office
DAG   Deputy Adjutant General
DAH   Disordered Action of the Heart
DC   *Daily Chronicle*
DG   *Daily Gleaner*
DMS   Director of Medical Services
EEF   Egyptian Expeditionary Force
FO   Foreign Office
FP   Field Punishment
GHQ   General Headquarters
GOC   General Officer Commanding
ICS   Institute of Commonwealth Studies
IWM   Imperial War Museum
JFL   Jamaica Federation of Labour
JIM   Jamaica Infantry Militia
JMA   Jamaica Militia Artillery
JT   *Jamaica Times*
JWC   Jamaica War Contingent
LOC   Line of Communications
MH   Ministry of Health
NAACP   National Association for the Advancement of Colored People
NAD   No appreciable disease/no abnormal discovery

NCO	Non-commissioned officer
NCPM	National Council for Public Morals
NSFU	National Sailors' and Firemen's Union
PRO	Public Record Office
RAMC	Royal Army Medical Corps
RFC	Royal Flying Corps
SSC	Secretary of State for the Colonies
SSW	Secretary of State for War
UNIA	Universal Negro Improvement Association
USS	Under Secretary of State
USSCO	Under Secretary of State, Colonial Office
WD	War Diary
WIC Ctte	West Indian Contingent Committee
WICC	*West India Committee Circular*
WIR	West India Regiment
WISCO	West Indies Sugar Company
WO	War Office

Introduction: Jamaica May 1938

On Friday 29 April 1938 sugar workers and unemployed labourers besieged the pay office of the West Indies Sugar Company (WISCO) at Frome in Westmoreland parish, after a misunderstanding over wage payments. In an attempt to disperse the crowd, a white manager fired his revolver into the air before fleeing by car to raise the alarm in Kingston. Hundreds of Jamaicans, desperate for work, had travelled from all over the island and were gathered in a makeshift encampment near the WISCO plantation. They had heard that WISCO, a subsidiary of Tate and Lyle, was paying high wages to workers constructing a new plant on the rundown estate, earmarked in a scheme to revitalise the cane sugar industry. However, wages turned out to be much lower than rumoured – the sugar company took full advantage of Jamaica's chronic unemployment crisis, engaging much of the workforce casually by the day.

In the days that followed, tensions rose as police reinforcements rushed to Frome. A crowd gathered once more on Monday 2 May, this time with bloody consequences. The pay office was stormed again and the demonstrators, pursued by armed police with fixed bayonets, tore stones from a wall to use as missiles. The police responded with bullets, cutting down eighteen demonstrators, killing four of them. The crowd fled into the adjacent cane fields, setting them ablaze as they ran.[1]

Hearing of the events unfolding in Frome, a demonstration, several thousand strong, assembled in Kingston that evening. At its head was the illustriously named and flamboyantly attired, St William Wellington Wellwood Grant,[2] a veteran of the First World War who had served in the eleventh battalion of the British West Indies Regiment (BWIR). The demonstrators marched on the offices of the *Jamaica Standard*, a paper recently established by expatriate financiers, critical of Jamaican planter interests. Dressed in a bright orange shirt, Grant led a delegation to the *Standard*'s editor, William Makin, demanding he print a vehement condemnation of the sugar industry and withdraw earlier remarks that Alexander Bustamante, Grant's associate, was not the man to lead Jamaican labour. They left satisfied with the draft editorial Makin had read back to them.

Over the next two months, strikes and riots took hold all over the island, threatening to topple the colonial regime. Special constables were sworn in, the

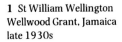

1 St William Wellington
Wellwood Grant, Jamaica
late 1930s

white garrison was reinforced by Royal Marines and the cruiser, HMS *Ajax*, rushed from Bermuda, stood offshore. Colonial order was eventually restored, not by armed force, but by the acting Governor's announcement of a new land settlement scheme to address the unemployment crisis.[3] Throughout this period, Grant was at the forefront of demonstrations and strikes. On 24 May he was detained alongside Bustamante when a sharp-eyed police inspector saw the two men walking past his office and decided to arrest them on the spot for sedition. Bustamante surrendered without a struggle, but Grant attempted to make a break for freedom and had to be subdued by several constables who viciously beat him. The two men were imprisoned for four days until they were released after further mass protests and the intervention of Bustamante's cousin, and future People's National Party leader, Norman Manley.[4]

In 1944, Jamaica was granted the universal franchise and greater legislative accountability, as the Colonial Office and Governor Richards tried to head off demands for outright independence, raised in response to wartime retrenchment and repressive legislation.[5] During the years since the labour rebellion, Grant's position was eclipsed by the struggle between Manley and Bustamante that dominated Jamaican politics for the next three decades, bequeathing a party political system characterised by violence and clientalism that persists to this day.[6] Perhaps Jamaica might have been better served if Grant had remained at the forefront of island politics. Grant's past was every bit as colourful as that of his former associate, ex-moneylender and first Jamaican Prime Minister Bustamante.[7] But he could claim a tough political pedigree, linked to pan-African and working-class struggles, spanning over two decades, compared to the relatively limited political experience of Bustamante and Manley. Furthermore, his racial background and somewhat itinerant lifestyle were more closely tied to those of the Jamaican masses for whom economic uncertainty and casual employment were a permanent feature of daily life. Tellingly, Grant also shared in the experiences of First World War veterans who, throughout the 1920s and 1930s, were at the forefront of political and economic struggle in Jamaica.

After his military service in the First World War, Grant emigrated from Jamaica to the United States of America where he was active in the Tiger division of the Universal Negro Improvement Association (UNIA) until 1934. He gained a reputation as a rough and ready street politician, often resorting to blows in place of argument. His style eventually proved too much for Marcus Garvey, who expelled him from the ranks of UNIA at the 1934 convention in Jamaica. Remaining in Jamaica, Grant nevertheless continued to espouse a pan-Africanist position from street corners,[8] often dressed in elaborate military costumes and wearing medals earned during the war and his membership of the Tiger division. In 1935 he instigated attempts to raise Jamaican volunteers to oppose the Italian invasion of Ethiopia. His association with Bustamante began in 1937, when he invited the prolific newspaper letter-writer to speak from his street-corner platform. Although at this point Grant veered towards the cause of labour, his relationship with Bustamante was always uneasy due to his continued espousal of pan-Africanism and Ethiopianism. The two men split in October 1939 when Grant far-sightedly proposed that Manley and Bustamante should sink their differences and that the Bustamante Industrial Trade Unions should adopt a more democratic programme.[9] However, Grant continued his joint activities as a union militant among the Jamaican dock workers and as an advocate of Ethiopianism.

What experiences did men such as St William Grant undergo in the First World War that contributed both to their militancy and an adherence to

[handwritten margin notes: War = nationalism / Colonial Subjects affected in / multiple ways]

symbols of military service? The war provided a major impetus to the rise of nationalism and popular discontent throughout the British Empire. But colonial subjects were affected in diverse ways. Economic hardship caused by wartime shortages and the demand for military raw materials was not a universal experience. Irish agriculture, for example, received a boost during the war years. Nevertheless, England's adversity proved to be nationalist Ireland's opportunity. Compulsory drafting into the carrier corps was a major grievance in East Africa. The terms and conditions of military labour and the impact of the war on the peasantry were keenly felt in Egypt. Indian nationalism was reinvigorated when declarations of loyalty and support for recruitment did not lead to concessions toward self-government.[10] Given the diversity of these experiences, it is necessary to explore both the symbolic and material impact of military service, to provide further insights into why the war proved so pivotal an event in the subsequent history of Empire. I felt a case study of the experience of Jamaican volunteers – rather than a broader West Indian study, which might not be able to take sufficient account of territorial distinctiveness – would provide a good starting point for subsequent comparative analysis.

The war provided colonial subjects with a masculine rhetoric and imagery, as well as material experiences, that could be appropriated, contested or reinterpreted with long-term consequences for the Imperial order. Laura Tabili has analysed the impact of the war on demands for citizenship and argues 'the war simultaneously strengthened troops' bond with the monarch and conferred a sense of entitlement that was ultimately subversive of the imperial order'.[11] Tabili captures the mood and outlook of many veterans, not only those who settled in Britain, but those who returned to their homelands after the war.

> Even though war experience was negative and disillusioning in many ways, it became part of the collective legacy of British colonized people, marshalled to support interwar demands. Appropriating the language of imperial unity, British justice and fair play, and the reciprocal obligations of military service and patriotism, colonial subjects pressed the central government to reconcile their demands with the rhetoric of empire.[12]

Jamaican servicemen, in common with most other non-white soldiers, were generally denied full participation in the military arena. But as well as the civic, fraternal and judicial metaphors acquired from Imperial appeals and homilies during the war, an appropriated language of military sacrifice and achievement left a heavy imprint on Jamaican nationalism.[13]

Within narratives of nation, the immortalised deeds of 'great men' laid the foundations for allegiance and service to the state.[14] But the promise of _possibility of immortality held up as a possibility reward for common men._

immortality was also held out to the lesser man to persuade him that his obligation to serve the nation – the duty of male citizenship – would be rewarded. George Mosse has argued that the ideal of the volunteer soldier-citizen has its origins in the French Revolution, as the volunteer became central to the identity and interests of the nation and was no longer viewed as a mere servant of the state.[15] The stereotypical citizen-volunteer was an educated and respectable idealist, who fought and died defending not only national integrity, but national ideals. The symbols of the national volunteer movements in Europe linked military authority with the pursuit of freedom that allowed the free-born, independent male to escape the confines of civilian life. The tradition crossed the English Channel after the involvement of Byron and other English volunteers in the Greek War of Independence. Although Byron, like Rupert Brooke nearly a hundred years later, died of disease, rather than a battle wound, he was subsequently immortalised as a fallen hero within the national canon. The masculine self-sacrifice of the volunteer came to be associated not only with the nation but with a noble cause.[16] By contrast, conscripts, who in the case of the British Army came to comprise over half of the five million men enlisted during the First World War, suffered a degree of stigma and invisibility.[17] Volunteering was a public gesture of active masculinity and commitment to the national project, whereas '[t]he conscript was the passive subject of a bureaucratic hand'.[18]

When the subject races of Empire came forward as volunteers in the First World War, in many cases they were aspiring to the model of the citizen volunteer, hopeful that wartime sacrifice would confer improved standing. However, martial narratives linking male sacrifice to citizenship and national interests and ideals are not unique to European societies. As Mimi Sheller has shown in the case of Haiti, martial roles and narratives arose out of a need to protect the integrity of the newly independent state and to ensure the 'elevation of the black man out of the depths of slavery into his rightful place as father, leader, and protector of his people'.[19] Not only did the Haitian revolution draw on the tradition of male armsbearing citizen of the American and French Revolutions but also on the black warrior figures of Boukman and Makandal.[20]

In her study of Australian national identity, Marilyn Lake has argued that the soldier-citizen achieved symbolic procreative power through his sacrifice for the nation. Australian military sacrifice on behalf of the Empire, particularly during the ill-fated Gallipoli campaign, was appropriated within the narrative of an emerging Australian nation.

[C]ollective death would bring forth immortal life, the birth of a nation. Though women might breed a population, giving birth to babies, only men, it

George Mosse

seemed, could give birth to the political entity, the imperishable community, of the nation. Men's deeds – their Landing at Gallipoli on 25 April 1915 – were rendered simultaneously sacred and seminal. 'A nation was born on that day of death.'[21]

Although the 'digger' came to occupy an honoured place in the Australian national iconography, this tended to obscure the failures of land settlement schemes and the ostracisation of those ex-servicemen at odds with the post-war Australian vision. The Australian government granted official recognition to the Returned Sailors' and Soldiers' League as the conduit for post-war assistance and commemoration events. Veterans who opposed the subsequent glorification of war, or who demanded greater welfare provision were ejected from membership.[22]

National movements in the colonies often articulated their demands and aspirations by appropriating for themselves the signs and symbols by which ideals of Empire were communicated. The early Jamaican nationalist movement deployed discourses of armsbearing to lay claim to independent citizenship and nationhood. There was certainly an acceptance of these values in black Jamaicans who came forward as volunteers to defend the British Empire. But, as a sense of Jamaican national identity began to emerge, it was the ex-servicemen's exclusion from both the material and symbolic rewards of military manhood that became a key issue in nationalist agitation: the non-recognition of male sacrifice that became a significant component of the nationalist narrative.

The feeling that non-white military sacrifice has not been recognised on equal terms has continued in the post-independence period. West Indian servicemen, alongside their Indian counterparts, were commemorated in memorials at home and on the great battlefield memorials, such as the Menin Gate at Ypres.[23] However, it can be claimed with some justification, that their sacrifices were quickly forgotten. Immigrant communities from the former Empire have subsequently reclaimed their legacy, partly as a means of asserting entitlement to citizenship and recognition in contemporary Britain. This resulted most notably in the construction of the Memorial Gates on Constitution Hill in recognition of the Asians, Africans and West Indians who served in both world wars, that were unveiled by Queen Elizabeth on 6 November 2002.[24]

The continuing discrimination experienced by black and Asian men in the British forces today may be explained, in part at least, by the historic treatment of colonial volunteers in the First World War. The Ministry of Defence and the Commission for Racial Equality entered into a partnership agreement in March

1998 to address the issue of poor recruitment and retention levels of black and Asian servicemen. Ethnic minority recruitment to the services remains at under 2 per cent, compared to a presence of at least 5 per cent in the population as a whole. This is despite a high profile investigation by the Commission for Racial Equality into the Household Cavalry, which had recently conducted its own campaign to attract black recruits, including a recruitment drive on the streets of Brixton.[25] Ironically, to meet ethnic minority quotas and shortfalls in home recruitment, the British armed forces are now recruiting extensively in the former colonies. In 2002, 240 men were recruited from Jamaica alone and one in six combatant troops were not born in Britain.[26]

The absence of memory and continuing issues of racism in the present day services are sufficient reasons in themselves to undertake a reappraisal of the historic contribution of black servicemen and women. Over the past thirty-five years, against a backdrop of national independence, the Civil Rights and Black Power struggles of the 1960s and 1970s and the development of social historical perspectives on warfare, scholars have also endeavoured to uncover and reassess the contribution of non-white servicemen. A growing body of literature has traced the extent of black and Indian involvement in the world wars and the degree to which the British Empire depended on this contribution on the road to victory. The segregation and exclusion that non-white volunteers experienced at the hands of the Imperial military hierarchy has become all to clear, underlined by the reluctance to employ black men on the front line.[27] We are also beginning to have a greater understanding of the impact of the war on nationalist and independence movements, and indeed on the servicemen themselves.[28]

But some key questions remain partially unanswered. Why, for example, was there such reluctance to deploy non-white troops in the First World War, particularly on the Western Front? Yes, there were the obvious fears that training large numbers of black colonial subjects might present a problem to post-war Imperial rule, and yes, helping to defeat a white enemy could certainly undermine notions of white superiority and invincibility. But we also need to look closely at how white and black identities – in the military context, particularly masculine identities – were imagined in relation to each other and how these wartime identities had the potential to disrupt those of the pre-war Imperial race and gender order.

The military body was the territory on which the desires and ideals of nation and Empire were mapped out. It symbolised the capacity of these joint endeavours to maintain power, chiefly in relation to the bodies which Imperial domination had marked out as inferior.[29] As Connell points out, '[t]he constitution of masculinity through bodily performance means that gender is vulnerable when the performance cannot be sustained'.[30] This is perhaps no more so than in the context of war where ideals of masculinity and the male body are considered to undertake the supreme test.[31] Ideals of masculinity may be undermined as the wayward body develops a separate trajectory that falls short of the ideal. The tendency of the body to intervene into gendered discourses shows that the corporeal body has significance that cannot be reduced solely to ciphers or emblems. Equally, rather than determining historical processes, the body is vulnerable to them, thereby exposing the flaws of essentialism and biological determinism. At these conjunctures, dominant ideals of masculinity are potentially open to reassertion, redefinition or rejection.[32] Imperial confidence had been dented by earlier crises such as the Indian Mutiny, Crimean War, Morant Bay Rebellion and the South African War. Fears were expressed for the future of the Empire, the fitness of the English to govern and to field an army. Each of these events heralded concerns about the physical ability of the British to contain the subject races which in turn dictated more physical and authoritarian models of masculinity.[33]

Underlining the relational nature of masculine identities, Mrinalini Sinha, in her study of gender identities under the Raj, has argued that the Empire was a constant frame of reference for white masculinity. The masculinity of Empire was not merely a continuation of post-enlightenment representations of gender. Masculine identities in the metropole and colonies were mutually constituted. Pre-existing masculine identities within subject societies became interwoven with popular and anthropological misconceptions and prejudices as discourses of dominator and dominated emerged.[34] In the context of this study, while existing representations of race and masculinity – the legacy of slavery and plantation society – were significant in the treatment and experiences of black volunteers, the war threw up unique relationships through which race and masculine identities were redefined.[35]

In its early stages, the First World War could be depicted as an extension of the Empire spirit, an escape from humdrum urban life and a spur to manhood. As it dragged on, white masculine values of rationality, progress and civilisation – central ideals of Empire – were brought into doubt. Many people had come to believe in the onward march of progress and sensed that European society had reached a point of near-perfection, a central theme in the literature and popular discourses that emerged from the war era.[36] The war disrupted the apparent certainties of the past when one knew what it meant to be British and to be a man and the threatening images of black and rival masculinities appeared more contained. Even today, historians of the war have struggled to construct 'an understandable continuity with earlier British history and to imply that the war makes sense in a traditional way'.[37]

A word of caution is needed at this point. The tendency to see the First World War as a major departure – a descent into barbarism, contamination and chaos – has led to a focus on what was dramatically different about the war, its alienation from normal experience. While it is important to recognise that there were disruptions and discontinuities, it is also necessary to see this within the broader historical pattern of constantly renegotiated gender and racial hierarchies. The experiences of the war intensified, rather than initiated, gender and racial categories already in process. As Susan Grayzel has shown in her study of the role of women in wartime, there were considerable continuities in debates around motherhood and sexuality from the pre-war years: '[T]he war did not shatter gender relations and identities in such ways that they needed to be reconstructed in the post-war period. Rather, such "reconstruction" was a constant and ongoing process from the first day of the war.'[38]

Two further significant questions arise from these considerations: how did the uncertainties around disrupted masculine identities impact on the day-to-day treatment and experience of black volunteers? Furthermore, how did the resulting experiences transform the minds of black soldiers, shaping some into radical thinkers and political activists? But before these issues are examined it is first necessary to trace some of the anxieties besetting metropolitan society and the Imperial military machine as Jamaicans and other West Indians presented themselves as volunteers.

Notes

1 Ken Post, *Arise Ye Starvelings: The Jamaica Labour Rebellion of 1938 and its Aftermath* (The Hague: Martinus Nijhoff, 1978), pp. 276–7; William Makin, *Caribbean Nights* (London: Robert Hale, 1939), pp. 53–7.

2 The following portrait of Grant is drawn from Makin, *Caribbean Nights*, pp. 69–70; Post, *Arise Ye Starvelings*, pp. 219, 239, 277, 279, 288, 290–1; Robert A. Hill (ed.), *The Marcus Garvey and Universal Negro Improvement Association Papers*, VII (Berkeley: University of California Press, 1990), pp. 309–10.

3 Governor Denham died after an operation on 2 June and was temporarily replaced by Charles Woolley until the arrival of the new governor Sir Arthur Richards in August.

4 The arrest of Bustamante and Grant was fortuitous for Manley's political career, for until that point he had been seen as a tool of the sugar industry, having previously acted as a lawyer for WISCO.

5 Ken Post, *Strike the Iron: A Colony at War: Jamaica 1939–1945*, 2 vols. (Atlantic Highlands, New Jersey: Humanities Press, 1981).

6 Amanda Sives, 'Violence and Politics in Jamaica: An Analysis of Urban Violence in Kingston, 1944–1996' (University of Bradford, unpublished PhD thesis, 1998).

7 See Post, *Arise Ye Starvelings*, pp. 252–3 for some details of Bustamante's background and intriguing past.

8   Victoria Park, Kingston one of Grant's favourite speaking venues, was renamed St William Grant Park shortly after his death in 1977: Hill, *Marcus Garvey and Universal Negro Improvement Association Papers*, VII, p. 310.

9   Post, *Strike the Iron*, pp. 63–4.

10 For an early, but excellent, overview which also draws some comparisons with the French Empire see Rudolf von Albertini, 'The impact of two world wars on the decline of colonialism', *Journal of Contemporary History*, 4:1, 1969, 17–35.

11 Laura Tabili, *'We Ask For British Justice': Workers and Racial Difference in Late Imperial Britain* (Ithaca: Cornell University Press, 1994), pp. 18–19.

12 Ibid., p. 28.

13 Jeremy Krikler, 'The Commandos: The army of white labour in South Africa', *Past and Present*, 163:3, 1999, 202–44, provides an interesting insight into the adoption of military language, iconography and tactics in post-war white South African labour organisations.

14 Graham Dawson, *Soldier Heroes: British Adventure, Empire and the Imagining of Masculinities* (London: Routledge, 1994), pp. 1, 11–12, 13–15.

15 George L. Mosse, *Fallen Soldiers: Reshaping the Memory of the World Wars* (Oxford: Oxford University Press, 1990).

16 Ibid., pp. 15–32.

17 Ilana R. Bet-El, 'Men and Soldiers: British Conscripts, Concepts of Masculinity, and the Great War' in Billie Melman (ed.), *Borderlines: Genders and Identities in War and Peace, 1870–1930* (London: Routledge, 1998), p. 74.

18 Ibid., p. 76.

19 Mimi Sheller, 'Sword-Bearing Citizens: Militarism and Manhood in Nineteenth-Century Haiti, *Plantation Societies in the Americas*, 4:2/3, 1997, 241.

20 Ibid., p. 242.

21 Marilyn Lake, 'Mission Impossible: How Men Gave Birth to the Australian Nation – Nationalism, Gender and Other Seminal Acts', *Gender and History*, 43, 1992, 306.

22 Alistair Thomson, 'The Anzac Legend: Exploring National Myth and Memory in Australia,' in Raphael Samuel and Paul Thompson (eds.), *The Myths We Live By* (London: Routledge, 1990).

23 The Menin Gate lists six members of the British West Indies Regiment. The Jamaican War memorial was unveiled on 11 November 1922 (see figure 11).

24 *Guardian*, 7 November 2002, p. 1.

25 MOD Press Release No. 264, 2 October 1999; MOD Factsheet, 'Equal Opportunities in the Armed Forces'; *Guardian*, 11 November 1998, p. 8, and 20 July 1999, p. 12. For a discussion of the perception of the armed forces among potential black recruits in Britain see Asifa Hussain, 'Careers in the British Armed Forces: A Black African Caribbean Viewpoint', *Journal of Black Studies*, 33:3, 2003, 312–34.

26 *Sunday Mirror*, 14 July 2002, p. 39; *Observer*, 21 July 2002, p. 6.

27 See for example C. L. Joseph, 'The British West Indies Regiment 1914–1918', *Journal of Caribbean History*, 2, 1971, 94–124; David Killingray, 'All the King's Men? Blacks in the British Army in the First World War, 1914–1918', in Rainer Lotz and Ian Pegg (eds.), *Under the Imperial Carpet: Essays in Black History 1780–1950* (Crawley: Rabbit Press, 1986); Albert Grundlingh, *Fighting their Own War: South African Blacks in the First World War* (Johannesburg: Ravan Press, 1987); B. P. Willan, 'The South African Native Labour Contingent', *Journal of African History*, 19:1, 1978, 61–86; Geoffrey Hodges, *The Carrier*

Corps: Military Labor in the East African Campaign, 1914–1918 (New York: Greenwood Press, 1986); Christopher Somerville, *Our War: How the British Commonwealth Fought the Second World War*, (London: Weidenfeld & Nicholson, 1998); Ben Bousquet and Colin Douglas, *West Indian Women at War* (London: Lawrence and Wishart, 1991); F. W. Perry, *Commonwealth Armies: Manpower and Organisation in Two World Wars* (Manchester: Manchester University Press, 1988).

28 See particularly W. F. Elkins, 'A Source of Black Nationalism in the Caribbean: The Revolt of the BWIR at Taranto, Italy', *Science and Society*, 33:2, 1970, 99–103; Glenford Howe, *Race, War and Nationalism: A Social History of West Indians in the First World War* (Kingston, Ja.: Ian Randle, 2002); David Omissi, *Indian Voices of the Great War: Soldiers' Letters, 1914–18* (London: Macmillan, 1999); Timothy H. Parsons, *The African Rank and File: Social Implications of Colonial Military Service in the King's African Rifles, 1902–1964* (Oxford: James Currey, 1999).

29 Richard Dyer, *White* (London: Routledge, 1997), pp. 30–40.

30 R. W. Connell, *Masculinities* (Cambridge: Polity, 1995), p. 54.

31 Niall Ferguson has argued that the acute sensory tuning demanded and caused by battlefield conditions gave the soldier a unique sense of self and realised many key masculine impulses – 'clarity, energy and freedom': Niall Ferguson, *The Pity of War* (London: Allen Lane, 1998), p. 361. Joanna Bourke has gone somewhat further, suggesting that killing and violence, as well as being central to military masculinity, were actually enjoyed by many men on the front-line: Joanna Bourke, *An Intimate History of Killing: Face-to-Face Killing in Twentieth-Century Warfare* (London: Granta, 1999).

32 Connell, *Masculinities*, pp. 54–5, 61, 64, 71–2.

33 On imperial masculinity see Joseph Bristow, *Empire Boys: Adventures in a Man's World* (London: Harper Collins, 1991); Graham Dawson, *Soldier Heroes*; J. A. Mangan, *The Games Ethic and Imperialism: Aspects of the Diffusion of an Ideal* (London: Viking, 1986); Jonathan Rutherford, *Forever England: Reflections on Masculinity and Empire* (London: Lawrence & Wishart, 1997).

34 Mrinalini Sinha, *Colonial Masculinity: The 'Manly Englishman' and the 'Effeminate Bengali' in the late Nineteenth Century* (Manchester: Manchester University Press, 1995), pp. 1–2, 8–11.

35 For a comprehensive discussion of mutually constituted identities in the Jamaican context see Catherine Hall, *Civilising Subjects: Metropole and Colony in the English Imagination, 1830–1867* (Oxford: Polity, 2002). See also Patrick Bryan, *The Jamaican People 1880–1902* (Basingstoke: Macmillan, 1991).

36 Paul Fussell, *The Great War and Modern Memory* (Oxford: Oxford University Press, 1977), p. 8.

37 *Ibid.*, 9. This perception of the war is still evident in recent studies, despite the efforts of revisionist historians who have attempted to salvage a sense of meaning and purpose from the slaughter. Rekindling the memory of the 'Lost Generation', John Keegan has argued that the war was 'a tragic and unnecessary conflict ... [which] damaged civilisation, the rational and liberal civilisation of the European enlightenment, permanently for the worse and through the damage done, world civilisation also': John Keegan, *The First World War* (London: Hutchinson, 1998), pp. 3, 8. See also Ferguson, *Pity of War*, pp. 21–30. For an overview of the revisionist critique of First World War histories see Alex Danchev, '"Bunking" and Debunking: The Controversies of the 1960s', in Brian

Bond (ed.), *The First World War and British Military History* (Oxford: Oxford University Press, 1991), pp. 263–88.

38 Susan R. Grayzel, *Women's Identities at War: Gender, Motherhood, and Politics in Britain and France During the First World War* (Chapel Hill: University of North Carolina Press, 1999), p. 244.

1 Degeneration and male hysteria: the wartime crisis of white masculinity

The first day of the Battle of the Somme resides in popular memory as the worst day in the history of the British army. The assault on the Somme was conceived as part of the grand Allied strategy to attack Germany on all fronts and, more immediately, to relieve pressure on the French forces at Verdun. It degenerated into a four-and-a-half month cycle of attrition marked by only minor break-throughs.[1] A relentless week-long artillery barrage against an eighteen-mile stretch of the German front line was expected to pave the way for a rapid break-through by the British forces. Haig, the British commander-in-chief, was confi-dent the Germans would crumble under the onslaught and the infantry would simply walk forward and occupy enemy positions with little opposition. At around 7.30 a.m. on the morning of 1 July 1916, thousands of Kitchener's volunteers were ordered to advance over shell-churned clay turned into a quagmire by several days of torrential rain. Each man was burdened with full kit, equipment and supplies weighing around sixty pounds.

Only a fraction of the British troops reached the German lines. The British shells had failed to cut the German wire and the defending troops had sheltered from the bombardment in heavily fortified bunkers. From these they emerged to cut down wave upon wave of the British attackers with withering machine-gun fire. By the end of the day nearly 60,000 men had been killed or wounded – a daily toll not matched even in the appalling conditions of Passchendaele in the Summer and Autumn of 1917. In the northern sector of the front, poorly co-ordinated artillery support meant that any ground gained was usually swiftly retaken by German counter-attack. In the South, the British were unable to consolidate some limited gains due to lack of reserves and cavalry support.[2]

As the casualties mounted in the ensuing weeks, a preoccupation, evident during previous Imperial military crises, emerged once again to impinge criti-cally on attitudes to the recruitment and deployment of black volunteers from Jamaica and elsewhere in the British Empire. The appalling casualty rates on the Western Front raised the fear that Britain would not be able to field sufficient recruits to make good the losses. This anxiety became deeply entangled with the related concern that the psychologically wounded, whose numbers rose dramatically during the Somme offensive, were having a destructive effective on both available manpower and the masculine image of the British soldier. The

2 Recruits at the Etaples base in France photographed for the Adjutant General's office, July 1918, illustrating the extreme youth and underdeveloped physique of many conscripts

Somme campaign served to highlight both the physical and mental fragility of the racial stock. Remarking on the condition of the infantry during the Battle of the Somme, Captain J. C. Dunn, a medical officer with the 2 Royal Welch Fusiliers, stated:

> The average physique was good enough, but the total included an astonishing number of men whose narrow and misshapen chests, and other deformities or defects, unfitted them to stay the more exacting requirements of service in the field ... Route marching, not routine tours of trench duty, made recurring casualties of these men.[3]

The potential for the apparent shortcomings of the British Tommy to concomitantly strengthen the aspirant national identities of subject nations, black or white, was clearly evident in the wartime re-articulation of Australian national and masculine identity. It was a commonly held view among the 'diggers' of the Australian Imperial Force (AIF) that the British Tommy was an inferior soldier, who was frequently to be found leading the retreat. This outlook had been engendered during the failed Gallipoli campaign which for many

Concern regarding fitness level of recruits

Anzac troops exposed the flaws in British military organisation and prowess. But the view really took hold on the Western Front where the AIF were confronted with the extreme youth, the pallid complexions and small stature of many British troops. The bushman myth that underpinned Australian national character was essentially a strain of social Darwinism. The bushman was everything the Tommy apparently was not – combative, energetic, self-reliant and independent – characteristics bred through exposure to the tough natural and social environment of Australia. Despite the heavy reliance on Australian units in many key campaigns, by the end of the war the British authorities had become extremely concerned at the effect the negative Australian portrayal of the Tommy would have on post-war colonial relations. Counter-propaganda was initiated to cast the Tommy in a more flattering light.[4]

Australian attitudes to the British soldiery were not entirely without foundation. In 1917, the army introduced a new classification system for the medical inspection of recruits. Over 41 per cent of those examined were regarded as unfit to serve overseas or in home garrisons; 10 per cent were rejected outright. Manpower was now at a premium and these figures mask the regularity with which official guidelines were overlooked by medical examiners under pressure to fill quotas.[5]

Concern about the fitness of recruits revived Imperial doubts that had emerged at the turn of the century when the British failed to swiftly defeat the Boer forces in the South African War. In 1899, around 40 per cent of recruits were found unfit within two years of service. Added to outright rejections at the recruiting stage, the rate of wastage among volunteers was closer to 60 per cent. The declining stature and poor health of military recruits was purported to be particularly evident among men from the industrial towns and cities.[6]

This apparent decline in the nation's manhood placed a question mark over the future of Imperial order, a pessimistic metropolitan response evident in earlier crises. In 1871, six years after the Morant Bay Rebellion in Jamaica had shaken Imperial confidence, Charles Kingsley visited the West Indies and observed that the black peasantry appeared more robust than the 'short and stunted figures' of the urban poor.[7] Shortly after the South African War, the leading eugenicist, Francis Galton, on seeing male bathers at the Serpentine in London's Hyde Park, feared 'they were less shapely than many of the dark-coloured peoples whom I have seen'.[8] Urban living and Irish, Eastern European and Jewish immigration were held to have undermined the Anglo-Saxon race, which since the mid-nineteenth century had been regarded as the dynamic force behind British global domination.[9]

In the wake of the South African War, the Inter-Departmental Committee on Physical Deterioration was appointed to investigate the causes underlying the high rejection rate of recruits. In contrast to the eugenicists, the Commission, which reported in July 1904, doubted hereditary conditions were responsible, blaming instead poor environment and food, excess drinking and ignorance. The Commission also found that standards of health in the urban slums were often no worse than those pertaining in deprived rural areas. This evidence discredited those who believed the solution lay in a return to a pastoral golden age free from the debilitating effects of urban life. The incomplete and often contradictory heredity theories advanced by the eugenicist movement at this time strengthened the influence of progressive Liberals and Fabians who believed tackling environmental factors was the answer to the nation's ills. The Inter-Departmental Committee's report gave rise to a series of interventionist measures including medical provision and meals for schoolchildren. The emergent Mothercraft movement, which aimed to inculcate sound domestic and nurturing skills among working-class women, was also encouraged.[10] Despite the predominance of reform and welfare solutions in the Committee's recommendations, a fatalistic eugenicist-inspired mood persisted, fearful that the British race was fast approaching dissolution. These smouldering doubts were rekindled during the early days of the world war when it became clear the fitness of recruits had scarcely improved since the turn of the century.

A related turn-of-century apprehension was the belief that the fruits of Empire and industry had paradoxically encouraged complacency, lethargy and moral enervation, further enfeebling the population and undermining Imperial effectiveness. Among the chief proponents of this viewpoint was the populist journalist Arnold White who had been among the first to draw public attention to the poor quality of military recruits. Prodigal living and the rejection of family life had, White argued, conspired to undermine national 'stamina', and was reflected in the political world where he perceived a notable loss of manly resolve.[11]

'Soft living' and material progress, blamed by White for the demise of family life, were linked to another factor that, from the eugenicist perspective, threatened to undermine the British nation. Through more widespread use of contraception the middle, upper and respectable working classes were forsaking the larger family in the pursuit of better living standards and greater personal freedom. As a result, many eugenicists argued, the quality of the race was deteriorating as the allegedly inferior lower orders continued to reproduce at higher levels.[12] As wartime casualties mounted, the matter took on a renewed urgency. The war, rather than proving the might of the nation, was increasingly seen to aggravate the problem of racial degeneration to the extent that the process of 'natural selection' was reversed. Men perceived as the cream of the population were being decimated on the front line, while their racial inferiors were rejected by the medical boards.

The war also compounded concern about the higher rate of male infant mortality, which some in the medical profession described as 'male infanticide'. The eugenicist, Caleb Saleeby, asserted that male infant mortality had increased since 1914, and suggested the surplus female population be dispatched to the colonies.[13]

The National Council for Public Morals (NCPM) was founded in 1911 to address the issue of the differential birth-rate and the purported degeneration of the race. It counted among its members socialists such as Ramsay MacDonald and Beatrice Webb, several bishops and peers and representatives of the non-conformist clergy, as well as leading eugenicists such as Saleeby and Sir John Gorst. During the war the NCPM conducted a crusade for the moral welfare of servicemen and launched a campaign against the cinema industry which it presented as a threat to public decency. But the most significant element of the NCPM's wartime work was the establishment of a National Birth-Rate Commission 'for the Promotion of Race Regeneration – Spiritual, Moral and Physical'. After over two years' research, the Commission presented its findings to government on the 28 June 1916, three days before the Somme campaign began to exact its dreadful toll.[14]

The chief witnesses reiterated the view that selfishness and the desire for material comfort was leading to smaller families, not only among the upper classes, but also among the respectable working class. The Commission insisted that greater material comfort be rejected in the interests of nation and Empire and demanded:

> [t]he gradual building up of a spirit of self-sacrifice or rational foresight which shall make it possible for parents of the good classes ... to have again the larger families ... The extra baby must be weighed against the motor car, and must be recognized as of more immediate and future value than ... any other thing not absolutely essential to well-being.[15]

Ethel Elderton, who had published a report on the birth-rate for the Eugenics Society in the first weeks of the war, also attacked the use of contraception and abortion by the middle and artisan class, and feminists who had campaigned to liberate women from the burden of continual childbirth. Elderton urged women of respectable background to devote themselves entirely to motherhood to avert the demise of Britain's global domination that could only result from a disproportionate rise in the poor urban population.[16]

> It is not only that any fall in the birthrate has endless importance for Great Britain as the mother of greater nations, but ... the present fall is harmfully differential; any such differential fall means racial degeneration ... Many of us

can see now that if the movement continues unchecked for another forty years, it means national disaster, complete and irremediable, not only for this country but for Britain across four seas.[17]

The 'dysgenics of war', an expression used by Caleb Saleeby in his evidence to the National Birth-Rate Commission, meant that the 'pick of our men' rushed to volunteer and almost certain death or injury on the battlefield, leaving behind those of poorer physique to reproduce. Saleeby proposed measures be taken to enable soldiers to marry at short notice before leaving for the front. Increased separation allowances for soldiers would encourage the rearing of children, he argued, even if the fathers were subsequently killed.[18] Other eugenicists went to more macabre lengths and suggested women should marry even the most severely wounded and maimed veterans as they were still capable of passing on their noble 'germ-plasm'.[19]

From the eugenicist perspective, rather than demonstrating the nation's masculine prowess, the war was contributing to the national malaise. As the fittest men were killed off, the process of natural selection would be undermined. Drawing on evidence from the Napoleonic and Franco-Prussian wars, Havelock Ellis, the eugenicist and sexologist, suggested the war would lead to reductions in height and an increase in hereditary conditions.[20] Ironically, when the eugenicist influence surfaced in the military, rather than working to spare the lives of the 'pick' of the men, it tended to be deployed against men considered to be of poor stock who were either rejected outright or relieved of front-line duties. In extreme cases, as Oram has shown, eugenicist practices served to justify the weeding out of undesirables through the imposition of the death penalty.[21]

Army medical records provide ample proof of eugenicist-inspired prejudice as well as illustrating the tendency of contemporary science to associate mental capacity and character with facial features and head shape, even though the scientific popularity of phrenology had waned by the 1830s and 1840s. In the process, however, as the following examples show, a reliance on such interpretations and classifications only served to underline the increasing difficulty the metropole was facing in recruiting sufficient men regarded as the best stock. The reports abound with phrases otherwise reserved for the subject races such as 'childish and simple minded'. A medical sheet for a private in the Army Service Corps recorded the following comments. 'Voluntary attention deficient. Judgement feeble and erroneous. His head and face are asymmetrical. Lobes of ears malformed. Articulation somewhat defective. He is simple and degenerate. In my opinion he is mentally deficient and unfit for any service in the Army.'[22]

Other cases illustrate the effects of the harsh social and economic conditions of the time but were still replete with terse designations of inferiority. One man whose recorded age was thirty-three, had the 'physical condition ... normal for a man of fifty years of age'. He was unable to read and write, had a double squint and poor co-ordination. The examining doctor observed that '[i]n my opinion this man is a feeblemind of degenerate type'.[23] Not only were the men classed as degenerates believed to be a threat to the efficiency of the army, their very loyalty to the state was brought into question. In the words of E. Mapother, a Medical Superintendent of the Maudsley Neurological Hospital, '[T]he intellectually defective is incapable of endurable patriotism; in fact, of any ideal so abstract as his country'.[24]

Fears of racial degeneration and the effects of the differential birth-rate provided sufficient doubts about the efficiency of British manhood in wartime. But the bewildering array of psychological responses to war manifested by thousands of soldiers also brought into question the intellectual claims of white masculinity founded on rationality, stoicism and self-control. Most significantly, many traumatised soldiers displayed symptoms of 'hysteria' – a diagnosis usually reserved for women or homosexuals. As Elaine Showalter has argued, 'English psychiatry found its categories ... built on an ideology of absolute and natural difference between women and men ... undermined by the evidence of male war neurosis'.[25] Showalter suggests male hysteria during the war was

> a disguised male protest not only against the war but against the concept of 'manliness' itself. While epidemic female hysteria in late Victorian England had been a form of protest against a patriarchal society ... epidemic male hysteria in World War I was a protest against the politicians, generals, and psychiatrists. The heightened code of masculinity that dominated in wartime was intolerable to surprisingly large numbers of men.[26]

If the arbitrary boundaries separating male and female behaviour were shattered, then those imposed between white men and non-white subjects of Empire could also be breached.

From the mid-1890s, British society had become increasingly preoccupied with the apparent growth in nervous ailments among the general population. Attention was drawn to the stress that modern industrial society placed upon individuals subjected to the demands of 'brain work' and poor environment.[27] The war exposed the 'nervousness' of white masculinity as never before. As the 'flower of British youth' was cut down on the fields of the Somme the scale of psychological casualties reached an unprecedented level. Ben Shephard's interpretation of the surviving statistical evidence suggests that up to 50,000 men exhibiting symptoms of trauma presented for treatment in the last six months of 1916. During this period the Somme offensive claimed over half a million casualties from the British and Empire forces.[28]

During the war as a whole, Sir John Collie, who was placed in charge of pension arrangements for shell shock cases, believed that around 200,000 soldiers were discharged from the army on psychiatric grounds. This figure obviously does not include men 'successfully' treated and sent back to the front line. The scale of shell shock casualties is also indicated by the massive increase in psychiatric facilities both within the army itself and, as a knock-on effect, within emergent civilian practice which was simultaneously forced to consider reform of the asylum system. By the end of the war there were twenty specialist army hospitals dealing with shell shock cases (there was only one in 1915), as well as numerous clinics and outpatient facilities.[29]

Traumatised men presented a bewildering array of psychosomatic symptoms, including involuntary movements, temporary paralysis or catatonia, loss of speech, blindness, or simple mental and nervous exhaustion, all of which could fall under the umbrella term 'shell shock', an expression that lingered in the popular imagination long after it was rejected by the army medical authorities. Other diagnoses may have suggested a physical complaint, when the underlying cause was psychological. Chief among these was Disordered Action of the Heart (DAH) a condition of which it was estimated that only 10 per cent of cases had an organic origin. The medical shorthand 'NAD' (No Appreciable Disease or No Abnormal Discovery) also appears very frequently in army medical records and may have on occasion been the diagnosis applied to men who presented as psychological cases.

Many in the army medical services could not come to terms with this state of affairs and advanced numerous theories that attempted to disassociate the young manhood of Britain from its apparent failure to live up to masculine expectation. Initially, it was held that the various conditions associated with shell shock had been brought about by close proximity to bursting shells or passing machine-gun fire. These diagnoses lingered in the public's perception and encouraged some sympathy towards shell-shocked veterans. The link with shell fire suggested a physical wound rather than mental instability which carried with it the stigmatic associations of the asylum or workhouse.[30]

However, Sir John Goodwin, the Director-General of the Army Medical Service, argued that the war had exposed the underlying nervous temperament of purportedly lesser men or those who manifested an insufficient quota of discipline, esprit de corps and regimental pride – the exemplars of military masculinity.[31] David Forsyth, an early exponent of psychoanalytic methods in the treatment of shell shock insisted that the urge to flee in the face of death was a strong and ineradicable, protective function, but one which could be contained 'by a still more powerful effort of will'.[32] A man with a neurotic disposition, however, did not possess the psychological resources to maintain self-control.

That 'shell shock' was indicative of a flaw in individual character, rather than a broader indication of masculine vulnerability, is evident in the treatment of a white Jamaican officer cashiered for homosexuality, routinely taken by wartime psychologists as predisposing a patient to neurosis. Ernest Dunn had served as a minor civil servant in Jamaica before enlisting as a private in the East Surrey Regiment at the start of the war. Although he was discharged on health grounds, he successfully earned a commission as a second lieutenant in the 3 Battalion of the Northumberland Fusiliers in March 1915. Dunn suffered concussion and shrapnel wounds to his left eye at La Bassée in August 1916, but after his physical injuries healed, Dunn was tormented by nightmares and insomnia and a rest-cure in Jamaica was prescribed. On his return, his general constitution had not improved and neurasthenic symptoms were still evident.

Dunn returned to his unit in July 1917, nearly a year after his original injuries.[33] Within weeks of his return, he was denounced by a fellow-officer, Second Lieutenant Yates, for mutual sexual acts while the two shared a billet. Dunn fiercely denied that such contact had taken place, both during and in the wake of the case. However, aside from the sexual aspects of the case, it is evident that Dunn was quite open about his need for comfort and emotional support due to his continuing fragile mental condition; a need to which his accuser seems to have initially responded positively. The military authorities seem to have been as much concerned about this display of male vulnerability and affection, and the boundaries of male friendship, as about the alleged instances of sexual contact. While comradely and platonic friendship between a younger and older male were highly regarded in the masculine culture of the period, any intimation of sexual contact was held to diminish such relationships. Although there was insufficient evidence for a courts martial, Dunn was stripped of his commission and dismissed from the army.[34] As a result, he also lost his peacetime position in the Jamaican civil service, although he subsequently enlisted in the Royal Naval Air Service for the remainder of the war without disclosing his recent army service.[35] Yates on the other hand had his commission reinstated on the personal intervention of Lord Derby, Secretary of State for War, on the grounds that he had been 'led astray'.[36]

Colonial Office officials felt that Dunn might also have been treated more harshly than Yates because of his Jamaican origins. White people who lived or served in the tropics had long been regarded as vulnerable to both physical enervation and moral decline. Some literary representations of Empire suggested the further one travelled from England, the more susceptible one became to homosexual urges or neurosis. But there is also evidence that some white volunteers from the colonies could expect preferential treatment. The writer Robert Graves encountered 'Young Jamaica', a planter's son awarded a commission senior to more experienced metropolitan officers at the recommendation of the Jamaican governor. This caused considerable resentment, especially when 'Young Jamaica' proved inadequate to the role.[17]

The pre-war concern with the degenerating effects of urban life also worked its way into medical interpretation. Men who in civilian life had worked outdoors as miners, shepherds or gamekeepers were seen as less prone to shell shock than artisans or clerks who were deemed more sensitive than the stolid and apparently less intelligent countryman. Those of artistic temperament were seen as particularly susceptible to nervous instability at the front.[38] In general, the victim of shell-shock was regarded as having lost all sense of self-control and discipline, if, indeed, he had not succumbed to outright cowardice. Slackness or outbreaks of petty crime within a unit were seen as the precursors to an increasing incidence of shell shock, which at times was regarded as having the infective qualities of organic disease. Indeed, medics argued that shell-shock cases should be isolated from military general hospitals to prevent the spread of what was regularly seen as a disciplinary, rather than medical condition. Among more intelligent men the wastage of 'nervous capital', – allowing one's thoughts free rein rather than living for the hour – was regarded as inevitably leading to the symptoms of shell shock.[39]

For many soldiers, the front-line experience and military life, rather than offering the much-vaunted opportunity to prove masculine prowess, produced instead feelings of heteronomy – subordination to military discipline and helplessness in the face of mechanised destruction. Some feminist scholars, notably Sandra Gilbert,[40] have suggested that this feeling of impotence was compounded by a sense that women were finding new and liberating opportunities in the wartime economy. The very nature of trench warfare, where men were pinned down for weeks, often without glimpsing the enemy and with little opportunity of firing a shot in anger, while subjected to shelling, compounded this feeling. David Forsyth, one of three British practitioners of psychoanalysis at the outbreak of the war, underlined the sense of powerlessness in the face of death as a major factor in psychological breakdown.[41] More significantly, Forsyth also established that many of his subjects began to experience psychological disturbance even before being posted to the front. In one instance, a man was rendered temporarily blind while still training in England.[42]

The vast array of psychosomatic symptoms gave rise to accusations of malingering. The prevalence of malingering itself cast doubt upon the sustainability of white masculine ideals. Malingering, which Bourke defines as the refusal to undertake risks attendant upon the obligations of citizenship, involved a man willingly presenting himself as emasculated in some way by feigning a mental or physical condition that would either act as an obstacle to enlistment or prevent a further posting to the front for men already mobilised. The authorities became concerned to ensure that every man lived up to the obligations of manhood citizenship. For the privileges they enjoyed, men were expected to render their bodies to more extreme fates than women or children.[43] Men suspected of malingering were subjected to ruthless treatment, as testified by a retired senior medical officer in the pages of the *Lancet*.

> During my 22 years service ... I can recall five cases of men having been brought to hospital suffering from sudden loss of speech due to shock. I found they were all cases of malingering and recovered their voice under an anaesthetic. Ether is the anaesthetic to give, and it is well to keep the patient under it for half an hour, and he will have plenty to say when he recovers.[44]

But while on one level the malingerer was rejecting masculine norms, on another he was asserting control over his body, placing it at the centre of his objection to enlistment. Men used various drugs or imbibed substances to mimic medical conditions, or neglected minor ailments in the hope that they would become more serious. Some men deliberately had their limbs broken to avoid the draft. Others resorted to even more desperate measures, such as the self-inflicted wound, which carried with it the risk of both serious injury and punishment.[45] Significantly, shell shock could be regarded as a mental self-inflicted wound which involved the 'voluntary and avoidable surrender by the soldier of his control over his emotions'.[46]

The scale of the problem made it harder to argue that the sufferers of nervous conditions were exhibiting evidence of flawed heredity. Members of the officer class were twice as likely to present, or at least be diagnosed, with symptoms of shell shock.[47] As Martin Stone has observed: 'the monolithic theory of hereditary degeneration upon which Victorian psychiatry had based its social and scientific vision was significantly dented as young men of respectable and proven character were reduced to mental wrecks after a few months in the trenches'[48] The very men who were upheld as the epitome of British manhood were failing the Empire in its hour of greatest need. In an attempt to protect the image of British manhood, shell-shocked officers tended to be diagnosed with neurasthenia. This term, coined by an American neurologist in 1869, implied mental exhaustion brought about by the pressures of modern life and devotion to duty, rather than an inherent weakness in character. As a correspondent to the *Lancet* claimed, in civilian life neurasthenia was most common among the professional classes 'all of whom are trying to perform three days' work in two days'.[49]

The term 'hysteria' was more usually applied to the working-class men of the ranks. Regarded as inferior in intelligence these men were regarded as less likely to respond to a talking cure. As a result, they were more likely to be 'treated' with the brutal and disciplinarian methods endorsed by Lewis Yealland and his colleague E. D. Adrian. Pinpricks, cigarette burns on the tongue and the application of electric shocks are all recorded as having successfully treated traumatised men who may have become temporarily mute or paralysed.[50] The pre-war tendency to link mental illness and mental impairment continued and a diagnosis of either type would be referred to the 'mental ward'. A man presenting in a confused or disorientated state with memory loss, or manifesting symptoms such as head tremors, jerking limbs or a stammer, could be designated 'mentally deficient (idiocy)', especially if he could, in the official jargon, 'only give a poor account of himself'.[51]

The letters of Raymond Asquith, son of the wartime Liberal Prime Minister, trace the declining image of British masculinity during the war. His familial connections and a promising career at the Bar meant that Asquith was pre-eminent among the 'lost generation'in many accounts and memoirs.[52] Among the foremost of Asquith's admirers was John Buchan, who commemorated his Oxford contemporary in *Nelson's History of the War*, the largest circulation war periodical. Buchan also devoted a chapter to Raymond Asquith in *These for Remembrance* privately published in 1919. Despite his own moments of doubt and anxiety, Asquith, a lieutenant in the 3 Grenadier Guards, was disdainful of fellow soldiers whose nerves had been torn to shreds. For Asquith, these men were the questionable types responsible for the decline of the race. Of a detachment of the Royal Welch Fusiliers, to whom he was assigned as an instructor, he wrote:

> The men were absurd and pathetic ... They were little black spectacled dwarfs with no knowledge, no discipline, no experience, no digestion, and a surplus of nerves and vocabulary ... They moaned and coughed and whined and vomited through the long night hours in a way that was truly distressing and paid so little attention to their duties that if they had been grenadiers I should have had to have had half of them shot. If they are a fair sample of K[itchener]'s army the repeated failures of our offensive are easily explained.[53]

A few months later, in May 1916, Asquith complained of the increasing irritability and war-weariness of the officers in his own regiment. However, he was quick to scotch suggestions that they might be falling prey to shell-shock and attributed the men's state of mind to boredom.[54] In early August, a month into the Battle of the Somme and a few weeks before his death, the psychological casualties mounted throughout the army. Although going to some length to distance his own feelings from the sense of panic gripping many men under his command, Asquith was forced to acknowledge the toll the war was taking on his own nerves to the extent that he wished to be relieved of his front-line post.

> This night I was up at the forward end of the trench, rather engrossed in directing the men's work, when suddenly I found myself surrounded by a mob of terrified figures from the battalion which was holding that part of the line ... [They] gibbered and crouched and held their hands over their eyes and generally conducted themselves as if the end of the world was at hand. It was very alarming; they had seen one of these damned rum jars [trench mortar] coming and I hadn't ... The explosion was as painful as a sound can be. In the moment immediately preceding it I made up my mind I was dead, and in the moment immediately following I said to myself 'I suppose this is shell shock at last, now I shall get home'. But it wasn't.[55]

If the war exposed the frailty of white masculinity at war, then it opened the possibility for a similar state of affairs in Imperial governance. Both strands of the masculine ideal placed a heavy burden upon soldier and colonial functionary alike. This is evident in the example of Lieutenant Leonard Ottley, Staff Officer Local Forces for Jamaica. During his service in Jamaica, Ottley had become a prominent figure. He served as commissioner of the Boy Scouts and delivered lectures on the war and scouting in which he extolled the value of discipline and training 'to bring out all the manly qualities dormant in the individual'.[56] When war broke out Ottley worked at frenetic pace, organising recruitment meetings, a training programme for the militia, and the mobilisation of the Jamaican war contingents. Unfortunately, these duties proved too much and Ottley suffered a nervous breakdown, which received wide public coverage registering the frailty of white masculinity. The *Zouave*, battalion journal of the 2 West India Regiment, in its 'letter from Jamaica' column, was 'sorry to say Ottley has broken down and is to be invalided home. The boy has had a very trying time since the war and – done good work'.[57]

Significantly, the symptoms Ottley displayed were very similar to the cases of neurasthenia more often associated with front-line service. His medical notes record neurasthenia and anaemia and show that Ottley was 'subject to headache and nervous twitchings of the hands'. He was also 'jumpy, intolerant of sudden noise, irritable and easily upset'. A medical board reported that Ottley was 'in a condition of nervous instability' and that he was not fit mentally or physically to remain in post. However, the medics could not resist the opportunity to lay part of the blame at the door of the Jamaican climate, reflecting the contemporary tendency to present the frontiers of Empire as at once enervating and invigorating. A return to the metropole where Ottley could enjoy 'country air and quiet rest' was prescribed.[58]

As if to restore this somewhat jaded image of white masculinity, breaking under the strain of both climate and wartime duties, the Jamaican press rushed to heap praise on Ottley as he left for home.

> As a worker he was a marvel. How he combined the multifarious and responsible duties assigned to him from time to time and duly executed them, has been the surprise of everybody. He did so with splendid courage and determination, never complaining at any time and but with a singleness of purpose. Whatever was assigned to him was considered a call to duty, and it was also a principle with him 'to do or die' ... No thought ever of himself. Is it any wonder that he has broken down and has had to seek rest and change?[59]

As a final flourish, reference was made to Ottley's role in the local scout movement and to the high esteem in which he was held by the boys – many of whom, it was reported, broke down in tears as 'Auld Lang Syne' was played when his ship departed.[60] During his sick leave, Ottley was promoted to captain. He eventually reached the rank of major in the post-war commission in Upper Silesia. He died from a liver abscess and septicaemia in August 1921.

Such loss of 'nerve' by a member of the colonial ruling class could have serious implications for imperial authority. This was well-illustrated during unrest among ex-servicemen in British Honduras shortly after the war. On the night of 22 July 1919, in the capital Belize, discontent fuelled by massive price rises and wage restraint erupted into violent protests. Workers and ex-servicemen laid siege to key government buildings and white residences. The Acting Chief Justice, George O'Donnell Walton, was ridiculed when he tried to address a group of demonstrators from his balcony, after which his composure and self-control rapidly declined. He publicly announced that the demonstrators should be shot, sought firearms for his own protection, and asked to be excused from trying cases related to the disturbances in case he was further targeted by protestors. The governor, Sir Eyre Hutson, became increasingly concerned about Walton's state of mind and, to 'remov[e] a danger to the Government', arranged quarters for the Acting Chief Justice on board HMS *Constance*, recently sent to the area to restore order. Hutson reported to Viscount Milner, Secretary of State for the Colonies, that Walton 'has undoubtedly lost status ... and the desired influence among both the European and negro inhabitants' and that his 'nerves appear to have given way'. He requested Walton's early transfer to another colony.[61]

The potential vulnerability of military and Empire masculinities also surfaced in advertisements for patent remedies and quack cures that adorned the pages of both the metropolitan and colonial press. The British Medical Association and a House of Commons select committee, reporting on the eve of the war, had exposed the negligible, and sometimes malign, effects of such products.[62] But for a colony such as Jamaica, which did not witness the return of large numbers of traumatised white troops, these advertisements were perhaps the most visible indication of white masculine anxiety until Jamaican troops went overseas. Most of the advertising campaigns predated the war and sought to exploit fears of the tropical climate or effects of overwork on the administrators of Empire. But by early 1915, many were reflecting and emphasising the toll of modern warfare in order to prove the efficacy of the product. Advertisements for the tonic, *Sanatogen*, a brand still recognisable today, targeted men 'doing hard mental work in a tropical climate'[63] and claimed to be 'the cure for jaded nerves' and nervous debility.[64] Meanwhile, an E. Norton of Chancery Lane, clearly alluding to sexual impotence, promised 'Weak, Tired and Nervous Men' he would send a leaflet with information to cure 'Nervous and Organic Derangements ... in a plain sealed envelope'.[65]

Another patent tonic, *Phosferine*, promised to cure, among other ills, 'nervous debility', 'mental exhaustion', 'hysteria' and 'brain-fag'. The manufacturer claimed 'a world-wide reputation for curing disorders of the nervous system'. A 'special travel and service note' recommended the product for 'men on active service, Travellers, Hunters, Explorers, Prospectors, Missionaries etc.'[66] Advertisements for *Phosferine* appeared regularly in the *Jamaica Times* with enthusiastic, illustrated endorsements by stereotypical characters that may otherwise have inhabited the populist novels of the war effort and Empire. One version captured the traits and personality of the 'heroic neurasthenic' in the front line who had previously strained to maintain a masculine composure in a hectic peacetime occupation; a rather ambivalent glimpse of the hero of Empire at home and abroad.

> I may say I am a continuous user of Phosferine and find it a great restorative after the nerve-racking atmosphere of the trenches, just as much as in Civil life after a hard day's work. Before enlisting, many a time my business, mostly brain work, would carry me sometimes into the small hours of the morning. At last I was told that I was on the point of a nervous breakdown and was recommended to try Phosferine, which soon brought me back to normal. But again, in the trenches under shell fire the old trouble very soon reasserted itself in the form of violent headaches and neuralgia. Again I tried the old remedy, and the same on the battlefield as in the office, Phospherine put me right.[67]

An advertisement for *Sensapersa* – 'A dependable remedy for nervous debility, impotency, sleeplessness, exhaustion, loss of memory, night emissions, wasting of parts, lost vigour and any form of neurasthenia' – claimed to have 'brought happiness, strength, vigour and vital power to thousands of men'. 'Procure a box today and be a new man',[68] the caption exhorted. This range of 'symptoms' might appear during war or peacetime and were routinely interpreted by contemporary medics as symptoms of male hysteria, effeminacy and poor self-control. However, they are also significant in that they appear repeatedly in the accounts left by the medical observers of shell-shock. The symptoms symbolised the feelings of powerlessness felt by many men in the face of mechanised destruction and military authority which were openly addressed in an advertisement for 'Junora, the wine of Health'.

> The Shock of Battle is tremendous in these times, the explosions, the shriek of the shell, the uncertainty of the happenings, death reaching a man from miles away sent by a man who cannot see his target to kill another who cannot see his attacker and in many cases does not know what struck him.[69]

These advertisements captured the deep sense of unease regarding the future of Empire and white masculinity. Although they promised restoration, the men of whom heroic feats were expected were portrayed as dependent on a quick cure, rather than of a stoic and manly character. As treatments for shell shock attempted to restore the nerve-wracked soldier from child to man[70] – to lift him from the level of the subject races – the demand for manpower threatened to erode these categories of Empire, juxtaposing black soldiers against the dented image of the British Tommy.

Notes

1 A new generation of revisionist military historians has suggested that although little was achieved territorially during the Somme offensives, the German army was sufficiently weakened to enable their defeat in 1918. Lessons were also learned by the British that allowed greater exploitation of advances in hardware and communications during the mobile warfare of 1918. See for example, Gary Sheffield, *Forgotten Victory: The First World War: Myths and Realities* (London: Headline, 2001), pp. 155–7.

2 Ibid., pp. 133–55; Keegan, *First World War*, pp. 310–21. Martin Middlebrook, *The First Day of the Somme* (London: Penguin, 2001).

3 Captain J. C. Dunn, *The War the Infantry Knew, 1914–1919: a chronicle of service in France and Belgium with the Second Battalion, His Majesty's Twenty-third Foot, the Royal Welch Fusiliers founded on personal records, recollections and reflections. Assembled, edited and partly written by one of their medical officers* (London: P. S. King and Son, 1938), p. 245. Dunn also gave evidence to the official post-war enquiry into shell shock.

4 E. M. Andrews, *The Anzac Illusion: Anglo-Australian Relations During World War 1* (Cambridge: Cambridge University Press, 1993), pp. 60–5, 150, 172–7. In fact, the Australian contingents included a significant number of men born in the metropole:

Jeffrey Grey, *A Military History of Australia* (Cambridge: Cambridge University Press, 1990), p. 91. Martial representations of Australian character were already evident during the South African War, 1899–1902: Luke Trainor, 'Building nations: Australia and New Zealand', in David Omissi and Andrew S. Thompson (eds.), *The Impact of the South African War* (Basingstoke: Palgrave, 2002), pp. 252–5.

5 J. M. Winter, *The Great War and the British People* (London: Macmillan, 1985), pp. 50–9.

6 Richard A. Soloway, *Degeneracy and Degeneration: Eugenics and the Declining Birthrate in Twentieth-Century Britain* (Chapel Hill: University of North Carolina Press, 1990), p. 41.

7 Douglas A. Lorimer, *Colour, Class and the Victorians: English Attitudes to the Negro in the Mid-Nineteenth Century* (Leicester: Leicester University Press, 1978), pp. 155.

8 *Sandow's Magazine of Physical Culture*, October 1903, p. 168.

9 Nancy Stepan, *The Idea of Race in Science: Great Britain, 1800–1860* (London: Macmillan, 1982), p. 42. David Feldman, 'The Importance of Being English: Jewish Immigration and the Decay of Liberal England', in David Feldman and Gareth Stedman Jones (eds.), *Metropolis London: Histories and Representations since 1800* (London: Routledge, 1989), pp. 57, 59, 72–3.

10 Soloway, *Degeneracy and Degeneration*, pp. 45–7, 140; Eileen Yeo, *Contest for Social Science: Relations and Representations of Gender and Class* (London: Rivers Oram Press, 1996), pp. 216–23.

11 Arnold White, *Efficiency and Empire* (London: Methuen, 1901), pp. 55, 108. For a more detailed discussion of debates around national efficiency before and during the South African War see Geoffrey Searle, '"National Efficiency" and the "Lessons" of the War', in Omissi and Thompson, *Impact of the South African War*, pp. 194–211.

12 See, for example, Ethel M. Elderton, *Report on the English Birthrate*, Part 1 England North of the Humber, Eugenics Laboratory Memoirs XIX and XX (London: Dulau and Co., 1914), pp. 232–6.

13 Evidence of Dr C. W. Saleeby in *The Declining Birth-Rate: Its Causes and Effects* (London: Chapman and Hall, 1916), pp. 415–17.

14 *The Times*, 5 June 1916, p. 5 and 29 June 1916, p. 5.

15 Evidence of Dr J. W. Ballentyne in *The Declining Birth-Rate*, p. 166.

16 Elderton, *Report*, pp. 232–6.

17 Ibid., p. 237.

18 *Declining Birth-Rate*, p. 415. See also Havelock Ellis, *Essays in Wartime* (London: Constable, 1916), pp. 28–9, 33.

19 Soloway, *Degeneracy and Degeneration*, pp. 144–5. 'Germ-plasm' was the agent of heredity passed through the generations according to the theories of August Weismann published in Britain in 1889. See William Greenslade, *Degeneration, Culture and the Novel* (Cambridge: Cambridge University Press, 1994), p. 198.

20 Ellis, *Essays*, p. 36.

21 Gerard Oram, *Worthless Men: Race Eugenics and the Death Penalty in the British Army During the First World War* (London: Francis Boutle, 1998).

22 Public Record Office Ministry of Health (hereafter PRO MH) 106/2300 No. 312427 W. J. Barnes ASC 3 May 1917.

23 PRO MH106/2304 No. 157010 J. Wilkinson 884 Area Labour Coy.

24 *Report of the War Office Committee of Enquiry into 'Shell-Shock'* (Cmd. 1734), (London: HMSO, 1922), p. 28.

25 Elaine Showalter, *The Female Malady: Women, Madness and English Culture, 1800–1980* (London: Virago, 1987), pp. 167–8.

26 Ibid., p. 172.

27 Ben Shephard, *A War of Nerves: Soldiers and Psychiatrists 1914–1994* (London: Jonathan Cape, 2000), pp. 7, 10–11. The incidence of post-traumatic disorders among servicemen serving in recent conflicts, particularly the Gulf War of 1991, and recent fictional accounts of the First World War, notably the *Regeneration Trilogy* by Pat Barker, have helped to encourage renewed academic and popular interest in shell shock. Other important recent studies include Peter Leese, *Shell Shock: Traumatic Neurosis and the British Soldiers of the First World War* (Basingstoke: Palgrave, 2002); Hans Binneveld, *From Shell Shock to Combat Stress: A Comparative History of Military Psychiatry* (Amsterdam: Amsterdam University Press, 1997); Anthony Babington, *Shell-Shock: A History of the Changing Attitudes to War Neurosis* (Barnsley: Leo Cooper, 1997).

28 Shephard, *War of Nerves*, pp. 40–1.

29 Martin Stone, 'Shellshock and the Psychologists' in W. F. Bynum, Roy Porter and Michael Shepherd (eds.), *The Anatomy of Madness: Essays in the History of Psychiatry*, Vol. II (London: Tavistock, 1985), pp. 243, 246–9, 251; David Forsyth 'Functional Nerve Disease and the Shock of Battle: A Study of the So-Called Traumatic Neuroses arising in Connexion with the War', *Lancet*, 25 December 1915, p. 1400; F. W. Burton-Fanning, 'Neurasthenia in Soldiers of the Home Forces', *Lancet* 16 June 1917, pp. 908–9. (For an example of the prevalence of NAD see the hospital register for No. 2 General Hospital, Havre PRO MH106/1015–64.)

30 *Committee of Enquiry into 'Shell-Shock'*, pp. 4–6, Chas. S. Myers, *Shell Shock in France 1914–18: Based on a War Diary* (Cambridge: Cambridge University Press, 1940), p. 13; Thomas Salmon, *The Care and Treatment of Mental Diseases and War Neuroses ('Shell Shock') in the British Army* (New York: Mental Hygiene War Work Committee, 1917), pp. 9–10.

31 *Committee of Enquiry into 'Shell-Shock'*, pp. 13–14.

32 Forsyth, 'Functional Nerve Disease', p. 1401.

33 PRO War Office (hereafter WO) 339/39693 medical sheets (Army Form A45) 31 August 1916–26 October 1917.

34 PRO WO339/39693 Statements of 2nd Lts J. Yates and E. W. Dunn, 20 September 1917. Robert Graves, *Goodbye To All That* (London: Penguin, 1960 [1929]) (particularly pp. 23, 39, 143) provides a good example of the nature of male comradeship and Platonism and the attendant attitudes towards homosexuality. The correspondence of Raymond Asquith, in which he details his role defending an officer accused in a similar case, also gives an insight into the attitudes and prejudices of the era. See letters to Lady Diana Manners, 27 August 1916 and K[atherine]. A[squith]. 2 and 12 September 1916; John Jolliffe, *Raymond Asquith: Life and Letters* (London: Collins, 1980), pp. 290, 295. Between 1914 and 1919, 22 officers and 270 other ranks were officially charged with committing 'indecent' acts: Ferguson, *Pity of War*, p. 349.

35 PRO AIR 79/2206 Service Record of Ernest William Dunn; PRO WO339/39693 Grindle, Colonial Office (hereafter CO) to E. W. Dunn 13 March 1918.

36 PRO CO137/729/30118 Minute 19 June 1918

37 PRO CO137/726//36598 Hewins to J. I. McPherson, MP, USS War, 13 September 1918; Graves, *Goodbye*, pp. 129–33; Philip Curtin, *The Image of Africa: British Ideas and Action, 1780–1850*, Vol. I (Madison: University of Wisconsin Press, 1964), pp. 58, 65,

71; Joseph Bristow, 'Passage to E. M Forster: Race, homosexuality, and the "Unmanageable Streams" of Empire', in Christopher E. Gittings (ed.), *Imperialism and Gender: Constructions of Masculinity* (Hebden Bridge: Dangeroo, 1996), pp. 151–4. As Wayne Cooper has discussed in the case of Walter Jekyll, mentor of Claude McKay and annotator of Jamaican folk songs, the colonies could provide a haven from the rigid sexual boundaries of late-Victorian Britain: Wayne F. Cooper, *Claude McKay: Rebel Sojourner in the Harlem Renaissance*, Baton Rouge: Louisiana State University Press, 1996, pp. 29–32.

38 *Committee of Enquiry into 'Shell-Shock'*, Evidence of Gen. Lord Horne, p. 16; Evidence of Lt. Col. E. Hewlett, p. 18; Evidence of A. F. Hurst, p. 26.

39 Ibid. Evidence of E. Mapother, Medical Superintendent, Maudsley Neurological Hospital 28, Evidence of Sq. Ldr Tyrrell pp. 31, 33–4; Myers, *Shell Shock*, pp. 95–6; G. Elliott Smith, 'Shock and the Soldier', *Lancet*, 15 April 1916, p. 814.

40 Sandra M. Gilbert 'Soldier's Heart: Literary Men, Literary Women and the Great War', in M. R. Higonnet and Jane Jenson (eds.), *Behind the Lines: Gender and Two World Wars* (New Haven: Yale University Press, 1987), pp. 197–8.

41 Forsyth, 'Functional Nerve Disease', p. 1400.

42 Ibid., p. 1401; see also Burton-Fanning, 'Neurasthenia', p. 907. A terminology emerged that distinguished between those who had developed symptoms in the firing line and who were therefore deserving of some public sympathy, and those whose symptoms had arisen away from the front. The latter were clearly to be regarded with more suspicion as either malingerers or of questionable manhood. At first, medical records for shell-shock cases were appended with 'W' – wounded – in instances where a man had been in the proximity of an explosion. These 'commotional' cases, however, accounted for only between 4 and 10 per cent of the total. The remaining 'emotional' cases were appended with 'S' – sick. Later not yet diagnosed NYD (Shell Shock) and NYD (Nervousness) were substituted respectively. By 1918, however, the problem had become so acute that the term 'shell shock' was dropped altogether in France and patients were sent for thorough diagnosis in the United Kingdom: Myers, *Shell Shock*, pp. 94–6, 101; Shephard, *War of Nerves*, p. 54.

43 Joanna Bourke, *Dismembering the Male: Men's Bodies, Britain and the Great War* (London: Reaktion Books, 1996), pp. 76–8.

44 Letter from Lt. Col. (late) J. McLaughlin, RAMC, *Lancet*, 22 January 1916, p. 212.

45 Bourke, *Dismembering the Male*, pp. 76–82.

46 Myers, *Shell Shock*, pp. 38–9.

47 Stone, 'Shell Shock', p. 249.

48 Ibid., p. 245.

49 Letter from 'G. P.', *Lancet*, 29 January 1916, p. 265.

50 Lewis R. Yealland, *Hysterical Diseases of Warfare* (London: Macmillan, 1918), pp. 7–10, 92, 197.

51 PRO MH106/2303 No. 3446 Charles Roake 12 KRRC and No. 327829 George Simpson ASC; PRO MH106/2304 157010 J. Wilkinson, 884 Area Labour Company.

52 *Nelson's History of the War*, xvi (London: Nelson, 1917), pp. 120–2; John Buchan, *These for Remembrance* (London: The Medici Society, 1919), pp. 63–82. The Nelson *History* was produced in twenty-four instalments between 1915 and 1919 and after revisions by Buchan, appeared as four book volumes in 1921 and 1922 under the title *A History of the Great War*.

53 To K[atharine]. A[squith], 17 December 1915, Jolliffe, *Raymond Asquith*, p. 227. It is
    important to recognise that Asquith's remarks were directed at conscripts or wartime
    volunteers, not the two prestigious regular battalions of the Royal Welch. Robert Graves,
    who alongside Siegfried Sassoon, served as an officer in the first and second battalions,
    complained, in more muted terms than Asquith, that the swelling of the regiment to
    twenty-five battalions in wartime threatened to undermine its good name: Graves,
    Goodbye, pp. 76–8.

54 To K. A. 28 May 1916, Ibid., p. 264.

55 To K. A. 4 August 1916, Ibid., p. 281.

56 *DG* 5 July 1915, p. 6 (quote); *Boy Scouts HQ Gazette*, November 1915, p. 207.

57 *Zouave*, April 1916, p. 58.

58 PRO WO374/51643 Proceedings of a Medical Board (Army Form A45) held 3 March
    1916 and 27 May 1916.

59 *DG* 28 April 1916, p. 3.

60 Ibid.

61 PRO CO123/295 X/N000129 Hutson to Milner, SSC, 31 July 1919.

62 *Secret Remedies – what they cost and what they contain – based on analyses made for the
    British Medical Association* (London: British Medical Association, 1912); *Report from the
    Select Committee on Patent Medicines* (London: HMSO, 1914).

63 *JT* 23 November 1914, p. 29.

64 *JT* 16 January 1915, p. 22.

65 *JT* 23 January 1915, p. 25.

66 *JT* 27 November 1915, p. 19.

67 Ibid.

68 *JT* 23 January 1915, p. 12.

69 *DG* 10 June 1916, p. 9.

70 Shephard, *War of Nerves*, pp. 74, 118.

2 'The cannon's summoning roar': Jamaica and the outbreak of war

Summer has come, and over wide spaces of sunlit country a deep silence broods. In the city and the towns there is but little movement; the mind feels itself occupied sufficiently with the mere exertion of will required to strive against the influence of the *deadening tropical languor*; nothing it would seem could startle this half-torpid community into *full-blooded* life, could awaken it to eager, compelling, *absorbing mental activity*. But in August, 1914, Jamaica was to receive a shock, the reflex of that which startled the world in those thrilling days that are now so far away. And Jamaica was to throw off its languor and its placid calm as sleep flies from the eyes of the soldier when he hears the cannon's summoning roar.[1]

So mused Herbert de Lisser, the editor of the Jamaica *Daily Gleaner*, opening his account of Jamaica's part in the war. Since the first colonial encounters with Africa and the Caribbean, the tropical environment was presented as a source of physical and moral enervation that sapped the productive capacity of all races.[2] But de Lisser's belief that war would provide an invigorating anti-dote were directed most specifically towards the black peasantry and working class. Described by Rupert Lewis as 'Jamaica's Kipling',[3] de Lisser echoed Thomas Carlyle, who, sixty years previously in *An Occasional Discourse on the Nigger Question*,[4] had castigated black West Indians for failing to place their productive efforts at the disposal of the plantocracy. In the first decades after emancipation, the black peasantry had achieved a degree of self-sufficiency through steady industry on their provision grounds. The peasantry tended to work on the plantations on a casual basis to provide a cash income. Carlyle epitomised metropolitan dissatisfaction with the more optimistic vision of the 'Great Experiment' in free labour finally shattered by the Morant Bay Rebellion.[5] He caricatured the black peasant as a simple, uncivilised soul happy to idle away each day, sustained by limitless supplies of 'pumpkin' the only remedy for which was the reintroduction of some form of coerced labour.

The view expressed by Carlyle was still deeply embedded by the time of the Great War. Canon Purcell Hendrick, the white Rector of Spanish Town, complained to the *Daily Gleaner* in 1916

> There can be no doubt that the labour problem in Jamaica is becoming a very serious one; indeed, the laziness amongst the lower classes is a curse, and the cause of much of the privation which they themselves have to suffer. Loafers abound in our streets, our prisons overflow with vagrants and thieves, whilst to get a man to come and take honest work and to stick to it is almost impossible.[6]

Hendrick bemoaned the practice of day labour whereby the labourer offered two or three days per week instead of the five or six required by the planters.

Responding to Hendrick's complaints, W. G. Hinchcliffe, a veteran trade unionist who had helped to found the Artisans' Union in 1899, provided an alternative analysis of Jamaica's ills. He became involved in the Universal Negro Improvement Association and spoke at its first anniversary celebrations in 1915 before splitting with Garvey in the December for reasons he never disclosed.[7] Hinchcliffe believed the plantation system, and socio-political structures that upheld it, lay at the root of the perennial poverty afflicting the mass of the Jamaican population. He highlighted how average wages for day labourers were the same as his grandparents had received at emancipation – 1s6d for men and 9d for women.[8] In the years since 1838, the white minority had become more diverse, both ethnically and occupationally, but it continued to constitute an elite, holding economic power and privilege over the black and brown population in inverse proportion to its size. At the start of the war, whites accounted for just 2 per cent of the Jamaican population. White power was sustained by the system of Crown Colony government that excluded the majority of the population from the franchise and elected office by high property qualifications.[9]

The brown middle class provided the most immediate challenge to white institutional authority. During slavery, brown people, usually the result of relationships between slave women and members of the planter class, were more likely to be manumitted. As 'free-coloureds' they became a small, but significant, element in Jamaican slave society, establishing themselves as the landowners who came to form the 'respectable' element of the Jamaican peasantry. Despite the high property qualifications in force after emancipation, the brown middle class formed up to one third of the House of Assembly before its dissolution in the wake of the Morant Bay Rebellion.[10]

The ranks of the brown middle class grew throughout the nineteenth and early twentieth century. To it was added a much smaller black component who had achieved success – against the odds – as landowners. A notable example was Thomas McKay, the father of the radical writer, Claude, who had accumulated over a hundred acres by 1912 and who was numbered among the one in every hundred black Jamaicans eligible to vote.[11] The development of colonial education was also a key factor, which saw brown men, and, to a lesser extent, their black counterparts, entering the lower echelons of professions such as the Colonial Civil Service and teaching. Aside from the professions, there was a significant black and brown artisan class among whom emerged the first trade union organisations in Jamaica.[12]

At the 1911 census, the black population stood at 630,200 or 76 per cent of the total. The majority subsisted as peasants, tenant farmers and wage labourers. The peasantry and tenant farmers, clustered on small plots, which by the turn of the century numbered over 100,000, had been responsible for the diversification of the Jamaican economy. They produced foodstuffs for home consumption and a large proportion of fruit, coffee and ginger exports. Despite this contribution to the Jamaican economy, the small cultivators faced constant pressure from high rents, disproportionate taxation and, from the 1890s, the monopolisation of land by the burgeoning banana industry. Increasingly, the peasantry was forced to supplement its income with employment on public works schemes or the sugar plantations. From the 1880s, these pressures on the peasantry precipitated its decline. The agricultural workforce, as a proportion of the Jamaican population, fell at the rate of around 4 per cent every ten years. At the same time employment opportunities in industry and domestic service remained static. The main alternative for the underemployed peasantry and working class was migration to the Panama Canal Zone, the United States of America, the Cuban sugar plantations or the fruit plantations of Central America. Indeed, between 1890 and 1920 there was a net emigration of around 120,000.[13] Under these circumstances, the chance to take the 'King's shilling' would have been a relatively attractive option.

When war was declared, Governor Manning immediately issued a Proclam-ation of Loyalty calling on all subjects, but especially ex-servicemen and constables, to present themselves for the defence of Jamaica to local police inspectors. The population was ordered to desist from activities likely to cause 'popular excitement',[14] a euphemistic allusion to deep-seated fears of black insurgency. Only two years before, Kingston had been gripped by a mass boycott of the Canadian-owned tramcar company after the announcement of a 14 per cent fare increase. Organised as a campaign of peaceful civil disobedience by the clerks of Kingston in February 1912, the boycott tapped into a mood of dissatisfaction prevailing among the Jamaican masses. Widespread unrest developed in which one man was killed by the police and the governor, Sydney Olivier, was stoned by a crowd.[15]

While the colonial authorities may have been preoccupied with potential unrest, public debate centred on the Jamaican contribution to the war effort. Letters began to appear in the press urging Jamaican men to volunteer. Fitz

Ritson, clerk to the Trelawny Parochial Board, wrote to suggest the formation of a local defence force to free regular troops stationed in Jamaica for service overseas. Fitz Ritson stressed support for the Empire and a desire to defend Jamaica, 'our dear country'.[16] Ivanhoe Harry, in a letter to the *Jamaica Times*, was more categorical, demanding Jamaica's menfolk should make the ultimate sacrifice for their island: 'Men of the Island of Jamaica, be not branded as cowards if you are needed for active service. Be courageous, be firm, be resolute, prepare to defend your country with your life's blood'.[17] Both these examples indicate Jamaican national identity was sufficiently developed to be mobilised as a tactic to recruit volunteers. This growing Jamaican national consciousness was also evident in cultural expression. In the poem 'My Native Land, My Home' written in 1912, Claude McKay pledged to shed his blood for Jamaica. In 1916, Bandsman W. D. Myrie of 2 West India Regiment, contributed a poem, 'Jamaica', to his regimental magazine that spoke

> ... of the land I Love,
> Jamaica the home of my birth,
> ... wherever I wander, for thee
> My love is abiding and strong.[18]

In the past, the call to arms to defend Jamaica and the Empire had been aimed at a very specific audience – the respectable, white property owner. However, as in other spheres of Jamaican life, non-whites were not content to sit back and be excluded from full participation in the island polity, especially when exclusion might pour doubt on their manhood. On 19 August 1914 a recruitment meeting was held for the Jamaican Defence Regiment. Two hundred volunteers attended, including several Indians who had seen military service before entering indentureship.[19]

The expectation in the metropole was that Jamaica, in common with many other colonies, would concentrate on supporting the war effort with raw materials, foodstuffs and funds. Consignments of fruit, preserves and cigarettes were regularly provided by individual and collective donation.[20] In a letter to the *Daily Chronicle*, 'A. E. B.' suggested Jamaica's 'loyal daughters' could assist the war effort by collecting medical supplies for the wounded and foregoing luxuries such as 'chocolates' and 'perfumes'.[21] While appeals such as these were clearly aimed at the wives and daughters of the white elite, the black majority were not excluded from wartime charitable efforts. The poet, Raglan Phillips, even composed a verse urging Jamaicans to 'sen[d] in Postal Order what you did [s]pen[d] [u]pon rum'.[22]

Although the official line was that Jamaica's contribution to the war effort would be limited to the supply of raw materials, many Jamaicans were not content to stop at home, minding the home fires. Local initiatives provided ample pomp and ceremony, but little activity other than bicycle patrols of the island on the lookout for spies or enemy ships. But the hearth was the place for women, old men and boys, not men eager to prove their masculine prowess. In the press and at public meetings potential volunteers were fed a steady stream of eulogies to the martyrs of Empire whose sacrifices helped to underpin manly ideals and conduct. Tom Redcam's poem, 'To Britain's Nameless Heroes', reprinted in the *Jamaica Times* in September 1914, recalled both the triumphs and setbacks for the Empire, such as the Afghan campaigns and the South African War. But it also assured the reader, that whatever the outcome, the volunteer slain in battle would achieve immortality, even if he did not grace the pages of the history books:

> Though ne'er recorded story may speak his humble name,
> Undying lives the Glory that crowns the nameless dead.

To a new generation of volunteers the war dead were offered as examples of steadfastness in the face of pain and fear. The Afghan and South African campaigns had involved black and Indian troops but the heroic dead were evidently white men who had adhered to the masculine ideals of fearlessness and self-control. But appeals to particular races or racial identities had the potential to became more generalised and blurred. These odes to military manhood, although pointed towards the white minority, could also be appropriated by non-whites intent on joining the war effort:

> From thee our race possessing the nerve that doth not fail,
> The will that doth not falter, the heart that doth not quail.[23]

The chief preoccupation of the colonial authorities throughout the war was internal security. However, to underpin allegiance to the Empire, the threat of a barbarous German invasion was kept alive in the public mind. Haiti was the main sphere of German influence in the Caribbean until the US intervention of July 1915. German companies had invested in the Haitian railway and shipped Haitian coffee to Europe. German interests had financed the Leconte and Simon revolutions between 1908 and 1912. Since then, rumours had circulated that Germany intended to establish Haiti as a protectorate and to use the island as a coaling station for warships. When around two hundred Haitians presented themselves for service at the French Legation in Port au Prince, they were rejected on the grounds that Zamor, the Haitian leader, had received German assistance to reduce public debts.[24]

The German presence in Haiti, coupled with long-standing white fears that Jamaica would undergo a Haitian-style revolution, helped fuel spy and invasion fears. In October 1914, a lieutenant in the defence forces spotted what he believed to be an 'aeroplane full of Germans ... followed by 2 war balloons' landing at Fellowship. This apparition was later found to have been the 'Evening Star seen through light cloud'.[25] Those with possible German origins were interned. Sigismund Bruhn, a shopkeeper, was arrested as an alleged German spy. Although he was able to prove he was actually a US citizen, he was swiftly deported upon his release.[26] Despite the fear of invasion, the only tangible contact with German forces occurred when a naval tender, the *Bethania*, was captured by H. M. S. *Essex* and escorted into Kingston harbour at the end of 1914.[27]

'Harry Morgan', a self-styled adventurer and writer, attempted to stir patriotic spirit by exaggerating the possibility of German invasion in a serial contributed to the *Jamaica Times*. The invasion narrative had been a recurring theme in metropolitan popular adult and juvenile literature since the Franco-Prussian War of 1870-71. The genre had initially emerged from a desire to encourage military reform to ensure adequate national defence. The swashbuckling pseudonym, 'Harry Morgan', was no doubt adopted to disguise the more Germanic-sounding Frederick Van Nostrand Groves. His tale, 'When the Germans Took Jamaica', lacked literary merit, but projected some significant concerns, primarily the wish to present Britain as guardian of the subject races in the face of German barbarism; a reiteration of the imperative of colonial stewardship that informed the Jamaican war effort.[28]

In Morgan's tale, Jamaica was laid waste by a German invasion supported by naval destroyers and aircraft. As armed resistance collapsed the population fled en masse to the countryside. However, the narrator and chief protagonist, Sir Horace Meadows, an ageing white patriarch and frontiersman stalwartly defended his womenfolk from the German menace. Meadows epitomised the stoical, straight-dealing, straight-punching Englishman who, even in these dire circumstances, could dispatch 'the Hun' with a single blow.

The German invader was described in terms previously deployed by whites nervous of black insurrection: 'the Kaiser's demonical hordes yell[ed] and shriek[ed] in fiendish glee' after shooting some prisoners and 'ended their orgy by hacking their corpses to pieces with ... short sabres'.[29] Fears of German regional intrigue and black revolt, centred on Haiti, merged. Morgan describes 'an armed contingent of 2,000 recruited in a neighbouring island ... commanded by German officers, clothed and equipped by the German Government'.[30] The narrator later reported that '[o]f the Haytians some 1,600 have been captured'.[31]

Subject to the depredations of Prussian militarism and without the staying hand of metropolitan influence the entire Jamaican population lost any vestige of self-control and became rapidly enfeebled. The white population was reduced to a rabble alongside the black: 'Up Slipe Road they came, dense mobs of terrified people, black and white alike wringing their hands and wailing piteously'.[32] The black soldiers 'of the once proud West India Regiment' fled 'wild-eyed'.[33] Meadows, having loaded a pair of 'army Colts' and strapped on 'a well-filled cartridge belt', barricaded his home before going 'to comfort and allay the fears of [his wife and daughter] who were by now sobbing piteously'.[34] Divine authority eventually interceded on behalf of the Empire and a great earthquake destroyed the enemy forces.

'When the Germans Took Jamaica' was taken literally by some readers. The *Jamaica Times* reassured readers it was a work of fiction,[35] but also published letters mocking the timidity of its more gullible audience. The population was expected to steel itself for conflict in a manful way without giving way to feelings of anxiety and doubt. As a correspondent, 'Not Frightened' declared, 'If people of vibratory [sic] tendencies see the enemy pouncing down upon them in every wind that blows, and in every descriptive exciting engagement, they should conceal such with themselves, and not intrude on others of sterner stuff'.[36]

That the press coverage of the war percolated to the mass of the population is evident in the large number of rural labourers and peasants who came forward as volunteers. By late 1915, when the War Office finally accepted proposals for war contingents from the West Indian territories, patriotic demonstrations and recruitment meetings were being staged even in the more isolated districts. After the war, a Colonial Office official remarked the majority of Jamaicans had no sense of attachment to Britain or the Empire other than 'a strong loyalty to the person and crown of the sovereign'.[37] But it was this very attachment to the monarch and popular interpretations of the ideals of Empire which sustained the Jamaican war contribution.

In the struggle for the abolition of slavery, the monarch was seen as a source of higher authority who could limit the power of the plantocracy and colonial officialdom. During the lifetime of Queen Victoria, early in whose full reign emancipation was achieved, Jamaicans displayed an open affection for the monarch.[38] Although this bond waned on Victoria's death, the imagined personal relationship between Jamaican subjects and the sovereign proved sufficiently strong to play a positive role in recruitment and support for the war effort in general. While the Colonial and War Offices felt their way uncertainly over the issue of the recruitment of black and 'coloured' soldiers, expressions of loyalty from these men were a key element in the founding of the British West Indies Regiment.[39]

Dying for the cause of King and Empire assumed a deep significance for volunteers welded to a vision of Empire characterised by justice and fair play.

But sacrifice in the pursuit of these values would also underpin demands for post-war economic and political reforms. The symbol of Empire and progress served as a yardstick by which black radicals measured their demands for equal treatment and articulated a desire to uplift the black race. As such, loyalty to this set of principles could transcend an attachment to the territory of Jamaica. Furthermore, the symbols of Empire remained open to numerous interpretations by individuals, communities or organisations who moulded them to their own ends.[40]

An affinity to Empire, or more specifically to the values which subject people ascribed to it, could act as a buffer against day-to-day discrimination and racism. Etienne Dupuch, the future editor and proprietor of the Bahamas *Tribune*, who served with the British West Indies Regiment recalled an incident in which a Sikh non-commissioned officer (NCO) was abused by a white private soldier. The Sikh deflected the racism and simultaneously belittled the white soldier, remarking "It is not for these that we fight ... It is for the grand British ideal".[41] Loyalty to abstract British ideals, as opposed to concrete experience, particularly equality before the law, suffrage and land rights, had been a central feature of pro-British sentiment among Africans and Indian migrants during the South African War. Such ideals, much vaunted by British leaders at the time, and existing limited rights as British subjects, stood in stark contrast to fears of dispossession under a Boer regime.[42] Many Jamaican volunteers adopted a similar approach by continuing to maintain an enthusiasm for the ideals of Empire, despite experiencing daily racism.

Jamaicans could point to examples where black West Indians had been compared favourably to other subject races and their participation in the defence of Empire had been welcomed. The role of the West India Regiment in the suppression of the Asante kingdom between 1873 and 1874, the overthrow of 'savage misrule and wrong', was frequently celebrated.[43] During the war, parallels were drawn between the past African and the present German foe. Tom Redcam referred, somewhat ambiguously, to England's enemies as 'Hate's dark-rolling millions'.[44] But another poet, C. C. Percy, describing the Kaiser, used the dialect insult, 'naygar', meaning a 'good-for-nothing' or 'uncivilised' African.[45] In the metropole, associations were also made between Germans and blackness. The *East Ham Echo*, commenting on appeals against conscription made by European immigrants in East London, reported how

> [t]he names of some of them were scanned rather suspiciously. Schwarz, or Schwarte, and Stein, for instance, have a German flavour ... 'Schwarz' is of course pure German, meaning 'black'; and we feel sorry for a Russian or Pole who has to bear that appellation of the Hun. He should get rid of it. It is allied

to our 'swart' and also to the Latin 'sordidus', meaning filthy, which all Huns are, body and soul.[46]

At the outbreak of the war, Lance Corporal James Grocer articulated the intense loyalty felt by many Jamaicans. In an article entitled 'What is the Union Jack', that appeared in the *Zouave*, the regimental magazine of the 2 West India Regiment, Grocer suggested the flag symbolised a benign and progressive Empire:

> the vial that contains the glorious essence of Civilization, ... the engine that is dragging to-day the train of blessing to man[k]ind the wide world over, irrespective of Class or Creed. It was, and is, and ever will be the attitude of the Union Jack to remove from Mankind the screen of despotism and tyranny which envelopes the poisoned and suffocating air, the regions that produce only the fruits of despair and death bringing in an atmosphere of hope and prosperity.[47]

Grocer expressed deep faith in the 'civilising' mission of Empire, that aimed to inculcate in the subject races the value of individual industry as the route to cultural progress. Grocer was influenced by his reading of *Self Help* by Samuel Smiles, the populist proponent of Victorian enlightened self-enterprise, who stressed 'manly character', attained by the 'honest and upright performance of individual duty' was the antidote to 'individual idleness, selfishness and vice'.[48]

The Empire could be portrayed as the guarantor of 'Emancipation' and 'Freedom' in the face of German barbarism – poignant symbols for a former slave colony deployed to perpetuate the myth that British benevolence had been responsible for abolition. Also significant in the context of Jamaican society was Grocer's belief that British ideals of liberty were sacrosanct within the Empire project. Citing Pitt the Elder, Grocer stated 'the humblest peasant in his cottage may bid defiance to any of the Forces of the Crown'. Linking these values to the outbreak of war and implicitly urging Jamaicans to be satisfied with an auxiliary role, Grocer declared 'Love, Liberty and Loyalty, are the trumpets that call us today to extend our powers, however feeble, to a gigantic cause, better known as a righteous war'.[49]

The fond imaginings of Britain as the emancipator of slaves and the guardian of freedom became a staple ingredient at recruitment rallies for the Jamaica contingents. At a meeting in St Mary and St Thomas in October 1915, Brigadier-General Blackden, commander of the troops in Jamaica, stressed the war was a fight for liberty. Were the men of Jamaica going 'to sit down and be slaves?'[50] The impact of demagogic statements such as these should not be underestimated. In post-emancipation society, economic independence and the personal autonomy associated with it were fundamental in defining black masculinity. Attempts by the plantocracy to limit black peasant initiative had always been fiercely resisted. Subordination to the dictates of the plantation economy – the loss of land and the imposition of poor wages – were viewed as deeply emasculating.

Previously the Jamaican masses were cast as the passive beneficiaries of British benevolence. Any efforts towards autonomous livelihood were frustrated by the plantocracy. But now the Jamaican populace was encouraged to take a proactive role in defending the liberties apparently bestowed upon them by British goodwill. At another meeting, in Kingston, Blackden demanded: 'What are we fighting for? Liberty ... Are we to say that [we] will shirk our duty? Are we to say that the liberty of the British Empire is the liberty to sit down and do nothing?' Implicit in remarks such as these was the belief that the war would stir the black population from 'tropical languor'. At the same meeting, Governor Manning urged all fit and able-bodied men of Jamaica to join the colours. He assured his audience they would reach England before the war was over and they would certainly get a chance to take part in what was sure to be a lengthy struggle. Manning asked volunteers to come forward and show their gratitude for what the Empire had done for them in the past and presented the spectre of a Prussian victory that would replace the 'benign rule of the Empire'.[51]

Poems appeared in the press in support of the recruitment campaign. In his poem, 'The Motherland's Call', Sydney Moxsy reiterated the fear slavery might be introduced in the event of a German victory and restated the role of the metropole as the upholder of black liberty.

> Strike Brothers strike! a blow for England's sake,
> Brave hearts that blow shall even stronger make,
> When England calls what British heart would shirk?
> She only calls in need for Empire's work.
> Colonial hearts in loyalty must stir,
> Face danger, death face all for sake of her.
> They rush to aid her and for England stand,
> No distance chills the love for Motherland
>
> No outward shade can dim the pluck within,
> Brave hearts may beat beneath a coloured skin,
> Who fear no death so long their land be free;
> The land they love, the Land of Liberty.
> No danger daunts who would his country aid,
> He'll fight for Country, home, for Wife and Maid.

What do you think, proud Sons of Liberty,
Your Land enslaved could you then happy be?
However much you hate such cruel strife,
Yet Death is better than dishonoured Life.
So die, if needs but try your land to save,
No craven life can equal patriot's grave.
Think not with fear of Death's untimely shroud,
But act like men of whom your land is proud.
Defend that land, don't seek alone renown,
Brave duty done is Life's immortal crown.
Fling off all selfish ties and 'play the man',
Your country serve and do the best you can.
He is no man who sneaks with some pretence
To shirk his duty in his land's defence.

That land is doomed which breeds a coward race,
Who money seek, but never dare to face
Their Country's foes; who fain at home would hide,
When need arises they should stem the tide,
That threats their land o'erwhelm, sweep all away,
Or make them slaves beneath a foreign sway.[52]

As Moxsy urged black volunteers to join a military fraternity of Empire his words blurred the distinctions normally drawn between black and white masculinity. England may have been the guardian of liberty, but the black 'Sons of Liberty' were also heir to a tradition of freedom crucial in the struggle for emancipation. As such, Moxsy believed black men were entitled to take up arms in self-defence and his allusions to 'country', 'home', and 'land' recognised a distinct Jamaican national heritage. Shortly after the war, Moxsy, a rationalist, provided one of the first elaborations of the concept of 'mental slavery' – the condition which Garvey later argued had prevented black people from reaching their true potential through an acceptance of doctrines of racial inferiority.

Marcus Garvey's Universal Negro Improvement Association (UNIA), established on the eve of the war, passed a resolution of loyalty to King and Empire at the Collegiate Hall, Kingston on 15 September 1914. The resolution affirmed that:

we the members of the Universal Negro Improvement and Conservation Association and African Communities League ... being mindful of the great protecting and civilizing influence of the English nation and people ... and their justice to all men, and especially to their Negro Subjects scattered all over the world, hereby beg to express our loyalty and devotion to His Majesty the King, and Empire ... We sincerely pray for the success of British Arms on the battle-fields of Europe and Africa, and at Sea, in crushing the 'common Foe', the enemy of peace and further civilization ... God Save the King: Long live the King and Empire.[53]

In a letter accompanying the resolution, Garvey averred 'Our love for, and devo-tion to, His Majesty and the Empire, stands unrivalled and from the depths of our hearts we pray for the crowning victory of the British soldiers now at War'.[54] Garvey's support for the war effort reflected the degree to which he had internalised certain values of Empire which he regarded as benchmarks for black self-improvement. Garvey may also have been influenced by the decision of some Irish Nationalists, widely reported in the Jamaican press, to suspend Home Rule agitation for the duration of the war in exchange for post-war concessions.[55]

Press allegations of German atrocities in France and Belgium may also have encouraged Garvey to support the devil he knew, particularly when it concerned the fate of fellow-Africans. As Raglan Phillips wrote of the Kaiser, 'Him burn [s]tore, house an' church too, man, woman, pickney all'.[56] Darnley, the Permanent Under Secretary of State for the Colonies, was sufficiently impressed by Garvey's loyalty to remark that 'I blush to think that I once suggested to Marcus Garvey that he should go the workhouse'.[57] It is not surprising that Governor Manning could declare 'I can confidently assert that there is no more loyal Colony that that of Jamaica ... [Jamaicans] are genuinely unanimous in their support of the Empire and of the Mother Country'.[58]

Although the Germans were presented as a nation of barbarians, the colo-nial elite did not wish to allow this to lead to criticism of the white races in general. The sentiment was often expressed that the Germans themselves were victims of 'Prussianism', an aberration that had caused the war through single-minded aggression and that departed from the distinctly amateurish traditions of 'fair play' associated with the British masculine tradition. 'Prussianism' was stereotypically ruthless, inflexible, militaristic and hostile to individualism. The British might stand at the pinnacle of civilisation, but the uncorrupted German, although portrayed as simpler and more rustic, was not far below. An article in the Jamaica Times stated '[t]he German as a man is an excellent fellow, home-loving, industrious and kindly, if a bit coarse'.[59]

The evils of Prussianism were derided in the Zouave in the first month of the war. 'The German Military Muddle' had arisen when masculine values were overridden by the application of Prussian military discipline. Total obedience and a thorough knowledge of military science were no substitute for the soldier 'who knows how to "muddle through" and how to "carry on" when in a tight place, without waiting for instructions'. German training 'eradicate[d] individualism' and resulted in 'iron-bound automatism'. Discipline alone was not sufficient. The officer 'is in exactly the same position as the father who has launched his son upon the battle of life. He must rely upon the past training of his son, certainly, but above all upon his 'individuality, courage, and devotion'.[60]

It was common knowledge that Kaiser Wilhelm was Queen Victoria's grandson and this also placed some limits on anti-German sentiment. Raglan Phillips, in his poem 'Victoria First Gran-Pickney' suggested Wilhelm had taken the wrong road due to his poor understanding of Christian principles, rather than his racial origins – 'Millennial people does preach dare is no hell, But him will mek fe him own'.[61] Presenting the war as a battle between good and evil reflected the tendency in Jamaican society to explain events through Biblical allusion.

A Jamaican nationalist undercurrent placed great emphasis on Biblical reinterpretation. The war represented the downfall of white claims to racial superiority and foreshadowed the collapse of western civilisation. This portentous interpretation became established during the stand-off between the European powers before hostilities commenced, and in the war's early months when politicians and military men still spoke of a war 'over by Christmas' – well before the Western Front came to be represented as an apocalyptic hell.

Other isolated voices spoke against the war in Jamaica. Non-conformists, unlike the majority in the Anglican clergy, used Biblical interpretation to condemn rather than justify war. In November 1914, John Bunting wrote to the *Jamaica Times* arguing the neutral nations should make petitions for peace which 'might ameliorate cruel feeling and bring about a better understanding and stop this wild butchery of souls'.[62] In March 1915, a letter, signed simply 'A Christian', referred to the message of Corinthians I, 6:7 – that it was better for men to suffer a slight than to engage in struggle – and called on ministers of all denominations to demand an end to the war. The white Jamaican writer, Albinia Mackay, in her poem 'War', contrasted heroic visions with the reality of broken homes, poverty and grief. Ultimately, however, she reluctantly supported the war which she blamed on 'German aggression'.[63]

However, the writer Frederick Charles Tomlinson developed the most sophisticated and consistent critique of the war. He counterposed a non-violent, rational black culture against the irrationality of a declining white civilisation, manifested by colonial oppression and now engulfed by world war. Tomlinson's writing was cryptic and couched in Biblical metaphor and he was often preoccupied by personal battles with publishers and colonial officials. His pamphlet, *The End of the Age*, charted his struggle with Chatto and Windus who had refused to publish his manuscript *A Study in White* (later re-titled *The*

Rainbow Book) since 1904. Tomlinson had previously published *The Helions*, a novel satirising race and class attitudes in Jamaica, in 1903. Tomlinson suggested the injustices directed towards him reflected those experienced by the black population in general. These in turn were reflected in symbolic episodes on the world stage, in which the promise of divine retribution was always present. For example, he linked the sinking of the Royal Mail Steamer *Lusitania*, in May 1915, to the interception by the Jamaican postal authorities of his own correspondence under wartime legislation.[64] Ultimately, Tomlinson believed these 'heavenly' interventions would bring about the demise of the Jamaican colonial regime – 'the mailed fist' – and the triumph of the rational, peace-loving black man.

Although he believed violent upheaval in Europe would benefit black Jamaica by the destruction of British power, Tomlinson's position was essentially non-violent. In contrast to colonial ideologies, he typified non-white Jamaicans as literate, intelligent and, above all, rational, in stark contrast to the irrationality of the European conflict and colonial representations of an 'excitable' black Jamaican populace. In *A Study in White*, Tomlinson had argued the rise of Japan would also undermine European domination, a prediction realised by its defeat of Russia in 1905.[65] Events within the Empire led Tomlinson to conclude world problems were being resolved by force of arms, rather than by logical discussion. In correspondence with the Jamaican Governor and his private secretary in July 1914, Tomlinson argued the Home Rule crisis in Ireland was a reflection of increased world tension and militarism: 'The "mailed fist" has taken advantage of the Situation in Ireland to inaugurate the War of the World. Observe the an[ti]thesis of the Literary to the Military'.[66]

Tomlinson recognised that colonialism and imperialism had always been dependent on armed force in order to establish dominion. As such, the Empire was incapable of calling a halt to the war. Tomlinson believed, however, that the pen – in other words reason – would ultimately triumph. Taking inspiration from the Book of Daniel, he presented the warring nations of Europe as the fourth and final beast in Daniel's apocalyptic vision. The oppressed of the world would be delivered into a New Age of justice and plenty.

> If the Nations of Europe once realised their JOINT LOSS through the wholesale slaughter of themselves, they would stop it – and stop it instantly. But they would have proved in so doing, The End of the Age on the other side. The 'Beast' in fact, would have given way to the 'Lamb'. That is where the shoe pinches.[67]

Tomlinson was not alone in his interpretation of this Old Testament vision. In 1903, J. Edmestone Barnes, a Jamaican writer and engineer, sought in Daniel and Ezekiel 'prophetic forecasts touching the economy and destiny of nations'.[68] He was prompted, in part, by the 'the recent exposure of [the] unpreparedness and physical weakness [of Britain] in the late Boer War to establish its paramount authority over a handful of uneducated farmers'.[69] He had reached the conclusion that by 1910 the Empire would face a tremendous struggle against the combined forces of Russia, Germany and France. Like, Tomlinson, Barnes believed war was inevitable given the increasingly belligerent stance of the European powers. But he differed from Tomlinson in that he believed the Empire could survive the struggle for 'the final supremacy of nations' through the collective efforts of its subjects. This was conditional on the adoption of two key policies. First, the policy of Free Trade should be reviewed so colonial industry might be protected and developed. Second, the equality of all races within the Empire should be accepted. Here, Barnes drew particular attention to the plight of black South Africans, comparing their lot to the early Christians persecuted by the Romans.[70]

For Tomlinson, the rise of Japan indicated that white military hegemony was on the wane. However, for many Jamaicans it was the early involvement of the Indian Army and French African soldiers which bolstered racial pride and encouraged volunteers to come forward. The deployment of non-white regiments in the European conflict was chiefly motivated by French fears, in the wake of the Franco-Prussian war, that Germany's greater birth-rate could only spell defeat in the event of renewed hostilities. West and North Africa was seen as an infinite 'reservoir of men' able to serve in both colonial and European wars. From 1909, the chief architect of African recruitment, Charles Mangin, drew up a series of racialised categories to delineate the ideal African soldier. Defined as relatively advanced but perceived to retain a primitive 'warrior instinct', the Wolof, Serer, Toucouleur and Bamabara of Senegal were regarded as ideal 'shock troops'. The French eventually deployed over 140,000 troops from Senegal, Mali and North Africa during the war. These troops were to prove particularly dependable after the near-collapse of the French army in 1917.[71] In the early stages of the war, the Jamaican press spoke favourably of the French African contingents. 'Singing' North African Zouaves were said to be 'boiling with impatience to get to grips with the foe'.[72] The deployment of French Algerians and tales of their 'gallant fighting' resulted in demands for the deployment of the West India Regiment in Europe.[73]

In September 1914, the *Jamaica Times* reported a House of Lords speech in favour of the deployment of Indian troops by the Marquis of Crewe. The Marquis asserted the pride of the Indian Army would be dented if her 'fine Indian troops' were denied a chance to be deployed in areas where black French troops had already made their mark.[74] As British Expeditionary Force casualties mounted, Indian troops were deployed from September 1914 to help stem the German advance through France and Belgium. By 1915, two divisions each of Indian infantry and cavalry amounting to nearly 30,000 men held a seven-mile stretch of the British lines.[75] The Jamaican press spoke glowingly of the Indian troops. 'Great Britain will throw her splendid Indian troops against the German forces', reported the *Daily Chronicle*.[76] By mid-September, Indian troops were rumoured to have 'smashed' crack Prussian units.[77] The *Jamaica Times* argued the Indians were far superior to the Germans and the equal of any other European people, remarking 'It seems to us almost a slur on our Indian troops to praise their success in the fighting in France as if it were a thing to be surprised at'.[78]

Jamaicans felt a close affinity with non-whites taking up the Empire cause. A Jamaican, who signed himself simply 'A Loyal Subject of the West Indies Island (jamaica)' [sic] sent a donation of $5 (£1) to Lord Kitchener 'for my brothers black and indian [sic] troop who are at the front fighting to defend our majesty's Empire'.[79] This was at a time when a labourer in Jamaica received around 1s 6d for a days work and the *Jamaica Times* had recently established a Shilling War Fund. The donation created a quandary for the War and Colonial Offices because they had not yet created a framework of support for black and Indian soldiers.[80]

The involvement of Indian soldiers in the war effort may have had a more subtle effect on black Jamaican volunteers. Forming around 2 per cent of the island's population, Indian indentured labour had a negligible demographic impact but significantly underscored images of black masculinity in Jamaica.[81] Black masculinity came to be defined, not only in terms of its relationship with the plantation and in *opposition* to white masculine ideals, but also in *relation* to images of Indian masculinity. Throughout the indentureship period, between 1845 and 1917, concerns were expressed that Indian labour was not suited to plantation labour. A culture that laid heavy emphasis on black physical prowess meant Indian labour was relegated to the 'water work' and 'dirty work'[82] black men refused that would have otherwise been done by women. Simultaneously, Indians were viewed as more capable of carrying out tasks requiring intelligence or dexterity – 'any delicate work ... such as pruning cocoa, and pruning bananas, ... that [could not] be safely left to the ordinary negro labourer.'[83] In the metropolitan division of labour the latter may also have been regarded as 'women's work'. In this setting some black Jamaicans may have felt a strong pressure to fulfil the manly obligation of war service.

In Jamaica, as in many frontier and settler societies, the right to take up arms was closely linked to the defence of property and racial privilege. Since the beginning of European settlement, the white rulers of Jamaica had depended on free and enslaved blacks to provide a component in the policing and suppression of the black majority. The black constabulary and the West India Regiment provided a much greater insurance against disorder than the largely white militias, whose chief qualification was their whiteness, rather than military effectiveness.

However, the right to bear arms to defend property and political privileges was fiercely defended by the white elite. From the late seventeenth century, the colonial power believed that a ratio of one white to every ten blacks was essential to keep the latter in check. At this time, white immigrants to Jamaica were granted thirty acres of land on the condition they served in the militia.[84] The 1879 Militia Law (amended in 1887 and 1891) raised the Jamaica Militia Artillery (JMA) and Jamaica Infantry Militia (JIM). Proposals for the reorganisation of the Jamaican militia forces during 1886 came amid fears the Sudanese wars would either reduce or remove the British garrison on the island. Membership was restricted to men over eighteen with a minimum income of £30, an annual income tax payment of at least £2, or property with a value of £50. Men wishing to join the mounted units had to provide their own horse. Although, like the franchise laws, this effectively squeezed out the majority of the black and brown population, some, with significant property, successfully enlisted. This caused consternation among elements of the white population who not only feared the availability of arms and training to non-whites, but recognised that their own dominance of society could be threatened by black and brown self-advancement. The elected members of the Legislative Council attempted to oppose the Militia Bill of 1891 using fiscal arguments as an excuse. However, the Colonial Office believed the class sympathies of the black and brown middle class would ensure their loyalty in the event of unrest.[85]

The JIM was disbanded in 1906 under the initiative of the metropolitan government, who believed any threat to Jamaican security could be met by regular forces. The JIM was maintained as the St Andrew Rifle Corps by public donation, which indicated both white fears of black insurrection and an assertion of the right of self-defence. At the outbreak of war the Rifle Corps was renamed the Kingston Infantry Volunteers and was called to active service in the island in late September 1914.[86]

Simmering black discontent in Jamaican society, most recently evident in the major disturbances linked to the tramcar boycott in the Spring of 1912, were an ever-present reminder of the need for white vigilance.[87] Any arming of the majority of the black population, either for home defence or service overseas, indicated a potential incorporation into Jamaican citizenship, as well as posing a potential threat to the colonial regime. The link between citizenship and arms-bearing was recognised by West Indian nationalists. Louis Meikle, a Jamaican member of the Trinidad-based West Indian Confederation Committee, laid out the aims of the organisation in August 1914 in the pages of the Jamaican *Daily Chronicle*. Alongside proposals to hold a referendum on confederation, to establish a national insurance scheme and institute free education stood a clause 'To suppress insurrections and repel invasion'.[88]

In the early stages of the war, vigilance and preparedness, watchwords of the frontier mentality, came to the fore. Appeals for volunteers reiterated the traditions of white arms-bearing and often referred to historic precedents where armed force had protected white privilege. Underlining the historical link between property and arms-bearing, the Jamaican government intimated it might remit property taxes on those volunteering for military service.[89] The ongoing anxieties of the white minority, rather than the minimal threat posed by Germany to British rule in Jamaica, often appeared to be the greater concern. A letter from 'Patriot' in the *Daily Chronicle* suggested that arms training should be compulsory and feared that a lack of arms training would leave Jamaica in a state of unreadiness. 'Patriot' pointed to Ulster, where Carson's Ulster Volunteers had been rapidly mobilised for the war effort. Ironically, Carson had taken up arms in defiance of the British parliament. But the inference was plain – national defence came second to defence of privilege by force of arms.[90]

But calls to arms no longer fell primarily on white ears. The existing black local forces could also be addressed within the language of the frontier. Major Edward Dixon, who had been elected as the member for St Andrews in August 1914, led suggestions that the West India Regiment (WIR) should be deployed in Europe. Dixon compared the veteran WIR favourably to the raw recruits in England 'who [had] declined to train themselves in time of peace'.[91] In other words, the well-prepared frontiersman, whether black or white, stood at the cutting edge of Empire masculinity when compared to the image of a more pampered, 'soft' masculinity in the metropole.[92]

Black Jamaica could also point to its past contribution and sacrifices, recollected in historical articles in newspapers, which relived the conquest of Spanish Jamaica and the defeat of eighteenth-century French ambition.[93] Frank Cundall, author of the official Jamaican history of the war, would recall how the arrival of the captured *Bethania* into Kingston harbour revived the memory of Rodney's triumphant entry into the port with captured French ships in 1782.[94] Delivering the address at the first reading of the Volunteer Defence Force Bill in August 1914, the Governor asserted:

> Jamaica will loyally and patriotically assume her part in maintaining the integrity of our Empire and will comport herself as gallantly today as she has done in the past. History relates that in days gone by this island has resolutely defended her shores and has taken no small part in the wars of the past.[95]

Under the guidance of its editor, Herbert de Lisser, the *Daily Gleaner* constantly reiterated the need for the steadying hand of white authority. But the paper's support for the raising of a Jamaican war contingent simultaneously promised that the contribution of manpower would elevate the place of Jamaica on the world stage. It was vital Jamaica should make a contribution, even if the war ended before the contingent was fully trained. 'It would never do for practically the whole Empire to be represented ... Jamaica standing out as the exception. We do not wish to feel ashamed of ourselves ... [The contingent] will have the fine moral consciousness of having offered to do their duty ... and Jamaica will share that feeling.'[96] More significantly, the raising of a contingent would raise Jamaica's position in Empire in 'the century of Imperial organisation'.[97] But the cool reception, in many metropolitan quarters, towards the proposed West Indian contingents would rapidly diminish the prospect of black Jamaican military endeavour being fully acknowledged or rewarded.

Notes

1   Herbert G. de Lisser, *Jamaica and the Great War* (Kingston: Gleaner Co., 1917), p. 1 (my emphasis).

2   Philip Curtin, *The Image of Africa: British Ideas and Action, 1780–1850*, Vol. I, (Madison: University of Wisconsin Press, 1964), pp. 58, 65, 71.

3   Rupert Lewis, 'Garvey's perspective on Jamaica', in Rupert Lewis and Patrick Bryan (eds.), *Garvey: His Work and Impact* (Mona: ISER, 1988), p. 230.

4   Thomas Carlyle, *An Occasional Discourse on the Nigger Question* (London: Thomas Bosworth, 1853).

5   Thomas Holt, *The Problem of Freedom: Race, Labor, and Politics in Jamaica and Britain, 1832–1938* (Baltimore: Johns Hopkins University Press, 1992), p. 280.

6   *DG* 22 June 1916, p. 4.

7   Robert A. Hill (ed.), *The Marcus Garvey and Universal Negro Improvement Association Papers*, Vol. I (Berkeley: UCLA Press, 1983), pp. 46, 148–9, 170–1.

8   *DG* 24 June 1916, p. 17

9   Bryan, *Jamaican People*, pp. 67–8; Patrick Bryan, 'The White Minority in Jamaica at the End of the Nineteenth Century', in Howard Johnson and Karl Watson (eds.), *The White Minority in the Caribbean* (Kingston: Ian Randle, 1998).

10 Holt, *Problem of Freedom*, p. 219.

11 Winston James, *A Fierce Hatred of Injustice: Claude McKay's Jamaica and His Poetry of Rebellion* (London: Verso, 2000), pp. 4, 10, 16.

12 Bryan, *Jamaican People*, pp. 217–33.

13 Ibid., pp. 131–51; Post, *Arise Ye Starvlings*, pp. 41, 106, 133. See also Aviva Chomsky, *West Indian Workers in the United Fruit Co. in Costa Rica, 1870–1940* (Baton Rouge: Louisiana State University Press, 1996); Velma Newton, *The Silver Men: West Indian Labour Migration to Panama 1850–1914* (Mona: ISER, 1984).

14 *JT*, 8 August 1914, p. 8.

15 James, *A Fierce Hatred*, pp. 81–7.

16 *DC*, 8 August 1914, p. 15

17 *JT*, 12 September 1914, p. 5

18 James, *A Fierce Hatred*, p. 91; *Zouave*, May 1916, p. 89.

19 *DC*, 24 August 1914, p. 11.

20 See, for example, PRO CO 137/708/2735 A. Cameron Mais to Colonial Secretary 29 December 1914; CO 137/708/1016 Manning to SSC 7 January 1915; CO 137/708/7081 Manning to SSC 12 February 1915.

21 *DC*, 20 August 1914, p. 3.

22 *JT*, 12 December 1914, p. 9. Phillips came to Jamaica as a penkeeper in 1871. He became a publisher and later encouraged the Salvation Army to send a mission to Jamaica. During the 1890s, he served the Salvationist cause as a staff officer. He later became a Baptist minister in Clarendon and St Thomas: Stephen A. Hill (ed.), *Who's Who in Jamaica, 1919–1920* (Kingston: Gleaner Co., 1920), p. 155.

23 *JT*, 12 September 1914, p. 1.

24 Robert and Nancy Heinel, *Written in Blood: The Story of the Haitian People 1492–1971* (Boston: Houghton Mifflin, 1978), pp. 351–3; *DC*, 31 August 1914, p. 4.

25 PRO WO95/5446 WD GOC Jamaica entry for 16 October 1914.

26 *DC*, 15 August 1914, p. 2; 25 August 1914, p. 3; 28 August 1914, p. 11.

27 Frank Cundall, *Jamaica's Part in the Great War 1914–1918* (London: West India Committee, 1925), pp. 20–1.

28 Michael Paris, *Warrior Nation: Images of War in British Popular Culture, 1850–2000* (London: Reaktion Books, 2000), pp. 86–7. Morgan also published an account of his travels in Cuba and Florida, *Odd Leaves From an Adventurer's Log* (Kingston, Ja.: F. N. Small, 1916).

29 *JT* 7 November 1914, p. 28.

30 *JT* 14 November 1914, p. 4.

31 Ibid., p. 29.

32 *JT* 7 November 1914, p. 28.

33 Ibid.

34 Ibid., p. 25.

35 *JT*, 14 November 1914, p. 15.

36 *JT*, 5 December 1914, p. 29.

37 PRO CO137/732/46378 Minute 19 August 1919.

38 James, *A Fierce Hatred*, pp. 93–5.

39 Howe, *Race, War and Nationalism*, pp. 37–40.

40 Patrick Bryan, 'Black Perspectives in Late 19th Century Jamaica: The Case of Theophilus E. S. Scholes', in Lewis and Bryan, *Garvey*, pp. 51–2.

41 Sir Etienne Dupuch, *A Salute to Friend and Foe: My Battles, Sieges and Fortunes* (Nassau, Bahamas: Tribune, 1982), p. 54.

42 Christopher Saunders, 'African Attitudes to Britain and the Empire Before and After the South African War', in Donal Lowry (ed.), *The South African War Reappraised* (Manchester: Manchester University Press, 2000), pp. 140–9; Goolam Vahed, '"African Gandhi": The South African War and the Limits of Imperial Identity', *Historia*, 45: 1, 2000, pp. 201–19.

43 *JT*, 23 January 1915, p. 17.

44 *JT*, 12 September 1914, p. 1.

45 'Dat War and de Kaysah', *JT*, 26 December 1914, p. 11; Frederic G. Cassidy, *Jamaica Talk: Three Hundred Years of the English Language in Jamaica* (London, Macmillan, 1961), p. 157.
46 *East Ham Echo*, 12 October 1917, p. 1.
47 *Zouave*, August 1914, p. 138.
48 'The Will and the Way', *Zouave*, November, 1914, pp. 170–1; quoted in Ilana Bet–El, 'Men and Soldiers: British Conscripts, Concepts of Masculinity, and the Great War', in Melman (ed.), *Borderlines*, p. 79.
49 *Zouave*, August 1914, p. 138.
50 *DG*, 20 October 1915, p. 14.
51 *DG* 12 October 1915, p. 13.
52 *DG*, 29 November 1915, p. 14. See *DG* 31 July 1919, p. 10 for Moxsy's letter on mental slavery.
53 PRO CO137/705 Marcus Garvey, Universal Negro Improvement and Conservation Association and African Communities League to RT Hon. Lewis Harcourt, MP, SSC 16 September 1914.
54 Ibid.
55 See for example *DG* 8 August 1914, p. 8
56 'Victoria First Gran–Pickney: How Him Turn Out Bad' by Raglan Phillips, *JT*, 12 December 1914, p. 9.
57 PRO CO137/705 Minute 26 October 1914.
58 PRO CO137/705 Gov. Manning to Lewis Harcourt MP, SSC 20 October 1914.
59 *JT*, 5 September 1914, p. 14.
60 *Zouave*, August 1914, p. 121. The Prussian stereotype was extended to British officers who were regarded as too autocratic. See for example A. P. Herbert, *The Secret Battle* (Oxford: Oxford University Press, 1982 [1919]), pp. 128–9.
61 *JT*, 12 December 1914, p. 9.
62 *JT*, 28 November 1914, p. 4.
63 *JT*, 14 December 1914, p. 37.
64 Frederick C. Tomlinson, *The End of the Age* (Kingston: Rainbow Printery and Publishing Co., 1915), p. 4.
65 Ibid.
66 Ibid., p. 7.
67 Ibid., p. 15 (upper case in original).
68 J. Edmestone Barnes, *The Signs of the Times: Touching on the Final Supremacy of Nations* (London: Henry P. Brion, 1903), p. 12.
69 Ibid., preface.
70 Ibid., passim.
71 Joe Lunn, '"Les Races Guerrières": Racial Preconceptions in the French Military about West African Soldiers During the First World War', *Journal of Contemporary History*, 34:4, 1999, 517–36. See also Anthony Clayton, *France, Soldiers and Africa* (London: Brassey's, 1988); Shelby Cullum Davis, *Reservoirs of Men: A History of the Black Troops of French West Africa* (Geneva: Librarie Kundig, 1934); Myron Echenberg, *Colonial Conscripts: The Tirailleurs Senegalais in French West Africa 1857–1960* (London: James Currey, 1991).
72 *DC*, 26 August 1914, p. 5.
73 *WICC*, No. 416 8 September 1914, p. 414.

74 *JT*, 5 September 1914, p. 6.

75 Omissi, *Indian Voices of the Great War*, pp. 2–3. Jeffrey Greenhut, 'The Imperial Reserve: The Indian Corps on the Western Front, 1914–15', *Journal of Imperial and Commonwealth History*, 12:1, 1983, 54–73.

76 *DC*, 31 August 1914, p. 1.

77 *JT*, 12 September 1914, p. 20.

78 *JT*, 31 October 1914, p. 15.

79 PRO CO137/706 A Loyal Subject of the West Indies Island (Jamaica) [sic] to Lord Kitchener 14 September 1914. An Indian Soldiers' Fund, to provide medical aid and other comforts for the Indian troops in Europe was established in early October 1914: *The Times*, 9 October 1914, p. 5.

80 PRO CO 137/706 Minute.

81 Ken Post, *Arise Ye Starvelings*, p. 41.

82 *Report of the Committee on Emigration From India to the Crown Colonies and Protectorates* (Sanderson Commission) (Cd. 5193) (London: HMSO, 1910), p. 325.

83 Ibid., p. 96.

84 Cundall, *Jamaica's Part*, p. 15.

85 Bryan, *Jamaican People*, p. 78–80.

86 *JT*, 10 October 1914, p. 4; Cundall, *Jamaica's Part*, p. 18.

87 James, *A Fierce Hatred*, pp. 81–90.

88 *DC*, 21 August 1914, p. 3.

89 Cundall, *Jamaica's Part*, p. 24.

90 *DC*, 5 August 1914, p. 7.

91 *JT*, 5 September 1914, p. 15.

92 This Jamaican image of the frontiersman was not dissimilar to that of the Antipodean bushman. See Chapter 1.

93 See for example, 'How Jamaica Followed the Flag' by T. H. MacDermott [Tom Redcam] which appeared as a series in the *JT* 5 June 1915, p. 7 and 12 June 1915, pp. 6–7.

94 Cundall, *Jamaica's Part*, pp. 20–1.

95 *DC*, 14 August 1914, p. 9

96 *DG*, 1 October 1915, p. 8.

97 Ibid.

3 The recruitment of Jamaican volunteers

In late October 1915, as the supply of volunteers in the metropole was exhausted, George V circulated an appeal for recruits throughout the Empire that appeared to contradict the racial considerations of colonial governments and the War Office. The previous April, the King had intervened to ensure the acceptance of West Indian contingents by questioning the wisdom of continued War Office obstruction. The 'Appeal' virtually coincided with the announcement, in the *London Gazette*, of the formation, by Royal Proclamation, of the British West Indies Regiment,[1] and suggested that his majesty's subjects would be admitted into the military fraternity on equal terms.

> At this moment in the struggle between my people and a highly organised enemy who has transgressed the Law of Nations and changed the ordinance that binds civilized Europe together, I appeal to you.
>
> I rejoice in my Empire's efforts, and feel pride in the voluntary response from my Subjects all over the world who have sacrificed home, fortune and life itself, in order that another may not inherit the free Empire which their ancestors and mine have built.
>
> I ask you to make good these Sacrifices.
>
> The end is not in sight. More men and yet more are wanted to keep my Armies in the Field, and through them to secure victory and enduring Peace.
>
> In ancient days the darkest moment had ever produced in men of our race the sternest resolve.
>
> I ask you, men of all classes, to come forward voluntarily and take your share in the fight.
>
> In freely responding to my appeal, you will be giving your support to our brothers who, for long months, have nobly upheld Britain's past traditions, and the glory of her Arms.[2]

The 'Appeal' was received in Jamaica and read out in the island's churches on Sunday 31 October.[3] It prompted press and literary declarations that reinforced the message that all races enjoyed equality in the fight against 'the Hun'. Tom Redcam, who penned numerous stanzas for the Jamaican press, captured the mood in his poem, 'Gentlemen, the King'.

> List to the words of the King!
> List to the summons they bring!
> Patriots, stand up for the right,
> Buckle your armour for fight! ...
> 'Sons of the Empire', rise,
> Sever your most sacred ties;
> For a greater is here,
> 'Tis our country's most dear,
> And her call let no stalwart despise.
>
> Heedless of race, rank, or creed,
> Heedless of glory or meed [reward],
> Mindful of Duty alone,
> Thousands before you have gone.[4]

Rose de Lisser directed a poem, 'The Appeal' at 'my brothers' and 'you women' of Jamaica. Familial language could create a sense of inclusiveness, while simultaneously implying a hierarchy of race, class and gender. De Lisser recognised that women played a significant role in encouraging masculine duty:

> God knows it is bitter to part;
> But your manhood shall never be lowered,
> No fear must be now in your heart.
> It is better to know they are fighting,
> For that which is dearest and best;
> Than to see them home playing the coward,
> In a languorous ease and rest.

However, de Lisser's apparently universal message was undermined by her call to 'Aside put your golf-stick and ball'[5] clearly aimed at the white elite.

The inclusive language of the 'King's Appeal' found an echo among the Jamaican masses. W. G. Hinchcliffe, articulated the dream of an inclusive Empire reinvigorated by the exigencies of war. He urged Jamaicans to go forward and take up the volunteer's mantle in the name of international brotherhood, before they were compelled in a less honourable way by conscription.

> We need no seer to tell us, nor any divine to inspire us with the fact that the time is now on us when brothers will be compelled to know each other as brother without thinking of race, nationality, colour, class, or complexion. Therefore, those who are not yet standing on the road platform of humanity, and are shirking the duty which the Empire demands of them, they need not be argued with, for the mandate will soon come down from the Throne. We cannot indulge in any arguments just now about 'class' and 'colour', 'spade' and 'shovel' ...

Yet the subject is one that has been causing innumerable troubles, and troubles which this universal war at the end will decide in favour of the British people and the African race. So it is just as well for the European, the middle man and the African, all to join hands and hearts together to strike the necessary death blow to Germanism, bearing in mind 'United we stand, divided we fall'.[6]

But inclusive language could not erase historical attitudes to the deployment of black soldiers or override anxieties surrounding white masculine performance during the war. Black men had been a visible presence in the British Army from the seventeenth century. They took part in colonial expeditions, filled garrisons in the Caribbean, and were deployed extensively during the American war of independence, as troops and auxiliaries. The West India Regiments, initially recruited from slaves during the American campaigns, comprised twelve separate regiments in 1798. The regiments became a crucial element of colonial power. During the Morant Bay Rebellion, the 1 West India Regiment supported the 6 Regiment of Foot (later the Royal Warwickshire Regiment) in the brutal, but successful, suppression of the uprising, earning the longstanding distrust and resentment of many Jamaicans.[7]

The West India Regiments also played a strategic role in the Imperial conquest of West Africa, particularly the Asante Wars of 1873–74 and the suppression of rebel tribes in Sierra Leone 1898–99.[8] The black soldier was said to outperform his white counterpart in West African conditions. Alfred Burden Ellis, a WIR officer and ethnologist, claimed that during the Asante War black troops marched two to three times the distance of white comrades and carried out the work of the European soldier while on half rations.[9] Ellis went on, 'The English-speaking negro of the West Indies is most excellent material for a soldier. He is docile, patient, brave, and faithful' and even when treated harshly, Ellis believed his men 'manifest[ed] their displeasure by passive obedience and a stubborn sullenness. [Whereas] English soldiers … under such circumstances, proceed to acts of insubordination'.[10] From Ellis's perspective these characteristics were conditional on white leadership to ensure that the black soldier's purported impetuosity and lack of self-control were kept in check. 'The bravery of the West India soldier in action has often been tested, and as long as an officer remains alive to lead not a man will flinch. His favourite weapon is the bayonet; and the principal difficulty with him in action is to hold him back, so anxious is he to close with his enemy.'[11] In 1906, four years after the South African War recruitment crisis, the travel writer, John Henderson, usually a more jaundiced observer, commented that the black Tommy of the WIR was 'conscious of [his] superiority' over the white troops stationed in Jamaica.

mid-nineteenth century → reduction in black soldiers

Could a white regiment have marched in the full glare of the noon sun through Ashanti and not dropped a man? Could a white man pierce jungle and fight through malarious tangled undergrowth, wading slimy swamps, swimming rushing rivers, and live? Can any company of white soldiers march with the swing of a West Indian Regiment when the black pipers shriek the quick-step?[12]

The historic role of the West India Regiments was recalled at Jamaican recruitment rallies. At a meeting in Gayle, in the parish of St Mary and St Thomas, Adam Roxburgh, a local magistrate, recollected how 'the officers who fought with the West India Regiment in the Ashantee war and at other battle fields, have bore testimony to the courage, the bravery and endurance of the Jamaica soldiers'.[13] Visitors to the island also spoke highly of the regiment. Sir Hamar Greenwood, Liberal MP for York, who witnessed the WIR giving assistance during the earthquake of 1907, declared 'Our Native Soldiers in Jamaica so worthily upheld the best records of the Soldiers of the King whatever colour they might be or in whatever climate they might serve'.[14]

Despite such praise, by the mid-nineteenth century the presence of black soldiers declined. Most of the West India regiments were disbanded by the late 1860s and in 1888 the remaining two were merged into a single West India Regiment which by 1914 comprised only two under-strength battalions.[15] From 1906, Jamaica served as the only depot for the WIR, whose two surviving battalions alternated garrison duty in Sierra Leone. Classed as a 'native' regiment, the men received poorer pay and conditions compared with other British army units, although they were required to undergo the same training. In their striking Zouave-style uniforms – tight blue waist-coats and red pantaloons – the men of the regiment had to be content that the main reward of military service was the attention they received from the populace of Kingston in their off-duty hours.[16]

In the wake of the Indian Mutiny of 1857, non-whites were increasingly caricatured as unreliable and potentially traitorous, as well as falling short of British ideals of heroism, military élan and steadfastness. The black presence in the metropolitan army waned and martial race theories were elaborated that circumscribed the racial groups from which colonial armies were recruited.[17] Influenced by contemporary scientific representations of difference, martial race theories held that some subject races possessed biologically determined soldier-like qualities. Anthropological interpretations of indigenous cultural and social practices were also influential, as were climatic explanations. After 1857, the main recruitment grounds for the Indian Army were redefined, the northern states replacing the South and East. Tropical climates were believed to dissipate manliness and so hill-dwellers from cooler climes, such as Nepal, were preferred over the plainsman of Southern India, in whom the practice of early marriage was also seen as evidence of doubtful military efficiency. The so-called Aryan races of North India were also regarded as superior as it was believed they shared a common Euro-Indian heritage. Often however, martial theories were pragmatically adapted to meet recruiting targets.[18]

Recruitment policy in Imperial Africa from the 1880s was also informed by martial race thinking. Men from remote, impoverished regions were preferred as they were held to be able to survive on irregular food supplies and to have natural scouting skills. Groups who had resisted colonial rule, such as the Nandi of Kenya were also favoured.[19] In all cases it was held that martial capability could only be fully realised under white tutelage and leadership.

Whatever concessions to non-white races were encompassed within martial race theory, white predominance could never be brought into question. As the nineteenth century progressed the model of white military masculinity upholding ideals of self-control and rationality became more entrenched. Wherever non-white units were raised in the Empire, they were led by white officers. Non-whites were only able to rise to the rank of NCO in the 'native regiments' as they came to be designated.[20] The one exception was the Indian Army where Indian officers could receive commissions from the Viceroy. Their main purpose was to advise white officers, particularly on cultural matters. However, Indian officers remained subordinate to their white counterparts regardless of rank as the latter held the King's commission. Furthermore, the proportion of Indian officers in relation to whites declined as the war approached. By 1914, each unit contained matching numbers of white and Indian officers, reflecting the feeling of the military establishment that units officered solely by Indians would not act decisively in the front line.[21]

Regardless of the perceived military capability of the martial races, British commanders were reluctant to deploy them against a white enemy. The fighting prowess of any white man could not be seen to be challenged. During the South African War of 1899 to 1902, the view of both British and Boer leaders was that the campaign should remain a 'white man's war'. Indian units amounting to nearly 10,000 men were limited to an auxiliary role, including medical support, transport and supplies.[22] A suggestion from Lord Roberts, the British commander-in-chief, that West Indian troops be employed in the most inhospitable climates was rejected by Landsdowne, the Secretary of State for War (SSW). The West India Regiment, stationed in Bermuda on a regular tour of duty, was barred from guarding Boer prisoners who had been sent there. Members of the regiment stationed on St. Helena did guard Boer prisoners until objections were raised by Lansdowne.[23] However, both sides departed from this position when it became expedient. The British, for example, used black auxilliaries to guard the chains of blockhouses that were regarded as essential to defeat the Boer guerrillas. In turn, the Boers, despite regarding any British deployment of black troops as uncivilised, routinely employed armed black and 'coloured' men in their columns.[24]

From the outset of the First World War, Colonial Office and War Office officials were confronted with a dilemma in relation to the acceptance of black volunteers. Black men, not only from Jamaica, but throughout the Empire, came forward to offer their services. Some were already resident in the United Kingdom, particularly those from a seafaring background. Others made their way to the metropole at their own expense or even stowed away. In Jamaica, Kingston City Council passed a resolution, forwarded to the Governor, demanding that all 'physically qualified' volunteers should have their passages paid by the Jamaican Government. In the Legislative Council, H. A. L. Simpson, Honorary President of the Jamaica League and Mayor of Kingston, put down a motion requesting that the Parochial Boards pay the fares of those travelling to the UK to enlist.[25]

The issue of black recruitment was most contentious in the army. The Royal Navy continued to employ men from all corners of the Empire, particularly as stokers and firemen. The *Daily Gleaner* carried a picture captioned 'Sons of Jamaica in Britain's Royal Navy', featuring three black sailors serving on HMS *Bristol*.[26] The *Manual of Military Law* of 1914 implied, but without absolute clarity, that 'any negro or person of colour' was an alien. 'Aliens' were barred from holding rank higher than NCO and their numbers restricted to one in fifty of the ranks. But the *Manual* also stipulated that a serving black man was 'entitled to all the privileges of a natural-born British subject'.[27] The *British Nationality and Status of Aliens Act* passed in the same year, in response to Eastern European migration, was less equivocal. The Act stated that 'Any person born within His Majesty's dominions and allegiance [was] ... a natural born British subject.'[28] As a consequence some legal protection was accorded to non-whites in the metropole. In a civil case heard during the war in West Ham, a landlord petitioned to evict a family that included a black man. Rejecting the landlord's application the magistrate stated 'a black man had as much right as anybody else to live in England, providing that he was a British subject'.[29]

Military law conceded that black volunteers were entitled to have their service rewarded with the rights of citizenship, but simultaneously attempted to limit the extent of such claims. The ambiguity of the regulations contributed to a situation where individual black volunteers were accepted or rejected on an ad hoc basis throughout the war. Military service and its implied reward would become increasingly contested values, particularly when postwar nationalist movements challenged the limited concessions granted to veterans who had served the Empire. These circumstances were anticipated in an article in 1916 that appeared in the *United Empire*, journal of the Royal Colonial Institute:

> The sons of the West Indies are worthy of the beautiful islands and the fighting ancestry from which they come. They are prepared to bear their portion of the burden of Empire, and to endure sacrifices for the ideals for which our armies are fighting, thus proving that they are entitled to greater recognition than ever before as a component part of our great Empire.[30]

On 28 August 1914 it was decided that Indian troops, originally intended for Egypt, should be deployed in Europe.[31] On the same day, a negative reply met tentative enquiries from the Colonial Office as to the desirability of West Indian contingents. Instead, it was asserted that the West Indian colonies would be of far more value to the war effort in their traditional function supplying primary products to the industrial centres of the Mother Country. This was despite the ready availability of men, including thousands of destitute West Indian migrant labourers in Panama awaiting repatriation to their homes. In addition to supplying vital raw materials such as foodstuffs, logwood and cotton, the West Indian colonies were expected to make heavy financial contributions to the war effort. Jamaica was scheduled to pay £60, 000 per annum for forty years after the end of the war to help reduce the War Debt.[32]

Many white military men believed black soldiers lacked sufficient self-discipline and rationality to be an effective force on the modern battlefield. In January 1917 it was suggested that black troops replace members of the Royal Engineers on technical tasks, releasing the latter for service in the firing line. The Assistant Adjutant General (AAG) to the War Office rebuffed the suggestion claiming 'coloured men would ... be most dangerous to the efficiency ... of the armies in France'.[33] Although they had played a significant role in many Imperial campaigns, black soldiers came to be regarded as objects of curiosity to be paraded at ceremonial occasions as a signifier of Imperial unity. Popular attitudes to the black man in uniform tended to be patronising and belittling, rather than overtly hostile. The black soldier was presented as childlike, entertaining, ineffectual and endearing as evident in the following remarks made about French African troops by a British Tommy:

> The niggers are hopeless ... Their slow thought-out movements – such as lighting a pipe, for example – often suggest a monkey to me almost as much as a man. And yet I am curiously fond of them. Wag your head towards them as you go by, and you win the richest smile in the world, white teeth, thick lips, black eyes, all combine in the most bewitching production. They do not bear pain like the brave French boys.[34]

Such images bolstered white martial self-esteem and Imperial arrogance. Even more supportive white commentators were concerned that the black soldier lacked the self-discipline and willing subordination that underpinned military masculinity. Alfred Horner, a padre attached to the sixth and ninth battalions of the BWIR, frequently praised the physical fitness of his men and believed that the majority displayed the 'Right Stuff' from which a soldier might be fashioned.[35] However, Horner was equally insistent that the West Indian recruit, having originated in the tropics, lacked the manly desire for profitable and self-disciplined enterprise. Echoing Carlyle and de Lisser, Horner lamented that

> [t]o the West Indian boy, whose life is cast in an easy mould, who works according to his own sweet will, whose wants are few and easily satisfied, the 'beginning of discipline' was not easy. As long as soldiering meant bands and uniform and a certain element of wild heroism all was well; but when it meant smartness, neatness and, above all, punctuality ... it was not so well.[36]

Faced with the dehumanising conditions on the Western Front, many white soldiers engaged in behaviour associated, in the Imperial imagination, with savagery. The majority of casualties on the Western Front were caused by high-explosive shells fired from behind the front line. Night-time raids on enemy trenches provided the most likely opportunity for hand-to-hand combat. Here the favoured weapons were clubs, knuckle-dusters, entrenching tools and Bowie knives, hardly the stuff of legend.[37] In a striking scene from *Memoirs of an Infantry Officer*, Siegfried Sassoon, described his men, their faces blackened with cork in preparation for a night attack, as 'shiney-faced nigger minstrels'. This temporary appearance provided a racialised alibi as the men armed themselves with knobkerries and hatchets.[38] Another British officer, Charles Edmonds, was appalled to see his apparently urbane sergeant collecting the teeth of dead Germans and laughing at grotesquely mangled corpses.[39] T. E. Lawrence's narrative of the war in the Middle East maintained its lasting allure partly because military tactics there permitted more traditional hand-to-hand encounters and chivalric codes of conduct.[40]

Other British soldiers attempted to transfer the blame for the erosion of decency and 'fair play' directly onto the presence of black soldiers. Robert Graves recalled that '[t]he presence of semi-civilized coloured troops in Europe was, from the German point of view, we knew, one of the chief Allied atrocities. We sympathized'.[41] In *Goodbye To All That*, Graves regaled the reader with the tale of a French North African soldier who arrived at the headquarters' mess carrying a German head and demanding his jam ration. He also related an account, heard from a French civilian, in which a retreating German column was set upon by a black French regiment: 'ces animaux leur ont arraché les oreilles et les ont mises a la poche!' ['these animals ripped their ears off and put them in their pockets'].[42]

Antagonism towards the German foe could be disrupted by other considerations that manifested a complex interplay of ethnicity, culture and religion. Graves and his fellow officers, for example, determined a racial hierarchy based on ascribed standards of hygiene. In descending order these were:

> English and German Protestant; Northern Irish, Welsh, and Canadians; Irish and German Catholics; Scots, with certain higher-ranking exceptions; Mohammedan Indians; Algerians; Portuguese; Belgians; French ... We put the Belgians and French there for spite; they could not have been dirtier than the Algerians and the Portuguese.[43]

Allegations of barbarity and racial inferiority deflected attention from atrocities committed by white troops and served to dismiss the military achievements of black and Indian troops that might otherwise undermine white claims to racial superiority. Discussing the deployment of black soldiers against the French in Africa, earlier in the century, Brigadier-General Sir James Willcocks had warned,

> It is always judicious ... never to give the black man an idea that you seek his assistance against other white men ... [W]ith our soldiers ... we always spoke as if all they would have to do would be to fight the other black soldiers and avoided reference to their white commanders ... First must come the white man to what ever race he may belong.[44]

Prevailing racial attitudes, inconsistencies in official policy and the approach of individual recruiting officers interacted to ensure that black and brown Jamaicans met with varying degrees of success in joining regular army units. Some were enlisted in the Army Service Corps, chiefly because the regiment served an auxiliary, rather than front-line role. A number of men served in infantry units. Many of these men elected to transfer to the British West Indies Regiment after its formation.[45]

James Slim, a Jamaican whose army papers describe him as black, enlisted in the prestigious Coldstream Guards before he was discharged under instructions from the War Office. As his conduct was good and no mention was made of a medical condition, it must be presumed that this was because of his colour. The *Jamaica Times* reported that Slim had served with the French Foreign Legion prior to enlisting in the British Army, although his army papers make no mention of this.[46] Another Jamaican, Egbert Watson, who described himself as a 'coloured West Indian from Jamaica' served in the Royal Garrison Artillery before being discharged on medical grounds after eighteen months' service.[47] Several newspapers carried pictures of a black Jamaican in the Staffordshire regiment joking with members of the Household Cavalry in Whitehall, before proceeding down Whitehall with a white comrade. And Edward Jones of Barbados, a recruit to the Cheshire Regiment, was pictured in the *Daily Mirror* atop the Lions in Trafalgar Square.[48]

Other black men travelling to the metropole to enlist met with a rather different response. At West Ham Police Court, whose jurisdiction covered the docks of Canning Town in London, nine men from Barbados were charged with stowing away on the S. S. *Danube* with the intention of volunteering in May 1915. Local police enquiries ascertained that they were likely to be rejected because of their colour. Although the case against them was discharged, the men's enthusiasm for the Empire cause did not protect them from the disparaging remarks of the bench. The magistrate, a Mr Gillespie, suggested they had stowed away '[i]n a dark corner ... to enlist in the Black Guards'; the play on the word 'blackguard' was calculated to insult the men's integrity as well as race.[49]

3 A black Jamaican private in the Staffordshire Regiment jokes with a cavalry trooper in Whitehall, Spring 1916

Despite these slurs the men insisted they would not return to Barbados – 'They had come to fight, and they were going to fight'. [50] A group of three Jamaican stowaways, including a sixteen and a fourteen-year old, who arrived with the same intention two years later were treated more harshly. Although they had worked their passage after discovery, all three were sentenced to seven days' imprisonment. [51]

Black professional men who sought commissions in the army were equally likely to be rejected. The Jamaican government veterinary officer, G. O. Rushdie-Gray was sent to England with the official blessing of Governor Manning and six weeks' paid leave, after official intimations that he would be accepted. Rushdie-Gray had also served as a vet to the West India Regiment. [52] Despite these credentials he was refused a commission in the Army Veterinary Corps. The Colonial Office and War Office tried to assuage Rushdie-Gray by offers of civil veterinary employment and, more eagerly, offered to pay his return passage. But the insult was compounded by the suggestion that if Rushdie-Gray had been of a lighter shade, he may well have been accepted. [53]

> Mr G[ray] called today, he is presentable, but black ... I am surprised at the Gov[ernor] recommending a black man without previously informing us of his colour. I have spoken to the Veterinary Dept. of WO and understand that there is no absolute bar against coloured men for commissions in the Vet. Corps, but that they did not expect Mr G to be the colour he is! [54]

The inconsistencies of official policy are well-illustrated by the fact that two lighter-skinned Jamaicans were able to enlist in the Royal Flying Corps (RFC). A former solicitor's clerk, Sergeant L. McIntosh, who was sponsored by his employer, became an aerial observer. After being wounded in a plane crash in 1916, he was reported to have become a flying instructor. McIntosh was pictured in the pages of the *Daily Gleaner* alongside Flight Sergeant W. 'Robbie' Clarke who submitted several reports of his exploits as an aerial photographer. Clarke was eventually shot down and seriously wounded over Ypres. [55]

The success of Clarke and McIntosh in enlisting in the RFC was particularly significant. The war in the air, in contrast to the Western Front, became an arena in which the rituals of personal engagement and heroic endeavour, myths central to the image of white military masculinity, were more easily maintained. In the air, unlike the ground war, technological advance had aided, rather than stifled this process. Air duels, portrayed as equal contests between individuals, were fought above the field of battle where technology and tactics had conspired to rob the combatants of such illusions. [56] Before enlisting in the Royal Field Artillery, Norman Manley, later to become Jamaica's Prime Minister, attempted to join the RFC, which he described as

4 Flight Sergeant
W. 'Robbie' Clarke

the last 'gallant' and 'sporting' arena of modern warfare. He was prevented
from enlisting by the cost of attending flying school.[57]

Official ambivalence towards black volunteers was further evident when
the British War Mission in the USA, headed by Lord Northcliffe, issued a series
of recruitment appeals to British subjects residing there during July 1917.[58]
Jamaicans and other West Indians in the USA were also exposed to the pro-
Allied sentiments of W. E. B. Du Bois and the National Association for the
Advancement of Colored People (NAACP). Black involvement in the war was
enthusiastically endorsed as an opportunity for racial advancement. As it had
been in Jamaica, a Germany victory was presented as a precursor of slavery. The
NAACP paper, the *Crisis* featured a special 'soldiers' issue' in June 1918. Racial
appeals were underpinned by the rhetoric of masculine sacrifice and duty. The

editorial asked, 'do you know what to the Negro people means the German Military Machine?' and continued:

> It means ... slavery chains for our wives , sweethearts, mothers, fathers and children, more galling and hopeless than those of ante-bellum days in the United States ... Let us keep our eyes ... on the star of our aspirations for racial betterment; let us play the game square and to the limit.[59]

The black volunteer was promised rich reward for his sacrifice, not only an improvement in the position of the black population in the USA, but political advances for subject peoples the world over.

> This war is an End and, also, a beginning. Never again will darker people of the world occupy just the place they have before. Out of this war will rise ... an independent China; self-governing India, and Egypt with representative institutions; an Africa for the Africans ... Out of this war will rise, too, an American Negro, with the right to vote, and the right to work and the right to live without insult. These things may not and will not come at once; but they are written in the stars, and the first step toward them is victory for the armies of the Allies.[60]

The recruitment of black Britons subjected to encouragement such as this, placed the British authorities in a quandary. When the USA entered the war in April 1917, men rejected by the British Recruiting Mission in New York could be conscripted into the US army, until the signing of the Anglo-US Military Service Conventions in spring 1918. This had the potential to cause confusion and resentment, that the British and US authorities feared would be exploited by black radicals in the USA and West Indies.[61]

Brigadier-General Wilfred White, head of the British Recruiting Mission, complained that no firm guidelines regarding the enlistment of 'men of colour' were in place and black volunteers were initially rejected. But in June 1917, it was agreed black recruits would be accepted on the understanding that they would form a separate battalion kept at full strength by ongoing recruitment.[62] General White appealed to the War Office for further clarification so that the equivocal recruitment policy did not become a contentious political issue. However, White made no attempt to conceal his own prejudices. His telegram to the War Office in February 1918 was headed 'Wooly [sic] headed niggers' and stated that as the military mission was unable to post black recruits to white battalions, '[t]hese "niggers" must therefore go to native units'.[63]

In June 1918, the War Office overturned its earlier policy and allowed black volunteers resident in the USA, Canada and the metropole to be recruited directly to regular British units. The policy encompassed men of black, East

Indian and mixed descent and stipulated that recruits agreed to eat standard British rations, to receive the same pay as other British soldiers and could understand and speak English. Drafts from the USA could not contain more than 10 per cent black recruits although a larger proportion was permissible for men drafted to the Army Service Corps as horse and motor drivers.[64] This meant that potential black recruits were turned away who would then be exempted from compulsory service in the US Army under the terms of the Anglo-US Military Service Convention.

Restricting the entry of black men to regular army units contained the numbers deployed in a combatant role. The War Office was adamant that recruitment terms agreed for the USA did not extend to US colonies or protectorates that were home to large numbers of West Indian migrants.[65] The British representative in Havana issued a press notice to state that the measures would 'exclude specifically Jamaicans and other coloured British subjects'.[66] The War Office also hastily moved to dispel any idea that black volunteers in Jamaica itself would also have the opportunity to apply for units other than the BWIR in order to have a greater chance of front-line duty. The Secretary to the Army Council, clarified the official view in a terse response to Colonial Office enquiries:

> I am to say that the intention of the Army Council was, and is, to provide a place in the combatant arms of the British Army for British subjects of colour resident in Great Britain and the United States and also for the better class British subject of colour or half caste resident in the Colonies for whom no appropriate combatant unit exists in the colony in which he resides. It was not, and is not, the intention of the Army Council to accept for units of the British Army natives of unmixed blood from Colonies for whose reception specially raised labour battalions have been formed, such as the West Indian and Mauritius Labour Battalions; or any British subjects, being natives and resident in Colonies which maintain appropriate combatant units such as ... Jamaica.[67]

Although the War Office adopted an almost implacable stance towards black recruitment throughout the war, greater encouragement for black volunteers did come from other quarters. By the second year of the war, it was clear that the pool of volunteers in the metropole was drying up and conscription was under consideration. The possibility of black recruitment began to receive greater attention. The National Sailors' and Fireman's Union (NSFU – a forerunner of the National Union of Seamen) was at the forefront of trade union recruiting campaigns and particular initiatives were aimed at the black membership, many of whom were based in the South Wales ports. These men comprised a long-standing community whose seafaring employment had brought them to the sailor's hostels of Cardiff and other ports from East and West Africa, as well as the Caribbean.[68]

Since 1908, the NSFU had waged a racist 'Yellow Peril' campaign against Asiatic seafarers, whom it regarded as a threat to conditions and wage levels, as well as potentially traitorous. The union was to pursue a more generalised campaign against non-white labour in the 1920s. However, during the war tentative support was offered to its black members, who were more readily accepted as British subjects and seen as less likely to undercut wage rates than Asian seamen.[69] In a letter to the *South Wales Daily Post*, a union official, George Gunning, complained that large numbers of unemployed black seamen of 'fine physique' were keen to enlist but had been turned down.[70] The official reason given was that the shipping companies wished to retain a pool of labour as many white seamen had volunteered. The length of time many black men had been unemployed and the complaints that cheap Chinese labour was being used in their stead suggested to Gunning that '[t]he ship-owners seem to ... be trying to starve the coloured seamen into submission, using... all the pressure they can bring to keep them from serving their country against German militarism'. He went on:

> These men bitterly complained because they were not allowed to join either the Army or Navy. They cannot understand why, and said that they were British born, proud of the freedom they get under the old flag, and also realising that if anything unforeseen should happen, if we should be beaten, that they would lose the same liberties as we should, and this without being given a chance to defend themselves. I think there is a good deal of logic in their argument. We should raise a strong coloured battalion of good fighting mettle, and thousands more to follow, only give them the chance ... I think it would be a brighter victory to crush this horrible militarism with our glorious voluntary system, and we can do it cheap by giving the millions of British subjects who are to-day debarred from enlistment this one and only chance of showing their patriotism for the flag that gives them freedom.[71]

The South Wales NSFU even compiled a list of black men of British nationality prepared to join the 'battalion of coloured men' then being formed.[72] This was most likely a reference to the BWIR whose first battalion had just arrived in England. Although most men were recruited in the Caribbean, West Indians already resident in the UK also joined the regiment. Eventually, the BWIR would became a catchall for non-white recruits from the Indian subcontinent and South Africa who enquired at recruiting offices in the metropole.

There was also a pragmatic desire to present an inclusive vision of Empire which also bolstered the more positive attitude towards black volunteers. This was highlighted in a court case shortly after the first West Indian contingents arrived in October 1915. Lawrence Bristow Graham appeared at Lewes Police Court and was charged with making remarks likely to jeopardise recruiting to His Majesty's forces. In a Hotel taproom in Seaford, Graham demanded of two privates in the British West Indies Regiment why they had enlisted for one shilling a day. Ministers such as Churchill, Asquith and Lloyd George were receiving £15,000 per year he pointed out. Graham had continued: 'Look at your King, he's a German, and so are all the rest of the family, why don't you lay down your arms and do no fighting'.[73] Graham was reported to have accosted other black soldiers in the street and suggested that white men should be left to fight their own battles. The West Indians were fools to fight for the Empire. Graham was sentenced to six months' imprisonment with hard labour. The local press applauded the sentence and accused Graham of belittling the patriotism of the soldiers of the BWIR who found themselves away from home in a strange country and climate.

But supporters of black enlistment had other motives. By the middle years of the war, black men, hoping to benefit from the employment opportunities created by the war, formed a more visible presence in some industrial cities. They were subjected to the attentions of a hostile press preoccupied with relationships between white women and black men. In Manchester, the press initiated a campaign to oppose the use of black men in munitions factories where they would readily come into contact with munitionettes who were themselves the focus of much official anxiety. Encouraging the black man to enlist instead was one solution, as 'Father of Four Girls', a correspondent to the *Daily Dispatch*, made plain: 'Compel some of us older men to go into the munitions factories before allowing this danger to exist. The place for many of these young fellows is in the army.'[74]

Pro-war enthusiasm in the West Indies and the need for manpower meant that the issue of black recruitment would inevitably have to be addressed by the War and Colonial Offices. The announcement, at the end of August 1914, that no contingents from the West Indies were to be accepted was greeted with disappointment.[75] The frustration felt by potential volunteers was expressed by a Barbadian who wrote to the West India Committee:

> We have put up sugar and money for the various subscriptions, but that won't win our battles. It's lives we desire to give as it's for the Empire that the Motherland is fighting, and it is only fair to give these colonies the opportunity of showing the true spirit of patriotism that they have always evinced in the past.[76]

In May 1915, the War Office finally conceded and communicated to the Colonial Office that West Indian volunteers would be accepted on the following terms: that they were passed fit before embarkation; had their transport costs to the UK paid by the colonial government and, on arrival, be enlisted as infantrymen for the duration of the war only.[77]

While the War Office had agreed in principle to West Indian drafts, local recruiters and middle-class supporters of the contingents were concerned that the prestige accruing from greater participation in the war effort should not be dispersed among the Jamaican population in general. Appeals for volunteers reached diverse audiences and were open to manifold interpretation, but recruiters attempted to articulate the call for recruits in such a way as to limit the response from the black masses.

At a rally in October 1915, Brigadier-General Blackden, the head of the Jamaican local forces, stated that 'The men of the Contingent were going to fight against the Germans, people of great scientific ideas – people who had discovered the latest methods of warfare. Therefore they wanted the best and most intelligent men'. He complained that it was often 'an undersized, ragged, barefooted set of fellows, who came forward probably to get a meal'.[78] In an attempt to discourage the black majority who were the mainstay of manual labour Blackden insisted:

> We ... want to see Jamaica represented by its most intelligent people ... although there is ... room for the muscle that drives the bayonet home, there is ... more room for the brain that can use the complicated weapons of modern warfare.[79]

Previously, Blackden had issued a circular stipulating enlistment regulations for the contingents that envisaged a certification system for skilled men to assist future deployment. The proposal was another attempt by Blackden to discourage the majority of the black male population from volunteering:

> for the good name of Jamaica ... these certificates should be sparingly given ... to really skilled men who have been examined by someone qualified to judge ... Preference should be given to unmarried men between 20 and 30 years of age who are in a position to feed and clothe themselves until embarkation.[80]

Blackden implied that the honour of military service should be extended to the respectable working class – the artisan or skilled workman – or successful peasant proprietors; men insulated, to some degree, from the uncertainties of the plantation economy. Military service was presented as a privilege that reflected standing in Jamaican society. However, a correspondent to the *Daily Gleaner*, under the apposite pseudonym 'Civis' [Citizen] expressed concern that the 'better class of men' were hesitant to volunteer as they were not confident

that hard-earned civilian status would be reflected in military rank. This sentiment proved to be well-founded when men of the black and brown middle class
presented themselves for commissions in the metropole.[81]

The white Jamaican elite were guaranteed high status in the military hierarchy as they were regarded as the 'natural' leaders of the colony. But in many
cases they proved less than enthusiastic volunteers. Jamaica represented a safe
haven from conscription, introduced in the metropole in March 1916. The
Jamaican Military Service Act of 1917 did provide for compulsory enlistment,
but, although a register listing men of military age was compiled, conscription
was never implemented. However, moral pressure was applied to ensure that
the Jamaican contingents were officered by white men. If the responsibilities of
privilege were forsaken, the black and brown-skinned middle-class might step
into the breach.

A *Daily Gleaner* editorial of November 1915 demanded, 'what are we to say
of the young men in this country who, with no dependants are living a life of
ease while the peasants come forward in their hundred to serve their sovereign.
Has position no obligations? Has it ceased to be the duty of Gentlemen to lead
where danger lies?'[82] A letter to the *Daily Gleaner*, signed, 'Arma Virumque
Cano' ['I sing of Arms and the Man'], the opening line of Virgil's *Aeneid*, argued
that the contingents should be officered by white men familiar with the West
Indian personality. Potential officers should be debarred from travelling direct
to the UK in the hope of gaining a commission in a more prestigious regiment.
Those who failed to volunteer should be shamed by the publication of their
names and photographs in the *Daily Gleaner*. 'Arma' invoked not only the
Roman heroic tradition but the chivalric discourse of Empire, and 'appeal[led]
to those men ... still sitting on the fence to come forward and "play the Game"'.[83]

This attempt to appeal to the ethos of athleticism that, since the last quarter of the nineteenth century, had served as a defining symbol of Imperial and
military effort, was elaborated by Harold Castle, who had played cricket for
Jamaica in the mid-1890s:

> It is up to you, young sportsman of Jamaica, to officer the men of Jamaica who
> are willing to fight for humanity and freedom. Never let it be said that the men
> who can play cricket, football, polo and tennis, and race, hung back when the
> greatest of all games, the fight for freedom and Empire was going on.
> Remember the true sportsman makes the ideal leader of men; he knows his
> team and they will back him through thick and thin ... What keeps you back?
> Are you ashamed to go with the Jamaicans? If that be so, let me tell you that
> the men of this country will make history. They have all the best attributes of a
> first class fighting man, and when trained thoroughly, will, as our General told
> us, 'be a credit to the Empire'.[84]

Castle later suggested that a special Jamaican brigade, along the lines of the public school battalions in the metropole, should be raised to encourage men from the middle and upper classes to enlist.[85]

These appeals, although targeted at the white echelons of Jamaican society, were also heeded by the black and brown middle class who saw themselves as the true representatives of Jamaica. This attitude, present even among those with nationalistic leanings, often emanated from relative economic success and greater exposure to metropolitan education and social values. W. G. Hinchcliffe acknowledged the contribution of peasant and working-class volunteers. He also fostered the view that military service would be rewarded with civil rights and improved circumstances for Africans and their descendants throughout the Empire. But Hinchcliffe simultaneously insisted the involvement of the black and brown middle classes was essential for an effective Jamaican contribution:

> Jamaica has not yet been truly represented to the British people ... until the more desirable class of men ... go forth ... I ... feel proud of the class of men that have already gone forth ... from huts obscure, and from 'the bush' ...While I am equally dissatisfied to know that they, and only they, have gone to be the historical representatives of this loyal and ancient mixed colony, I am glad to know that not withstanding, that on them the laurels will fall, which must eventually, lift the standard of the African race, and cause oppression into oblivion to fall.[86]

The 'desirable class of men' – the black and brown middle class – laid claim to a greater share in the privileges of Jamaican society and sought to place distance between themselves and the black masses. However, despite their attainments, they were routinely rejected from army commissions in both Jamaica and the metropole. Many found themselves stranded in London, penniless and unable to pay the return fare, having paid their own passage and resigned their Jamaican employment. In these circumstances they were forced to call at the Colonial Office for assistance.

Abraham G. Kirkwood travelled to England in 1915 having decided not to join the Jamaican War Contingent due to 'the mixed class of men enlisted'. His attitude was not unique. In July 1918, Jamaica's Governor Probyn supported a suggestion by the Barbados Recruiting Committee for a regiment of 'the better class of coloured men'. It was asserted these men were reluctant to serve alongside the black labourers and artisans who composed the bulk of the BWIR.[87] Although passed fit in Jamaica, Kirkwood was rejected at several recruiting depots in England. A Colonial Office official suspected that both racial and physical considerations had played a part in Kirkwood's failure to find a posting. 'I am not sure that he is unmixed European though he said his father was a Scotsman and his mother Canadian ... he is a rather depressed melancholy person, delicate looking and respectably dressed'.[88] Here, the official echoed the eugenicist-inspired belief that fusion of the races would result in physical and mental degeneration.

Governor Manning, was keenly aware of the embarrassing shortfall of white recruits in Jamaica but wished to address the matter in ways that would continue to exclude black and brown men and maintain an illusion of racial order. Appealing for guidance to Andrew Bonar Law, the Secretary of State for the Colonies, Manning stated:

> There are a certain number of young men, among applicants for commissions with the Jamaica contingent, who are not of pure European descent but who otherwise are qualified for commissions. I should like to have the discretion to recommend *certain of them* for commissions with the Jamaica contingent provided that *only those whose colour is not pronounced should be selected.*[89]

However, although the Colonial Office concurred that there would be 'difficulty in finding men qualified for commissions ... if ... selection is restricted to those of unmixed European blood',[90] the army insisted the Manual of Military Law be strictly adhered to. The Army Council, the military executive, were 'averse to any officers being appointed to commissions in the Jamaica Contingent who are not of unmixed European blood ... [any] deficiency will be supplied from the trained and partially trained officers in this country'.[91] Correspondents to the Jamaican press pointed out the injustice of this ruling by arguing that non-whites could reach the rank of major[92] in the Indian Army and that local officers would be better placed to understand and motivate the black rank-and-file. Local recruitment would also be assisted if men felt that they might gain a commission in the future.[93] A *Daily Gleaner* editorial complacently argued that, as some non-whites had managed to secure commissions despite the regulations, the racial barrier would eventually be eroded by default. Under these circumstances 'any young man with no real hindrance to enlistment is disgraced if he does not enlist'.[94] Black and brown Jamaicans were faced with two choices – volunteer and endure official obstruction and discrimination or be branded as cowards.

Notes

1 Joseph, 'British West Indies Regiment', 98–9; 'Fusilier', 'The British West Indies Regiment', *United Empire*, VII, 1916, 26.
2 *The Times*, 25 October 1915, p. 7.
3 DG 25 October 1915, p. 8; 26 October 1915, p. 13.

 4 Rev. J. W. Graham and Tom Redcam, *Round the Blue Light* (Kingston: Jamaica Times Printery, 1918), p. 5.

 5 *DG* 26 October 1915, p. 6.

 6 *DG* 27 May 1916, p. 4.

 7 Brian Dyde, *The Empty Sleeve: The Story of the West India Regiment of the British Army* (St. Johns, Antigua: Hansib, 1997), pp. 179–80. For the early history of the West India Regiments and the wider black presence in the British Army see John D. Ellis, 'Nineteenth Century Culture and Society: The Visual Representation, Role and Origin of Black Soldiers in British Army Regiments During the Early 19th Century' (Nottingham University: unpublished MA dissertation, 2000); Roger Buckley, *Slaves in Red Coats: The British West India Regiments, 1795–1815* (New Haven: Yale University Press, 1979).

 8 Dyde, *Empty Sleeve*, pp. 191–241.

 9 Major A. B. Ellis, *The History of the First West India Regiment* (London: Chapman and Hall, 1885), pp. 21, 23.

10 Ibid., p. 13

11 Ibid., 14–15

12 John Henderson, *Jamaica* (London: Adam and Charles Black, 1906), 64.

13 *DG*, 20 October 1915, p. 11.

14 *Zouave*, January 1911, p. 1.

15 Killingray, 'All the King's Men?', pp. 166–9.

16 *Zouave*, August 1911, p. 114. Henderson, *Jamaica*, p. 63. See Dyde, *Empty Sleeve*, pp. 245–6 and Bryan, *Jamaican People*, p. 270 for rivalry between police and soldiers.

17 Killingray, 'All the King's Men?', p. 166. Despite the desire to project racial homogeneity within the metropolitan army, Ireland and Scotland provided substantial numbers of recruits, a situation that continued up to and during the First World War. Martial race theories held that the Celtic races made natural soldiers, although the Irish came to be viewed with some ambivalence; at once childlike, unruly and emotional: Keith Jeffrey, 'The Irish Military Tradition and the British Empire', in Keith Jeffrey (ed.), *'An Irish Empire'? Aspects of Ireland and the British Empire* (Manchester: Manchester University Press, 1996), pp. 94–122; H. J. Hanham, 'Religion and nationality in the mid–Victorian army', in M. R. D. Foot (ed.), *War and Society* (London: Elek, 1973), pp. 159–81.

18 Lionel Caplan, *Warrior Gentlemen: 'Gurkhas' in the Western Imagination* (Oxford: Berghahn Books, 1995), pp. 88–90, 93, 103; David Omissi, *The Sepoy and the Raj: The Indian Army 1860–1940* (London: Macmillan, 1994), pp. 28–9, 32–4.

19 Timothy H. Parsons, *The African Rank and File: Social Implications of Colonial Military Service in the King's African Rifles, 1902–1964* (Oxford: James Currey, 1999), p. 54.

20 *Manual of Military Law* (London: HMSO, 1914), p. 471.

21 Omissi, *Sepoy and the Raj*, 159–62.

22 For Indian involvement in the South African War see Bill Nasson, *The South African War* (London: Arnold, 1999), pp. 141, 249, 282; David Omissi, 'India: Some Perceptions of Race and Empire', in Omissi and Thompson (eds.), *Impact of the South African War*, pp. 215–17.

23 PRO WO108/399 No. 245 Secretary of State for War to Roberts 6.4.00, No. 352A Roberts to SSW 10 October 1900, No. 352B SSW to Roberts 16.10.00; Dyde, *Empty Sleeve*, pp. 243, 248–9.

24 PRO WO108/399 Nos. 1004 and 1022 Kitchener to SSW 11 and 17 March 1902; Emanoel Lee, *To the Bitter End: A Photographic History of the Boer War 1899–1902*

(London: Viking, 1985), pp. 200, 202–3. See also Pieter Labuschagne, *Ghostriders of the Anglo-Boer War (1899–1902): The Role and Contribution of Agterryers* (Johannesburg: University of South Africa,1999); Peter Warwick, *Black People in the South African War* (Cambridge: Cambridge University Press, 1983); Bill Nasson, 'Black Communities in Natal and the Cape', in Omissi and Thompson, *Impact of the South African War*, pp. 38–55.

25 *DG* 5 October 1915, p. 8; JT 23 November 1914, p. 24; JT 24 October 1914, p. 15.

26 *DG* 9 July 1915, p. 6.

27 *Manual of Military Law*, London, 1914, p. 471.

28 *British Nationality and Status of Aliens Act*, 1914, p. 33.

29 *Stratford Express* 14 July 1917, p. 7.

30 'Fusilier', 'The British West Indies Regiment', p. 29.

31 Maurice Hankey, *The Supreme Command*, I (London: George Allen and Unwin, 1961), pp. 171–2, 205; Greenhut, 'The Imperial Reserve', 55.

32 Joseph, 96, 'The British West Indies Regiment', p. 111; DC, 6 August 1914, p. 9; *Jamaica War Contribution* (Cd. 8695), London, 1917.

33 PRO WO32/5094 WO Minute AAG to AG 23 January 1917.

34 Quoted in Bourke, *Dismembering the Male*, p. 149.

35 Alfred Egbert Horner, *From the Islands of the Sea: Glimpses of a West Indian Battalion in France* (Nassau 1919: Guardian), pp. 5–6.

36 Horner, *From the Islands of the Sea*, p. 7.

37 Bourke, *An Intimate History of Killing*, pp. 51–5; Bet-El, 'Men and Soldiers', p. 89.

38 Siegfried Sassoon, *Memoirs of an Infantry Officer* (London: Faber and Faber 1965 [1930]), p. 24.

39 Charles Edmonds, *A Subaltern's War* (London: Peter Davies, 1929), pp. 53–5. Trophy-hunting, which ranged from the personal effects of the dead to body parts, was seen as 'proof' of martial virility – a tally of killing power – across the racial spectrum; Bourke, *An Intimate History of Killing*, pp. 37–43.

40 Samuel Hynes, *The Soldiers' Tale: Bearing Witness to Modern War* (London: Pimlico, 1998), pp. 76–80.

41 Graves, *Goodbye to All That* (Harmondsworth: Penguin, 1960 [1929]), p. 155. There were claims that the German army offered 400 marks for the capture of live black soldiers in the early stages of the war. A German veteran, quoted in the *New York Times*, stated that 'throughout the war German soldiers lived in great fear, and even terror, of the negroes': *New York Times* 26 January 1919, p. 1. German representations of race were greatly influenced by the French deployment of black troops, especially when Senegalese battalions were deployed in the post-war occupation of the Rhineland. See Annabelle Melzer, 'Spectacles and sexualties: The "Mise-en-Scene" of the "Tirailleur Senegalais" on the Western Front, 1914–1920', in Melman, *Borderlines*, pp. 228–31; Benedikt Stuchev, review of *Von Wilden aller Rassen niedergemetzelt*, *Journal of Imperial and Commonwealth History*, 31:1, 2003, 128–9.

42 Graves, *Goodbye to All That*, p. 155.

43 Ibid., p. 152.

44 Quoted in Dyde, *Empty Sleeve*, p. 243.

45 See PRO CO318/339/6828 and /28543; CO318/340/32243 and /46561 include details of Jamaicans enlisting in England.

46 PRO WO364/3753; JT 3 April 1915, p. 1.

47 PRO WO364/4505; CO137/724/111885 Gunner E. Watson RGA to Secretary Dominion War Committee, CO 12 October 1917.

48 *Daily Sketch*, 7 March 1916 and *Daily Mirror*, 8 November 1915 cuttings in ICS/WIC/2/BWIR Album of Press Cuttings (hereafter BWIR Album); *Illustrated Western Weekly News*, 11 March 1916, p. 27.

49 *Stratford Express*, 19 May 1915, p. 3.

50 Ibid., 29 May 1915, p. 2.

51 *Stratford Express*, 12 May 1917, p. 3; West Ham Police Court Register of Charges 1917, p. 101, entry for 3 May 1917.

52 PRO CO137/715/20904 Manning to Bonar Law SSC 15 April 1916; *Zouave* November 1914, p. 181.

53 PRO CO137/715/20904 Minute 15 May 1916.

54 PRO CO137/715/20904 Minute 3 May 1916.

55 *DG* 14 June 1916, p. 4; 8 May 1916, p. 10; 19 January 1917, p. 9; 7 September 1917, p. 4.

56 Bourke, *An Intimate History of Killing*, pp. 56–8.

57 'The autobiography of Norman Washington Manley', *Jamaica Journal*, 7:1/2, 6.

58 *The Times*, 11 July 1917, p. 5; 12 July 1917, p. 5; 23 July 1917, p. 5.

59 *Crisis*, 16: 2, June 1918, p. 59.

60 Ibid., p. 60.

61 PRO WO32/4765 Ministry of National Service to Secretary WO 20 March 1918; Grindle, CO to USS, FO 22 March 1918.

62 PRO WO32/4765 'Enlistment of Men of Colour' (Copy) enclosed with Ministry of National Service to Sec. WO 20 March 1918.

63 PRO WO32/4765 General White, New York to WO (copy of Secret telegram) 19 February 1918.

64 PRO CO323/781/28914 WO to USS, CO, 13 June 1918; CO323/781/30020 WO to USS, Foreign Office (herafter FO), June 1918; CO323/781/31081 WO to USS, CO, 24 June 1918; CO323/782/41475 WO to USS, CO, 24 August 1918; WO32/4765 WO to Gen. White 17 June 1918 (copy telegram); Gen. White to WO 26 June 1918 (copy telegram); WO to Gen. White 27 June 1918 (copy telegram).

65 PRO WO32/4765 Cubitt, Sec. Army Council (hereafter AC) to USS, FO 3 July 1918.

66 PRO WO32/4765 Leech (Minister Havana) to FO 21 June 1918 (copy telegram).

67 CO323/782/41475 WO to USS, CO, 24 August 1918.

68 *Seaman*, 22 October 1915, p. 6 and 19 November 1915, p. 5.

69 Tabili, *'We Asked for British Justice'*, pp. 86–93.

70 Reprinted in *Seaman*, 19 November 1915, p. 5.

71 Ibid.

72 *Seaman* 22 October 1915, p. 6. The court trying the nine Barbadian stowaways had earlier heard that 'a Major Lucas was forming a coloured battalion at Cardiff': *Stratford Express*, 29 May 1915, p. 2.

73 *Newhaven Chronicle*, 18 November 1915, n.p.

74 *Daily Dispatch*, 8 August 1917, p. 3.

75 *WICC*, No. 419 20 October 1914, p. 481.

76 *WICC*, No. 421 17 November 1914, p. 571.

77 PRO CO137/712 WO to Sec. State, CO 19 May 1915.

78 *DG*, 20 October 1915, p. 14.

79   *DG*, 12 October 1915, p. 13.

80   *DG* 31 May 1915, p. 13.

81   *DG* 17 May 1916, p. 10.

82   *DG* 27 November 1915, p. 8.

83   *DG* 20 November 1915, p. 6.

84   *DG* 6 December 1915, p. 11.

85   *DG* 19 May 1916, p. 4.

86   *DG* 12 May 1916, p. 10.

87   PRO CO137/726/42533 Hutson to Barbados Recruiting Ctte 4 May 1918 (enclosed in Probyn to Long 31 July 1918).

88   PRO CO137/713 CO Minute 8 September 1915.

89   PRO CO137/711/54861 Manning to SSC 26 November 1915 (my emphasis).

90   PRO CO137/711/54861 Minute 27 November 1915.

91   PRO CO318/336/57697 Cubitt, WO to USSCO 14 December 1915.

92   Subedar-major was the highest rank normally attainable by an Indian: Omissi, *Indian Voices of the Great War*, p. xxi.

93   *DG* 3 December 1915, p. 4.

94   Ibid., p. 8.

4 Jamaican soldiers in Europe and the Middle East

'Neither women nor coloured troops could be used in Field Ambulances or convoys to replace the medical personnel. Strength, coolness and courage, in addition to technical training, are required.'[1] So declared Sir Arthur Sloggett, Director-General of army medical services in a War Office minute of January 1917, unaware that a black Jamaican, Joe Clough, who settled in England in 1906, served as an ambulance driver in France for much of the war.[2] Representations of black men and white women as irrational, emotional and deficient in self-control were restated in an attempt to prevent encroachment onto the white male domain of the front line. As Sloggett made these remarks imaginings of white masculine supremacy had been severely dented by the dramatic volume of shell-shock cases and other concerns regarding the physical and mental staying power of British troops, particularly after the Somme offensive. The exclusion of black men and white women from the front line became more imperative as part of a damage-limitation exercise to curtail the erosion of white masculine authority in both Imperial and metropolitan contexts.

Black recruits were subject to policies that perpetuated the racial division of labour on the plantations, tending to exclude them from military duties on the front line or in technical operations. When proposals were put forward that men of the British West Indies Regiment might replace men of the Royal Engineers to free the latter for the front line, a War Office official responded the use of 'coloured men would ... be most dangerous to the efficiency ... of the armies in France'.[3] To underline the point, a memo from the senior military authority, the Army Council, stated 'In any question of substitution it is essential that the difference between skilled and unskilled labour should be borne in mind.'[4] Such dismissive attitudes to black soldiers came from the highest level. Sir Douglas Haig, the Commander-in-Chief in France, categorised the BWIR as 'supplementary' troops, meaning that they should provide logistical support, rather undertake front-line duties. In fact, combat troops were ineffective without such assistance. The Army Council acknowledged that for every man in the firing line three more were required in support, to provide supplies and other ancillary services. Soldiers on the ground believed the ratio was perhaps as high as fourteen to one. The BWIR came to form a significant part of this infrastructure on the Western Front and later in Italy.[5]

Between May and October 1915 negotiations between the Colonial Office and the War Office established the terms for the acceptance of Jamaican and other West Indian contingents who formed the BWIR. Pay was set at standard British Army rates, while separation allowances for dependants were laid down at the reduced level already applied to the West India Regiment and presumed a lower standard of living in the colonies. By April 1916, three service battalions were assembled and, after training at Seaford Camp in Sussex, they were posted to the Egyptian Expeditionary Force. By the end of the war a further nine battalions were created. Jamaica provided 303 of the 397 officers and 9977 of the 15204 other ranks (76.3 and 65.6 per cent respectively) for the twelve BWIR battalions (for details of the Jamaican contingents see table overleaf). The next largest contingent came from Trinidad and Tobago, consisting of forty officers and 1438 other ranks (around 10 per cent of the total in each category).[6] Following the precedent in other black units, including the West India Regiment, the commissioned officers were white. Non-whites were restricted to non-commissioned rank.

As the first Jamaican War Contingent sailed for England on 9 November 1915, the island's press proudly proclaimed Jamaica's arrival on the world

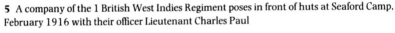

5 A company of the 1 British West Indies Regiment poses in front of huts at Seaford Camp, February 1916 with their officer Lieutenant Charles Paul

Dates and numbers of the Jamaican War Contingents

Contingent	Date	Officers	Men
First	8 Nov. 1915	12	722
Draft	24 Dec. 1915	2	53
Second	7 Jan. 1916	22	1100
Third	6 March 1916	25	1115
—	26 May 1916	12	—
Fourth	30 Sep. 1916	36	726
Fifth	30 March 1917	30	1656
Sixth	1 June 1917	33	1656
Seventh	20 July 1917	22	851
Eighth	26 Aug. 1917	31	1304
Ninth	2 Oct. 1917	18	985

Notes: A further 465 men were recruited but were not drafted overseas. Not all men who sailed with the JWC successfully enlisted in the BWIR.
Source: Stephen A. Hill (ed.), Who's Who in Jamaica, 1919–1920 (Kingston: Gleaner Co., 1920), p. 245.

stage. The men of Jamaica: 'young, virile, bubbling over with life, proud soldiers of that Empire on which the sun never sets ... [were] writing possibly the most glorious page in the long, and chequered story of this isle ... It was Our Day, Jamaica's Day ... Jamaica, as Jamaica was now in the war'.[7] Military training was perceived to have effected physical, moral and social improvement in the men – slouches and the downward gaze of social inferiority and deference were noticeable by their absence. Townsmen could boast they possessed the same conditioned physique as their peers from the countryside.[8] Indeed, the contingent was held to be matching metropolitan masculine ideals and by volunteering could claim a degree of equality. The men had captured the Jamaican public imagination, and combined with a sense of military camaraderie and purpose this bolstered racial pride.

This early optimism was swiftly dashed. Away from Jamaican shores the men would be faced by a military apparatus whose traditions and structures existed to maintain obedience and perpetuate the social order of Empire. In many respects the treatment meted out to the volunteers was presaged by the experience of the West India Regiment during its decline from the late 1880s. In common with other black troops in the Empire, the WIR was designated a 'native' regiment. Despite the regiment's admirable record, when its services could be dispensed with on the front-line, the men were regularly demoted to auxiliary or labouring duties. When stationed in Jamaica the WIR was deployed on fatigues to load and unload the kit of white regiments stationed on the island.[9] The term 'native' served to imply that the men to whom it was applied were not of front-line calibre and fit only to serve in subsidiary roles. 'Native' status was further compounded by the low standing occupied in the British military hierarchy by all men employed in a labouring role, regardless of race.

The WIR had played a key role in the West African campaigns of the last quarter of the nineteenth century. But the regiment was never deployed at battalion strength in the African campaigns of the First World War, even though small-scale 'bush-fighting', of which the regiment had great experience, was the norm. After a brief spell of duty in Cameroon, the first battalion returned to Jamaica for the duration of the war. This was in part due to the desire of the colonial authorities to have a force on hand in case of internal unrest. When it was proposed the 1WIR be deployed in the event of a Mexican or German incursion into British Honduras, the War Office stipulated 'that a portion of the contingent of the British West Indies Regiment in training at Jamaica is utilized for guard duties and held available to *maintain internal order*'.[10] Meanwhile, the second battalion, maintained at only half-strength, was deployed chiefly on lines of communication in West and East Africa. Shortly before the close of the war, the 2WIR arrived in Palestine to guard Turkish prisoners.[11]

The demarcation of black men as 'native' troops and the perpetuation of discourses questioning the ability of black men to meet the demands of modern soldiering, served to ensure most BWIR battalions were deployed as labour units. The exceptions were the first, second and fifth battalions who served in the Egyptian Expeditionary Force (EEF) throughout the war. This policy disregarded early assurances the regiment would be constituted as an infantry unit. During 1916 and 1917 the majority of the BWIR battalions were stationed in France and Belgium maintaining supplies to the artillery. Shells were unloaded from supply trains and relayed in stages via 'parks' and 'dumps' to the ammunition columns that serviced the batteries. This was hazardous work involving the risk of crush injuries and accidental detonation as well as enemy shellfire. The men were also engaged in road building, railway construction, concrete mixing and digging trenches.

From early 1918, several of the battalions were stationed at Taranto in Italy, a major logistical centre for the British forces in the Italian campaign. Here the men were even further removed from the front-line, carrying out the work of stevedores – loading and unloading ships, coaling the supply ships and carrying out general fatigue duties at the base camp.[12]

Members of the BWIR described themselves as 'King George Steam Engine',[13] a term reflecting the arduous nature of the work and the affiliation toward the monarch felt by many West Indian volunteers. The war diary of the sixth battalion notes that on one occasion sixty men unloaded 375 tons of ammunition in under two hours. Reverend John Luce Ramson, a padre attached to the ninth battalion, reflected that even members of the white Jamaican elite were forced to reappraise their earlier prejudices.

> The best comment on the work our men have done, and are capable of doing, is perhaps that made in my hearing by an officer, a Jamaican himself and afflicted in former days apparently, with the strange disease so common in the Island, viz. the habit of running down and disparaging anything Jamaican: he said 'I used to think that it could really be no good at all, no real help to the war I mean, getting these fellows over here, but, I tell you what, I have jolly well changed my mind!'.[14]

Although deployed as labourers, the BWIR men stationed in France and Belgium were regularly in the line of fire, but were denied the opportunity to fire a shot in anger themselves. The war diaries of BWIR battalions serving in France and Belgium show the men were regularly in exposed positions and suffered casualties as a result. One company of the fourth battalion, mainly composed of the sixth Jamaican war contingent, had to lay water pipes between

6 'King George Steam Engine' – Men of the British West Indies Regiment stacking 8 inch shells with Australian troops, Gordon Road, Ypres, October 1917

first and second line trenches. Here they were subject to shellfire and infantry attack without weapons for self-defence.[15] Several men of the fourth battalion were honoured for extinguishing fires in a blazing ammunition dump.[16] Letters from Jamaican servicemen indicate the men took up the euphemistic banter which came to characterise the apparently stoical, but often cynical British Tommy. J. E. R. Stevens, a white sergeant in the Jamaican War Contingent (JWC), referred to shells as 'iron rations' and 'souvenirs' as he recalled the scene when the regimental band was shelled on their parade ground: 'One fellow who evidently got a direct hit had his head blown off ... another had his legs off, so you see, it's not all beer and skittles, in this corner of the world.'[17] Eighteen out of twenty-four bandsmen were killed in this incident.[18]

Faced with these circumstances, some West Indian volunteers broke under the strain, as was tragically illustrated in the court martial report of a young Jamaican, Herbert Morris, executed for desertion, aged just seventeen. Morris served with the 6 BWIR, which had been raised in Jamaica between November 1916 and March 1917. Stationed close to the front line, Morris's battalion served a battery of eighty pound guns at 'Essex Farm' near Poperinghe, in the Ypres Salient. This battery formed part of the largest artillery formation yet seen, assembled by Haig, the British commander-in-chief, in preparation for the campaign of Third Ypres, (Passchendaele). In the fifteen-day barrage preceding the main Allied thrust on 31 July, 2297 British guns fired over four million shells – four times the number fired prior to the attack on the Somme. The Germans responded in kind and the 6BWIR experienced daily casualties.[19] Father Van Walleghem, a Belgian Catholic priest who lived in the area, recalled that the West Indians became 'enormously afraid of the guns' and were often bewildered and disorientated during the shelling.[20] Alfred Horner, who joined the battalion at the beginning of September related that 'a full range of Boche "heavies" comes our way, making the day and night alike a terror to all'.[21]

As the bombardment commenced, Morris went absent without leave until he was picked up at Boulogne and given fourteen days field punishment. On 20 August, having seen seven of his comrades become casualties, Morris absconded again, jumping from the lorry taking him to his battery. He was arrested, once more at Boulogne, when he entered a rest camp with no ticket of leave. Morris had clear symptoms of battle fatigue or 'shell shock'. He pleaded to the court 'I am troubled with my head and cannot stand the sound of the guns. I reported to the Dr. [sic] and he gave me no medicine or anything'.[22] In the absence of a medical officer to confirm Morris's statement, the court made no attempt to adjourn the case for medical reports. Morris had to rely instead on the testimony of two character witnesses who stated he had been a willing worker, was of above average intelligence and had given no cause for trouble.

The subsequent death sentence passed by the court was confirmed by Field Marshall Haig, and Morris was paraded in front of the battalion as an example. Having dictated a letter to Padre Horner for his parents, Morris was executed on the morning of 20 September 1917 by a firing squad composed of seven West Indians and three white soldiers.[23]

The case of Albert Morris is an extreme example of what could happen if a soldier fell into the hands of the courts martial, rather than being directed for medical treatment. Other black soldiers did undergo treatment for psychiatric manifestations of battle stress. Private L. Jones of the 4BWIR was admitted to Number 2 General Hospital, at Le Havre and was diagnosed as suffering from acute mania. He was reported to be:

> talking continuously and incoherently ... the general trend of his talk was partly religious and partly voicing his delusions of persecution ... He is unduly emotional and he readily weeps. He is confused mentally and he can give practically no account of himself ... He is rambling and inconsequent in his conversation in a childish and simple minded way.[24]

Eustace Shaw, of the same battalion, was admitted to hospital after attempting to murder a white Company Sergeant Major attached to the regiment in July 1918. There are no explicit references to Shaw's race or colour in the medical reports, which also indicate he was reasonably well-treated while in hospital. However, records do report he had become 'depressed and anxious under constant air-raids'.[25] On admission to hospital he was reported to be 'noisy and violent, threatening'[26] and apparently suffering from hallucinations. To the army medical services this was proof of black irrationality and lack of self-control. Later statements from the hospital were glad to report Shaw was 'cheerful and has insight into his previous state of depression. He has now been free from depression, delusion and hallucinations for several weeks and is usefully employed.'[27] But the medical staff doubted whether he would cope with a return to duty. 'He would relapse under stress of further military service.'[28] Shaw was subsequently discharged from the Nottinghamshire County War Hospital in January 1919. In spite of the marked improvement in his condition, he was held at Broadmoor until a passage was arranged for him back to Jamaica in early 1920 on a ship containing separate accommodation for 'coloured personnel'.[29]

Faced with these conditions, the men of the BWIR assumed the *nom de guerre*, 'King George Steam Engine', as a means of disassociating themselves from the inferior status marked out for them as labour battalions. Within the military establishment labour battalions were viewed as the place for men deemed of low intellect or poor physique – unsuitable material for the front line. The Military Service Acts of 1916 established that men unfit for the front line

Labour unit
Seen as inferior,
but necessary

could be enlisted for home garrison or non-combative duties. In January 1917 the War Office established the Labour Directorate to co-ordinate the work of all labour units, henceforth designated the Labour Corps. With mounting casualties, recruiting officers made sure no human raw material went to waste – Denis Winter cites the example of an infantryman who had a foot blown off being transferred to a labour battalion. As the Allied forces collapsed in the face of the German Spring offensive of 1918, white British labour battalions were armed and remained so for the duration of the war, taking their place in the firing line when necessary.[30]

Although labour units were regarded as an inferior species in the military hierarchy they were essential to military operations. The labour corps built railways and roads, dug trenches, constructed accommodation and handled supplies and freed frontline battalions from fatigue duties. By the Armistice nearly 125,000 men were serving in labour battalions on the Western Front, supplemented by over 20,000 South African labourers, 96,000 Chinese and smaller contingents from Egypt and India.[31]

Deployment to labour battalions served, on occasion, to punish men who failed to show sufficient combative spirit. Some commanding officers believed sufficient stigma was attached to the labour battalions to discourage soldiers from disgracing themselves on the battlefield. On the 3 July 1916, two days after the start of the Somme offensive, Lieutenant-Colonel G. C. Sladen, commander of 1/5 Royal Warwickshire Regiment, submitted a report on the battalion's failure to withstand a small-scale German attack. Sladen complained of the 'utterly useless men' who had failed to use their rifles and bayonets, resulting in unnecessary casualties. Sladen believed the men were fearful of confronting the enemy and were of poor physique and stamina.

A court martial recommended 100 of the men involved be deployed on labour duties unloading ships. Eventually, 130 were posted on permanent fatigues. Some commanders disapproved of this measure, arguing any man who desired a safer posting would indulge in similar behaviour. It was suggested instead the disgraced men should be distributed among the other battalions of the regiment. The spirit of despair would be diluted and the offenders would experience suitable disapprobation from their new comrades. But Sladen insisted the men should not stay in the front line. They would be retained as labourers for, in his words:

> these men are degenerates – a source of danger to their comrades, their battalion and the Brigade and this will not be lessened by distribution to Warwickshire Bns. They should be replaced by drafts. This will not be a dangerous precedent as the stigma (the transfer) will be a deterrent.[32]

Disarming a soldier or group of men formed part of a ritual humiliation process. The handing over of weapons was most obviously a mark of defeat by a vanquished opponent who henceforth placed himself at the mercy of his captor. Being disarmed, or denied the opportunity to bear arms in the first place, signalled a man had failed to meet his ultimate public duty and symbolically removed the status and rights linked to discourses of armsbearing. In the early days of the Somme offensive another Court of Enquiry was established to enquire into the failure of the 11 Border Regiment to carry out an attack. The battalion, which formed part of the Fifth Army group, had lost twenty-five officers and over five hundred other ranks killed or wounded on the opening day of the battle. When they received instructions for a fresh assault, a number of men reported to the medical officer, Lieutenant G. N. Kirkwood, with shell shock. Others refused to pick up ammunition supplies as they moved forward.

One officer reported to the Enquiry 'that there was great lack of the offensive spirit in the party'. Major-General Gough, commander of the Fifth army, thundered: 'It is inconceivable how men who pledged themselves to fight and uphold the honour of the country could degrade themselves in such a manner and show an utter want of manly spirit and courage which at least is expected of every soldier and every Britisher'. He ordered that the men be paraded unarmed in front of their brigade and told they had disgraced themselves and their battalion. Kirkwood, the medical officer was accused of having 'undue sympathy with the men' and was replaced. [33]

An indication of the low regard with which the labour corps were held within the military hierarchy is evident in remarks made by Lieutenant-Colonel J. H. Patterson, a key supporter of Jewish recruitment during the war. Led by Ze'ev Jabotinsky, advocates of a Jewish Legion within the British Army believed this would result in Allied support for the Zionist cause after the war. Their efforts met with little official enthusiasm until late 1916 when it became apparent the army would face a manpower shortage before long. In August 1917, the formation of the 38 Royal Fusiliers, an entirely Jewish unit, was announced. The battalion arrived in Egypt in February 1918 and undertook training in preparation for offensive action against the Turks. However, Patterson, by now commander of the battalion, received some disappointing news that threatened temporarily to put an end to his plans. 'It was nothing less than a proposal to break up the battalion and allow the men to join Labour Units! This was undoubtedly a clever move on the part of the staff to ... bring the derision of the world upon the Jew.'[34]

Men of all ranks in the British West Indies Regiment were also keen to shed the stigma associated with labour battalion duties. When his men were assigned to road-mending and construction duties Alfred Horner stressed: 'do

* Stigma attached to
labour battalion duties

not think, though, for a single second that we had become mere labourers and had lost either our military style or military bearing'.[35] The observance of martial custom was regarded as a symbol of the incorporation of the BWIR into the masculine military tradition:

> [t]he click of the 'Present' given by the British Guard in response to the 'Eyes Right!' of the B[ritish] W[est] I[ndies Regiment] is more than a mere exchange of compliments – it is a recognition that in the 'War of Wars' our own coloured lads earned the right of entry into that fraternity which was displayed by our Empire in arms against German tyranny.[36]

Underpinning Horner's view was the fact that all the men in the BWIR were volunteers. They could therefore be regarded as heirs to a tradition, evident from the time of the French and Haitian revolutions, in which the volunteer, as opposed to conscript, mercenary or pressed soldier, served in pursuit of an ideal or just cause. Significantly, the volunteers of the BWIR started to arrive in the UK as the Derby Scheme was being tested, shortly before the introduction of conscription in March 1916. Under the scheme, devised by the minister for war, men were canvassed in their homes regarding their willingness to enlist, providing a degree of moral, if not, legal compulsion.[37] The West Indian volunteers had arrived under no such duress – a fact they expected to be given due regard in the application of discipline, as Horner observed:

> the West Indian boy is generally fond of his officer and will do any mortal thing for him. Sometimes he understands and rather admires discipline, but it must be just and fair. He is always conscious of the fact that he is a free soldier, no conscript and no mere labourer.[38]

The exemplary ideals captured in images of the citizen-volunteer became apparent in rivalries between the BWIR and the West India Regiment. These emerged when the WIR suppressed disturbances involving the Jamaica War Contingent in Kingston during June 1916 and in Port Royal the following May. Several hundred enlisted men could be gathered at any one time in Jamaica, awaiting transports for Europe or the Middle East, where they would be formally incorporated into the BWIR.[39] Inter-regimental tension reached a climax when proposals were mooted in East Africa to merge a BWIR detachment with the 2WIR in March 1918. By early April the idea had been abandoned. Jacob van Deventer, the South African general commanding British troops in East Africa, advised the War Office that

> [i]f it is carried out serious trouble will result involving riot and probable murder ... Some disorder has already been threatened ... [The] feeling [is] so

general that it is impossible to fix responsibility on individuals. The units [are] well behaved in other respects.[40]

In a series of memos, Captain Martinez, commander of the BWIR detachment, identified the main objections to the proposed merger:

The WIR is classified as a 2nd Class Colonial Force, while the BWIR was originally classed as a service unit and later on as an overseas contingent ... The men of the B.W.I. Regt. are in the main *volunteers* from a somewhat higher social class than those of the W. I. Regt. The Colonial authorities ... were aware of this, and to stimulate recruiting an entirely new regiment was raised. [41]

The class and race tensions between the two regiments were compounded by the fact that the WIR was composed mainly of Jamaicans whereas the BWIR was more representative of the West Indies as a whole. Non-Jamaicans in the BWIR did not wish to be absorbed into what would become an overwhelmingly Jamaican force. Martinez reported a feeling among the men that the BWIR, not the WIR, was the official representative of the West Indian colonies in the war effort, a position that would be undermined if the regiment, or parts of it, were merged with other units.[42]

Volunteers in the BWIR also wished to avoid the designation 'native' regiment, historically applied to the West India Regiment to denote inferior status and resulting in poorer conditions of service. But equally, they wished to preserve distinctions that indicated the BWIR was comprised of the 'better class of man'. The lower status of the WIR was confirmed when it was announced that the regiment could accept volunteers rejected from the BWIR on grounds of illiteracy.[43] For their part, the regular soldiers of the West India Regiment insisted their experience and professional calling as soldiers merited higher status. Volunteers in the BWIR were dismissively termed 'recruits' or 'civilians'.[44]

When West Indian troops were deployed in the front line they performed as well as other units in the British Army. The perception among the military establishment that they lacked the stoicism, discipline and determination for combat conditions was exposed as false. Given that the West Indian contingents had to overcome official prejudice in addition to the 'enemy', their front-line performance suggested such characteristics were available in abundance and the men were extremely well-motivated. As Lieutenant Colonel Wood Hill, commander of the 1BWIR, remarked, 'It was fortunate for the manhood of the West Indies that two battalions of the British West Indies Regiment were able to participate in the fighting in Palestine and to prove to the world at large that the West Indies possess soldier-like qualities'.[45]

Jamaicans were first involved in front-line combat in Cameroon. A machine-gun detachment from the 2WIR was involved in a skirmish at Wum-Biagas in October 1915. The battalion magazine reported that when 'the machine gun Section ... was subjected to a very heavy fire ... the discipline and morale of the rank and file ... was all that could be possibly desired'.[46] During the campaign in the German East African territory of Tanganyika (now Tanzania) the bravery of the 2WIR detachments was remarked upon again. Skirmishes in September and October 1917 culminated in the Battle of Nyangao. Fought over two days, the battle proved to be the final and most bloody encounter of the cat-and-mouse struggle waged between the German forces commanded by von Lettow-Vorbeck and the British under van Deventer. The forces involved – around 1,500 Germans, mainly *askaris*, and 5,000 British – were small but casualty rates were high. The German and British forces lost 30 and 50 per cent of their strength killed or wounded respectively. The 2WIR was praised for its courage under fire and robust discipline maintained amidst fleeing porters and a demoralised section of the Cape Corps. Such was their bravery it was reported 'they have had to be reproved ... for exposing themselves un-necessarily'[47] to enemy fire.

In Palestine, the British West Indies Regiment got its first taste of action at Umbrella Hill on the Gaza–Beersheba line. In July 1917, the machine-gun section of the first battalion took part in several raids on the Turkish trenches.[48] Allenby, Commander-in-Chief of the of Egyptian Expeditionary Force, was sufficiently impressed to state in a dispatch to the Jamaican Governor, 'I have great pleasure in informing you of the excellent conduct of the Machine Gun Section ... All ranks behaved with great gallantry under heavy rifle fire and shell fire, and contributed in no small measure to the success of the operations.'[49]

In September 1918, as the Middle Eastern campaign drew to a close, the first and second battalions took part in several attacks on Turkish positions on the Bahr Ridge in the Jordan Valley under heavy artillery fire. The Turkish lines were breached by a furious bayonet charge that accounted for a 140 Turkish casualties, forty prisoners and fourteen captured machine guns. Sergeant M. C. Halliburton, Private (Acting Lance Corporal) Sampson and Private Spence of Jamaica received the Military Medal. Private H. Scott also of Jamaica received the Distinguished Conduct Medal for carrying a message for 700 yards under shell fire.[50] Chaytor, commanding officer of the combined Australian and New Zealand Army Corps (ANZAC) and West Indian force, remarked in a letter to Wood Hill: 'Outside my own Division there are no troops I would rather have with me than the BWI[R], who have won the highest opinion of all who have been with them during our operations'.[51] The performance was all the more remarkable for having been carried out in scorching heat and at a point when many men were falling prey to malaria.[52]

7 British West Indies Regiment troops preparing dugouts near Deir-el-Belah on the Gaza–Beersheeba line, where the regiment was deployed on offensive action in July 1917

The fact that front-line fighting experience was gained in the African and Middle Eastern theatres was particularly significant. The local terrain and relatively small size of the opposing armies produced different tactics from those associated with the Western Front where, until 1918, vast armies endured virtually static warfare. The Middle Eastern and African campaigns were characterised by small-scale engagements and greater troop mobility. Cavalry were also routinely deployed in the Middle East. This helped perpetuate the mythology of heroic hand-to-hand combat that tested each man on equal terms. Such imaginings proved unsustainable on the battlegrounds of the Western Front where the majority of casualties were caused by long-range artillery.[53] The specific circumstances of the Middle Eastern campaign presented Jamaican nationalists with tangible chivalric images, such as dashing bayonet charges, to underpin demands that military duty and sacrifice be rewarded with greater social and economic participation.

'Bayonet work' featured as a central component of army training out of all proportion to its military efficacy. Recruits were assured the mere appearance of British soldiers weighing in with cold steel would put an enemy to flight.[54] Shortly after the war an article by the boxing correspondent of *The Times* captured the significance of the weapon as a symbol of heroic combat and conquest. In the imaginings of Empire, the bayonet was a tool of superior civilisation – an extension of the rifle and 'not merely a spear'[55] – that had proved its worth by winning the war. It was most effective in the hands of the sons of Empire who engaged the hostile environments of the Imperial frontier and whose character and combativity had been moulded by manly pursuits, such as boxing. Before the war, claimed the correspondent, bayonet training had taken place in the gymnasium rather than the great outdoors, divorcing bayonet technique from the realities of combat. The war had seen a pragmatic change of emphasis that restated the link between 'bayonet work' and the 'noble art'.

> Quickness, footwork, a hard punch ... a fine parry ... were identical and vital both to boxing and bayonet training ... the spirit of attack, of endurance, of self-control ... of refusal to give in – in short the 'ethical' side of boxing – was found to be essential in effective bayonet work. Colonel R. B. Campbell, DSO ... was among the earliest to appreciate the changed conditions. [He was a] first-class boxer, a hard athlete, an open-air man, as opposed to a mere gymnast.[56]

Twenty years after the war, Jamaican veterans submitted statements to the Moyne Commission, set up in the wake of industrial and social unrest throughout the West Indies during the 1930s. By this time many found themselves in the depths of poverty. In a submission to the Commission, Sergeant W. Johnson called for equitable treatment for the ex-servicemen and deployed the bayonet as a symbol of heroism and military efficiency that merited just reward:

> See and know the existing conditions of the Ex-soldiers who did services for our most Bratanic Majesty King George V and Supreme Lord of Jamaica, of which we dearly has given our lives as a supreme sacrifice for King and country of which we fairly did our duty and, do it well, by returning with Victory on the point of our Bayonet [all sic].[57]

However, this attachment to noble images of combat had caused divisions within the ranks of the BWIR, reflecting in turn the prejudices of pigmentation and class upon which the West Indian hierarchy depended. When the regiment was denied pay increases granted to the British army under Army Order 1 of 1918, it was suggested by some men that demands for its extension to the BWIR should only be for those who had fought on the front line in Palestine. The first and second battalions, it was asserted, had not only distinguished themselves in hand-to-hand fighting, but were drawn from the 'better class of men'. The subsequent battalions serving as military labour on the Western Front and in Italy were purportedly comprised of lower-class labourers, regarded as unworthy either to fight in the front line or to claim the full reward of military service.[58]

Writing to the *Daily Gleaner*, the white Jamaican sergeant, J. E. R Stevens, scoffed at members of the labour battalions who claimed front-line status.

> I see some idiots are writing home, and talking of being in the trenches, being up to the front line, etc. but that's all rot. We are miles from the trenches; under shell fire of course. But then, the Boche has guns of a range of sixteen to twenty miles. There is not the remotest possibility of us ever going up to the trenches, except those we have made, for protection from shell fire.[59]

But in the next breath Stevens was forced to concede that modern weaponry placed every soldier in the firing line. 'We all had the wind up a bit ... and we lived in dugouts for quite a few days ... I can't imagine a more disagreeable and frightful sound than the shriek of a shell passing nearby. It simply seems to yell with delight at the prospect of hitting you'. Another *Daily Gleaner* correspondent underlined how the fixation with heroic images of hand-to-hand fighting discounted the true role of labour battalions, underlining how the arbitrary demarcation between front-line and auxiliary roles served to create a racial and gender division of labour during wartime. Stressing how the duties of the BWIR battalions were as dangerous as holding the line, Lieutenant Leonard Mackay rejected the view often held by those with little insight into modern warfare that 'infantry work [was] the one essential thing'.[60]

Many black soldiers in the BWIR endeavoured to create a more proactive image for themselves than that associated with the auxilliary roles designated by the War Office. This desire was well-illustrated by Alfred Horner, who although visualising the black soldier as a child awestruck by white technological power, still captures the pent-up frustrations and the longings of his men to assert a degree of autonomy and historic purpose.

> There are humorous incidents even amidst the roar of the guns, and one of them is always afforded by the insatiable desire which our lads have to pull the cord which fires the gun. The fact that he is in a peculiar sense the author of the devastating noise which follows seems to create in *le soldat noir* a certain sense of satisfaction. Our boys will almost promise anything for this privilege, and often amusing bargains are struck with the British gunners. It is the personal element which they desire, the feeling that they themselves are actually striking at the enemy; and when we hear that coloured soldiers in other armies have shown remarkable aptitude in the attack, we, who are in the know, feel certain that the same desire to be personally 'in at the thing' animates our own boys too.[61]

Non-combatant troops could go to great lengths to associate themselves with front-line action and heroic deeds. In October 1915, the *Daily Gleaner* published a photograph and story relating the exploits of a black Jamaican, Alonzo Nathan, while serving in a British regiment. In the studio photograph, Nathan struck a brotherly pose with a white comrade. Captioned 'A Native of Falmouth Fought at Chapelle', the accompanying article claimed Nathan and his companion had enlisted together and were both wounded during the battle of Neuve Chapelle in March 1915, Nathan receiving a bayonet thrust to the head. They were both reported to be recovering from their wounds in a military hospital in Aldershot.[62] However, Nathan's service papers show he enlisted in the Army Service Corps (ASC) at Aldershot, but not until the end of August 1915, before which he served as a ship's fireman. Nathan was still in England in December 1915 when he was examined by a military court for insubordination. Before the formation of the BWIR, black volunteers who successfully enlisted were often posted to the ASC as the unit was chiefly involved with supply and logistic support, rather than front-line duties. Nathan, like many other black men assigned to the ASC, later transferred to the BWIR in the belief he would fulfil his ambition to see front-line action.[63]

Nathan's case illustrates the tendency of many men involved in the conflict, whatever their actual role, to portray their participation as one involving direct and intimate contact with the enemy. Where this was denied, personal frustrations could be assuaged and the expectations of a civilian audience could be met by imagined narratives that drew on discourses of heroic masculine endeavour.[64] It is significant that Nathan's 'experiences' were drawn from a letter to his Jamaican guardian, who he clearly went to some pains to impress as he wrote 'My career has been from sailor to soldier'.[65] The Jamaican press were keen to appropriate 'soldiers' tales' that encouraged the impression its volunteers entered the war at centre-stage on equal terms with their white comrades.

Imaginings of noble deeds and sacrifice occupied a pivotal space in narratives of nationhood, with the promise of immortality held out to those who died defending the interests of the nation. Sacrifices in pursuit of the wider cause of Empire could also be enlisted by an emergent nation to legitimise demands for the transition from subjecthood to statehood. Jamaican cultural nationalism incorporated military sacrifice into its canon from the first days of the war. H. S. Bunbury, an Anglo-Irish poet living in Jamaica, suggested in 'A Chant for Our Contingent' that fallen Jamaicans would find immortality, setting an example for others to respond to the call of the Empire 'over the ocean'. Those who did so stepped beyond the domesticated male ties of home and family to fulfil their manly public duty – defence of nation and Empire.

... They give without pause, without measure
Their love, their delights and their lives
Surrender, to save us, the treasure
Of children, of mothers, and wives
Their sweetheart, their mothers and wives

Shall we, for our part, be behind them?
Shall we be less ready to give
Our souls? And in sacrifice find them
And, dying eternally live
Immortal in memory live?

... They rest, but their spirit still lights us
It leads us the way we must tread
If noble ambitions incites us
To do and to be as our dead
Our dear and most wonderful dead.[66]

In 'Jamaica Marches On', which was set to music as a marching song for the contingent, Tom Redcam suggested military service would lay the basis for a future Jamaican nation.

Tramp, Tramp, Tramp
We tread the road to Glory,
Tramp, Tramp, Tramp
Jamaica marches on.
Wide through the world we'll bear our Island story
Tramp, tramp, tramp
Jamaica marches on.
On, on we go,
Up on the road of Glory,
There Honour calls and Duty's banners fly
On Times great roll we'll write our Island story
Tramp, Tramp, Tramp
Jamaica marches by.[67]

Colonial legislation during the war also started to delineate a Jamaican nation. The Jamaican Military Service Act, passed to establish eligibility for military service in the event of conscription, also served to designate aliens. This was ostensibly in relation to subject-status within the British Empire, but could also be interpreted to distinguish Jamaicans from non-Jamaicans. The Act stipulated a £50 fine or 3 months, imprisonment with hard labour for those who failed to register and represented an attempt by the island legislature to enforce the responsibilities of citizenship upon the menfolk of Jamaica, even while they were denied political rights. The small Chinese community, descendants of around 1,000 indentured labourers who arrived in the 1850s, was revitalised by fresh migration from 1911.[68] Community spokesmen feared the immanent conscription of Chinese men between 16 and 41 who were registered, and presented a petition of protest. In response, Governor Manning stated the 'Chinese in common with persons of other alien nationality, although required to register under the Law, will not be liable to be called upon or required to perform military service'.[69] The alien status of the Chinese community, applied despite its sixty-year presence, persisted into the 1930s and beyond. Submissions to the Moyne Commission for example contained frequent references to the allegedly sharp business practises of Chinese shopkeepers, commonly termed 'alien traders', and demands were made for their entry into Jamaica to be limited.[70]

Writing in the *United Empire*, journal of the Royal Colonial Institute, 'Fusilier' boasted the blood sacrifice of the West Indian volunteers 'weld[ed] together the ties of Empire between Imperial and Colonial arms'.[71] Alfred Horner spoke of the 'many happy hours ... spent cementing a friendship with the British Tommy which should bring forth its fruit yet in the great reorganisation of Empire which must take place after the war'.[72] But these idealised images were never free from the familial power relationships imagined by Horner as he anticipated the feelings of West Indian recruits landing in the metropole:

> it was the awe-inspiring thought, almost incapable of being understood by the non-colonial, that here at last was England, that this was their first view of that wonderful 'Motherland' of which they had heard and read ever since they had been children, that great mother whose children they were, whose flag they served under, and whose quarrel they had in loyalty made their own'.[73]

Horner continued this maternal and infantilising metaphor in his portrayal of the rousing reception the men received at the quayside and railway stations. In his eyes, the crowds of cheering and curious onlookers were 'welcoming, as a mighty mother, the offering, however feeble, of her smallest sons ... forg[ing] another priceless link in that golden chain of affection which binds the Empire together'.[74]

Incorporation into the brotherhood-in-arms of the Empire was therefore conditional and contingent on the place each man occupied in the hierarchies of race and class, often expressed through the trope of family. Frank Cundall, in his Jamaican history of the war, reproduced a glowing eulogy to the combined ranks of Allenby's forces who had crushed the Turks in the Holy Land and which had involved the legendary bayonet charge of the BWIR:

From all over the Seven Seas the empire's sons came to illustrate the unanimity of all the King's subjects ... English, Scottish, Irish and Welsh divisions of good men and true fought side by side with soldiers of varying Indian races and castes ... our dark-skinned brethren in the West Indies furnished infantry who, when the fierce summer heat made the air in the Jordan Valley like a draught from a furnace, had a bayonet charge which aroused an Anzac brigade to enthusiasm (and Colonial free men can estimate bravery at its true value) ... The communion of the representatives of the Mother and Daughter nations on the stern field of war brought together people with the same ideals, and if there are minor jealousies between them the brotherhood of arms will make the soldiers returning to their homes in all quarters of the globe best missionaries to spread the Imperial idea. Instead of wrecking the British Empire the German-made war should rebuild it on the soundest of foundations – affection, mutual trust, and common interest.[75]

But these words show that even heroic actions, which the West Indian soldier could rightly claim as evidence of unstinting front-line service, did not dissolve the racial categories of the Imperial military order.

Notes

1 PRO WO32/5094 Minute *DG* to AG 22 January 1917.
2 John Brown, *The Unmelting Pot: An English Town and its Immigrants* (London: Macmillan, 1970), pp. 23–4.
3 PRO WO32/5094 WO Minute AAG to AG 23 January 1917.
4 PRO WO32/5094 Memorandum from Military Members of the Army Council to Commander-in-Chief, British Armies in France 6 February 1917.
5 WO32/5094 C in C, British Armies in France to WO 4 March 1917; Denis Winter, *Death's Men: Soldiers of the Great War* (Harmondsworth: Penguin, 1979), p. 236.
6 Joseph, 'British West Indies Regiment', pp. 100–4, 124.
7 *DG* 10 November 1915, p. 1.
8 Ibid., p. 3.
9 Dyde, *Empty Sleeve*, pp. 247–8.
10 PRO WO106/868 'Suggested Cablegrams in the event of German/Mexican incursion into Belize' (n.d., but probably late March 1917) (my emphasis).
11 Dyde, *Empty Sleeve*, pp. 253, 260–1.
12 PRO WO95/338 WD 3BWIR passim.; WO95/495 WD 6BWIR entry for 2 July 1918; Lt. R..J Blackadder, ts. diary (IWM 88/11/1), p. 40; WO95/4262 WD 7BWIR entry for 7 January 1918; Rev. J. L. Ramson, *'Carry On' or Papers from the Life of a West Indian Padre in the Field* (Kingston: Educational Supply Co., 1918), pp. 33–7.
13 Ramson, *'Carry On'*, p. 47.
14 Ibid., p. 35.
15 Sir Etienne Dupuch, *A Salute to Friend and Foe* (Nassau: Tribune, 1982), pp. 71–2.
16 PRO WO95/409 WD 4BWIR entry for 7 December 1917.
17 *DG* 10 September 1917, p. 3.

18 Ramson, 'Carry On', p. 37.

19 Keegan, First World War, pp. 385–7; PRO WO95/495 WD 6BWIR entries for July and August 1917.

20 Diary of Father Van Walleghem, In Flanders Field Museum, Ieper, Belgium (kindly supplied and translated by Dominiek Dendooven).

21 Horner, From the Islands of the Sea, p. 28.

22 PRO WO71/594 Defence statement by Herbert Morris.

23 PRO WO71/594 Army Form B122 and Evidence of Lt. L. R. Andrews, 14422 Sgt. Goldson, 7453 Cpl. J. Russell, 6325 Sgt. Simpson 2 D[urham] L[ight] I[nfantry]; Ramson, 'Carry On', pp. 18–20.

24 PRO MH106/2302 L. Jones 4878 4BWIR Medical Case Sheets October 1917.

25 PRO WO364/3655 Army Form B 179A 4338 Pte Eustace Henry Shaw.

26 Ibid.

27 Ibid.

28 Ibid.

29 Ibid.; PRO CO137/735 WO to USS, CO 17 December 1919.

30 Winter, Great War and the British People, p. 54; Winter, Death's Men, pp. 194, 197.

31 PRO WO137/37 'Report on the Work of Labour with the BEF During the War'.

32 Wellcome Institute RAMC 446/18 memorandum '1/5th Royal Warwick Regiment'.

33 Ibid. 'Extract from proceedings of a Court of Enquiry into failure of a party of 11th Border Regiment ... to carry out an attack, on 10th July 1916'; PRO WO95/2403 WD 11 Border Regiment, 1–10 July 1916.

34 J. M. Patterson, With the Judaeans in the Palestine Campaign (London: Hutchinson, 1922), p. 64.

35 Horner, From the Islands of the Sea, p. 39.

36 Ibid., p. 3.

37 Bet–El, 'Men and Soldiers', p. 83.

38 Horner, From the Islands of the Sea, p. 63.

39 PRO WO95/5446 WD GOC Jamaica entries for 5–6 June 1916 and 16 May 1917.

40 PRO CO318/347/17779 GOC, East Africa to WO, 9 April 1918.

41 A. A. Cipriani, Twenty-five Years After: The British West Indies Regiment in the Great War 1914–1918 (Port of Spain: Trinidad Publishing Co., 1940), pp. 55, 57 (my emphasis).

42 Ibid., p. 57.

43 DG 26 November 1915, p. 10.

44 Cipriani, Twenty-five Years After, p. 57.

45 Lt Col. Wood Hill, A Few Notes on the History of the British West Indies Regiment (unpublished ts, 1919), p. 5.

46 Zouave, February 1916, p. 32.

47 PRO WO95/5370 WD 2WIR entries for 6 and 9 November 1917.

48 ICS WIC/3/BWIR War Diary, 1st Battalion of the British West Indies Regiment, 1915–19, pp. 75–8.

49 Cipriani, Twenty-five Years After, p. 20.

50 PRO WO95/4732 WD 1BWIR entries for 19–21 September 1918; The Times, 6 December 1918, p. 8.

51 PRO WO95/4732 Chaytor to Wood Hill, 18 October 1918.

52 W. T. Massey, Allenby's Final Triumph (London: Constable and Co., 1920), pp. 204–5; Cipriani, Twenty-five Years After, p. 34.

53 Hynes, *The Soldiers' Tale*, pp. 76–80.
54 Bourke, *An Intimate History of Killing*, pp. 44–7, 51–5, 58–62.
55 *The Times*, 15 June 1920, p. 6.
56 Ibid.
57 PRO CO950/93 Memoranda from British West Indies Regiment Association, Sgt. C. W. Johnson to Royal Cm. (n.d.).
58 PRO CO28/294/56561 Challenor Lynch to Colonial Secretary, Barbados, 9 October 1918.
59 *DG* 10 September 1917, p. 3.
60 *DG* 10 September 1917, p. 6.
61 Horner, *From the Islands of the Sea*, p. 32.
62 *DG* 11 October 1915, p. 1.
63 PRO WO364/2665 discharge papers for Alonzo Nathan.
64 Bourke, *Intimate History of Killing*, pp. 8–10, 33–7.
65 *DG* 11 October 1915, p. 1.
66 *DG* 16 October 1915, p. 13. The song followed the tune of 'My Bonny Lies Over the Ocean'.
67 *DG* 1 May 1916, p. 11.
68 In the 1921 census 3,696 Chinese were recorded living in Jamaica: Samuel J. Hurwitz and Edith F. Hurwitz, *Jamaica: A Historical Portrait* (London: Pall Mall Press, 1971), p. 162.
69 PRO CO137/724 Summary of Petition dated 7th June 1917 received by the Chinese Minister in London from the Chinese Club in Jamaica (translation); CO137/722 Gov. Manning to Long SSC 29 September 1917.
70 See for example PRO CO950/87 Memorandum from Chinese Residents in Jamaica, 5–6; CO950/944 Serial No. 173 Memorandum from A. G. S. Coombs, Jamaica Workers' and Tradesmen's Union, 15 CO950/945 Serial No. 183 Memorandum of St George's Citizens' Association, 3.
71 'Fusilier', 'British West Indies Regiment', 29.
72 Horner, *From the Islands of the Sea*, p. 21.
73 Ibid. , p. 12.
74 Ibid., p. 14.
75 W. T. Massey, *How Jerusalem Was Won: Being the Record of Allenby's Campaign in Palestine* (London: Constable, 1919) quoted in Cundall, *Jamaica's Part in the Great War*, pp. 57–8.

5 'Their splendid physical proportions': the black soldier in the white imagination

Alfred Horner, padre to the six and ninth battalions of the British West Indies Regiment, often watched while the men drilled on the parade ground.

> This they rather liked; and indeed, with the splendid physical physique which our men possess generally, it was only natural that they should enjoy it. I have often wished that our men could have worn something different from the ordinary fighting kit of the British soldier. It does hide their splendid physical proportions so ... We held a boxing competition, and several officers ... were absolutely astounded at the fine figure and splendid outlines of our men. They look sometimes a little heavy and ill-built in their heavy kit, but remove that and – well, it makes all the difference.[1]

Horner's words bore a striking similarity to those used to describe Eugene Sandow, the physical fitness performer and entrepreneur, some thirty years previously. 'When in evening dress there is nothing specially remarkable about this quiet mannered, good natured youth; but when he takes of his coat and "prepares for action" the extraordinary development of the arms, shoulders and back muscles is marvellously striking ... the muscles stand out under a clear white skin in high relief.'[2] But there was a significant difference, in that the object of the gaze was now black. At a time when black soldiers were otherwise viewed as inferior military material, too lacking in self-discipline and intelligence to serve in the firing line, what significance can be attached to Horner's eroticised imaginings? What implications did such representations of black physicality hold for metropolitan society during the war?

Richard Dyer's study of the black performer and intellectual, Paul Robeson, whose rise in popularity occurred shortly after the Great War, highlights how blackness was regularly taken by the white observer to signify life, vigour and closeness to nature.[3] Walter Jekyll, a mentor of the poet Claude McKay, moved to Jamaica 'to reconnect with some form of unspoiled "natural" life',[4] turning his back on what he regarded as a jaded metropolitan culture. Qualities projected onto a subject race, usually simple and essential, rather than acquired and complex, could be appropriated to inject fresh energy into the Imperial project. The ideal of the frontiersman or scout, for example, cast in reaction to the fear of metropolitan enfeeblement, was inspired in part by the martial qualities perceived in the North American Indian, the Zulu or Asante warrior.[5]

In contrast to the demands made of white men during the First World War, blackness represented unrestrained expression of sexuality, feeling and emotion. These perceived qualities stood in stark contrast to white society, typified by emotional and sexual repression, and now subordinated to mechanised warfare and military discipline. For some disillusioned whites, black people became 'a repository of all the qualities ... considered lacking in the dominant society' during the war.[6] In the process, representations of blackness focusing on the alleged sexual licentiousness of black men were reconstituted. Although the Empire provided ample opportunity for sexual adventure and exploitation by members of the Imperial apparatus,[7] as Kobena Mercer has shown, the control of sexuality and sexual appetite were seen as central to the civilising mission. '[O]ne is civilised at the expense of sexuality, and sexual at the expense of civilisation. If the black, the savage, the nigger, is the absolute Other of civility then it must follow that he is endowed with the most monstrous and terrifying sexual proclivity.'[8]

Over-sexualised images of black men could re-assert the primacy of white civilisation apparently at its nadir amid the carnage of the Western Front. But imagining, in black people, the repressed instincts of humankind created a chimera that had to be contained. Naturalistic representations of blackness

8 West India Regiment and their fitness instructor before the war

signified chaos and violence, overt sexuality and physical prowess – delicate issues when many elements of white society longed for a return to order and unchallenged masculine virtue and efficiency. As white men returned from the war mentally and physically emasculated, the black body served as 'a reminder of what the body can do, its vitality, its strength, its sensuousness'.[9]

Women's writing of the war expressed a wish for men who were bodily and spiritually whole. American troops, who arrived in the later stages of the war were viewed as sexually potent supermen compared to the war-weary Tommy, as Vera Brittain testified:

> They looked larger than ordinary men; their tall, straight figures were in vivid contrast to the undersized armies of pale recruits to which we had grown accustomed ... they seemed, as it were, Tommies in heaven ... I pressed forward with the others to watch the United States entering the war, so god-like, so magnificent, so splendidly unimpaired in comparison with the tired, nerve-wracked men of the British Army.[10]

As a military nurse, Brittain had experienced the shattering consequences of war on the flower of British youth. Mentally exhausted by the competing demands of family and nation, Brittain's mind was wracked by images of 'dying men, reeking with mud and foul green-stained bandages, shrieking and writhing in a grotesque travesty of manhood'.[11] Her eroticised, miraculous vision of the US troops occurred during the German offensive of March 1918 when the British army in Flanders was almost pushed into the sea. These American soldiers were white, and wearing similar uniforms could be mistaken for British Tommies. But it was when desire became focused on black subjects of Empire that British manhood was most acutely brought into question.

As Alfred Horner's remarks suggest, the desire for inspiring masculine images was not restricted to women. Arriving in England in July 1917 with drafts from Jamaica and the Bahamas, Horner experienced the changes in the metropole he had left in 1913 with feelings of loss and sadness: 'Khaki, the women workers and alas! the uniform of the wounded, everything, in fact, reminded one constantly and in every way that this was a different England'.[12] Some West Indian volunteers worked as stretcher-bearers on the Western Front and like Brittain and her colleagues in the Voluntary Aid Detachments witnessed the wretched state of white manhood at first hand, as Horner recounted:

> Except in the heroism of the poor wounded lads and the loving devotion of the regimental stretcher-bearers and the M[edical] O[fficer] ... there is nothing to edify. Gone are the cries of victory, gone are the feelings of what may be termed the 'joy of battle'; here matted hair, clotted blood, pale blue faces and here and there the silence of the Great Sacrifice reign supreme.[13]

These circumstances, in which the physical and mental vulnerability of white soldiers were exposed, did not automatically imbue black soldiers with a sense of superiority. As Sharon Ouditt has shown, nurses treating the wounded often became traumatised and imagined their own disfigurement.[14]

Horner's background gave him a specific perspective on the apparent degeneration of white masculinity. Before being posted to the Bahamas as Rector of St. Johns, Horner passed through St. Paul's Missionary College, Burgh, a seminary for the Church Missionary Society after earning a licentiate in Theology at Durham. Described as a 'man's man' with a military bearing acquired from a brief spell in the army before entering the church, Horner was an ebullient proselytiser of 'muscular' Christianity, that since the 1860s, had lent an air of moral and physical superiority to missionary efforts in the Empire.[15] Disenchanted by his wartime experiences, Horner's response to the physique of the Jamaican soldier, manifested not only homoerotic desire, but a yearning for spiritual and physical wholesomeness. What was at issue was the symbolic significance of the black soldier. Medical rejections of Jamaican volunteers during the war ran at around 60 per cent, similar to rates in Britain during the South African War. Of 26,667 volunteers for the Jamaican contingents of the BWIR, 13,940 were rejected as medically unfit and a further 2,082 were discharged or died before embarking overseas.[16]

Pre-war concern with the detrimental effects of urbanisation gave renewed vigour to a nostalgic romanticism that yearned for the 'natural', 'innocent' and 'unspoilt'. Such desires are evident in the works of the Uranian poets whose influence may be found in some homoerotic poetry and prose of the war. Wartime writers such as Siegfried Sassoon and David Jones were enthralled by golden or blonde-haired young men who represented, for them, the bravery and purity of an earlier, more certain era.[17] The Uranians, however, expressed a greater predilection for the sunburnt, muscular, youth engaged in hard physical labour. In his epic poem, 'Towards Democracy', written in 1883 and revised in 1902, Edward Carpenter, the Utopian socialist, spoke of the 'thick-waisted hot coarse-fleshed young bricklayer', and 'the begrimed stoker'.[18] While a poem attributed to Horatio Forbes Brown mused:

> Dearer to me is the lad, village born, with sinewy members
> Than the fine face of a pale town-bred effeminate youngling.[19]

The 'lowly' object of the Uranian gaze represented the 'other' *within* metropolitan society. The Uranian perspective, while celebrating, rather than denigrating the lower classes, nevertheless borrowed from the racialised class categories of the later nineteenth century. The lightest skin stood as a mark of high-born status, far removed from the physical labour outdoors. While the industrial 'abyss' of 'darkest' Britain, housing the degenerate urban poor, was viewed as simultaneously dangerous and alluring.[20] Through this lens the dark-skinned subject *without* was also a potential object of desire imagined as a child of nature, untroubled by the cares of civilisation and with an innate spirituality. This re-articulation of old categories offered some reassurance in contrast to the modernist vision more commonly associated with the war and described at length by Paul Fussell. Coupled to the historical association of black skin and physical labour on the plantation, there was even more scope for the objectification of the black form.

When the West Indian contingents arrived popular attention quickly focused on their physique. When a small detachment paraded at the Lord Mayor's show in November 1915, the *Standard* referred to them as 'big men all',[21] the *Daily News* as 'huge and mighty men of valour'.[22] Military records regularly remarked on the 'exceptional' or 'fine' physique of both the BWIR and the WIR.[23] A local paper in Seaford, reported the 'splendid impression' made by the BWIR volunteers, encamped in the south coast town between October 1915 and March 1916, and declared 'Some of them are magnificently proportioned'.[24] A Barbadian, Private Harman, was said to be six feet eight inches and wished to join the Life Guards. At this time the army had started to raise white British 'bantam battalions' to accommodate men who did not meet the minimum height requirement of five feet three inches.[25] The *Daily Sketch* pictured 'A Dusky ... Lady-killer' in the 'King's khaki'.[26] As Ouditt has argued '[u]niform had a certain mystique – it was a prize, a symbol of one's coming of age, of having entered the Symbolic Order.'[27] Particularly during the early years of the war, men in khaki, including black men, were seen as a source of sexual temptation for women.[28]

Yet the preoccupation with the black soldiers' physique could be a means of reasserting, as well as undermining, white hegemony. Alfred Horner's recollections of his men on the parade ground and in the boxing ring were admiring and not a little envious. But moulding the black subject to white yearnings and desires enforced control when elsewhere masculine certainty appeared in tatters. Horner's vision evokes the slave market as black soldiers became objects of toil and entertainment for white men; their strength a consequence of nature, rather than self-disciplined training. Horner's preference for the black male form unencumbered by uniform reduced the men to a primitive state, placing the black soldier firmly in the position of Other relieved of the obligations *and* rewards of white masculine civility.

Displays of physical strength on the parade ground or the boxing arena simultaneously provided the opportunity for black men to contest the marks of racial inferiority. Pre-war metropolitan concern at the prospect of a black man

9 A 'Dusky lady-killer'? A British West Indies Regiment soldier poses with two Belgian women in the ruins of Ypres shortly after the war

defeating a white opponent in the boxing ring anticipated the desire to exclude black men from the front line. Sport had become a metaphor for white racial dominance within the Empire. The games ethic embodied the purported ideals of English masculinity and the Imperial enterprise – team spirit, fair play, skill and stamina. In the wake of uprisings against colonial rule, such as the Jamaican Morant Bay Rebellion of 1865, and growing competition from other world powers, a more aggressive Imperial mindset started to replace the model of moral leadership. Sporting imagery came to embody the ideas of Social Darwinism, as the processes of natural selection were symbolically acted out on the playing field.[29]

In 1911, the contest between the black American boxer, Jack Johnson, and Bombardier Billy Wells was cancelled, after the freeholders of Earls Court obtained an injunction prohibiting the fight. The leading Baptist minister and moral crusader, Frederick Meyer, who headed the opposition to the match, used the race issue to underpin a campaign whose ostensible complaint was the link between boxing and gambling. But the broader racial significance of the protests was evident in the support received from leading Imperial figures including Lords Roberts and Baden Powell.[30] Anti-fight protestors were particularly anxious that cinematic copies of the fight would circulate throughout the Empire and undermine Imperial authority if the white soldier, Wells, was defeated by the black champion.[31]

In May 1914, the match at Olympia between 'Gunboat' Smith and Sam Longford, the black Nova Scotian, was abandoned after Home Office pressure.[32] *The Times* summed up prevailing Imperial and metropolitan attitudes: '[T]he chances of a contest of this kind is eagerly read by half-educated natives ... the black man's victory is hailed as a proof that the hegemony of the white race is approaching the end.'[33] The paper feared the unrest in the USA and the West Indies following Johnson's world title victory at Reno, Nevada in 1910 would recur throughout the Empire. During the Johnson affair in 1911, the paper had shown less hostility to bouts between black and white boxers.[34] However, with war looming the black man needed a firm reminder of his place in the world order.

In the metropole, protagonists of the 'noble art' – unlike the disreputable tradition of pugilism – 'boxed' rather than 'fought', skill being valued above brute force. Ironically, as a result, British boxers seemed increasingly vulnerable to American and French opponents.[35] British boxers were urged to master the more aggressive 'American' technique of 'infighting' that 'develops the individual's natural gifts, makes him a fighter from the first, and never sacrifices for the sake of traditional form, or rather formalism, that priceless asset, the punch that comes by nature so much more often than by art'.[36]

It was one thing for a white man to exploit his 'natural gifts' and quite another for a black man to do likewise. Eschewing competition with black opponents, white observers argued black fighters were naturalistic, raw, and untutored. A report in the *Zouave* bemoaned how:

> There are many men in the battalion, obviously cut out by nature to box, who do not evince as much interest in the sport as one might wish ... in most cases the will was good though the knowledge may be weak ... one may say that the boxing was characterized by hard hitting rather than by technical skill ... As we have said ... with a little instruction some of the men might be easily turned into very first class boxers. They can apparently take a very much more severe punishment than the average European, without the ill effects, though appearances are rather deceptive in this respect ... Most of the blows ... appeared to have enormous force behind them ... but there was a lack of knowledge of the science of hitting which must have materially reduced the force of the blow ... [The men] paid more attention to the spectacular than to the useful part of the art.[37]

Black soldiers were generally excluded from the recreational facilities provided for their white counterparts. However, there were occasions when BWIR teams competed with white opponents, despite the pre-war opposition to such contests. The three BWIR battalions stationed in the Middle East, for example, took part in joint cricket competitions and athletics meetings. During the 1917 season, the BWIR cricket team competed in a league comprised of local civilian and military teams organised by the Alexandria Cricket Club. The BWIR team, playing on many occasions without white officers, won twenty-eight out of thirty-one matches.[38] Another notable BWIR sporting triumph was achieved shortly before the end of the war when a team from the crack Italian dreadnought, *Duilio*, was defeated in a tug-of-war contest.[39]

But black sporting triumph did not always shatter the racial categories of Empire. As Vasili argues in his study of the footballer, Walter Tull, one of the few black men to serve as an officer during the war:

> winning ... could be seen as, ultimately, a pyrrhic victory ... defined in such a way as to confirm the scientific taxonomies of 'race': it was their 'animalism', a sub-human characteristic, that allowed them their physical prowess, possession of which necessarily excluded ownership of civilised cultural traits such as a highly evolved intellect or refined sensitivities.[40]

When the black subject was forced into a more passive role, the white imagination could more readily concede a degree of common humanity. In August 1917, Private Hubert Clarke, a Jamaican volunteer was executed after assaulting two military policemen in a field punishment compound at Kantara, Egypt. James Johnston Abraham[41] was the medical officer called to attend the execution and to certify death. Abraham left an account at odds with military reports characterising Clarke as violent, ill-disciplined and almost sub-human. In Abraham's depiction, Clarke dwarfed, physically and spiritually, the nervous observers of the execution and the hesitant firing party as he waited to die:

> The prisoner was standing close to the wall, a magnificent bronze Hercules, clad in a pair of khaki shorts only, his hands fastened behind his back. The firing-party, men from a Labour Battalion, stood huddled some twenty feet away. Their faces looked white and drawn in the gathering light. I glanced at my little Quartermaster. His face, usually ruddy, was blanched. I turned towards the A[ssistant] P[rovost] M[arshall]. He was nervously fingering his revolver. We were all in a state of extreme nervous tension. Then I looked at the prisoner. The light was coming up from the East. It glistened on his bronze skin and the whites of his eyes, and I was startled to see there was a look of beatitude on his face. His white teeth sparkled. He was completely at ease.[42]

Abraham's vision has an epiphanic quality, the Christ-like black soldier raised to a privileged, blessed state. According to Abraham, Clarke's 'eyes seemed to glow with an inner joy',[43] as he received the last offices of the Baptist chaplain. Physical features more usually a focus of ridicule or disgust – dark skin, teeth and eyes – appear in a more positive aspect. References to the soldier's glistening skin, retain an eroticised, fetishistic quality, but Abraham, rather than connoting toil or sexual exertion, conjures up a heavenly, religious image of lightness and ennoblement, echoing wartime homoerotic verse, such as Leonard Green's *Dream Comrades* that imagined Christ as a beautiful youth, 'brown-breasted with the kisses of the sun'.[44]

Remarking on the soldier's courage, an army chaplain related to Abraham how, after a week of constant ministry, Clarke 'had repented of his sins, and believed he had been forgiven. He was ready therefore to face his God, "fortified by the rites of Holy Church"'.[45] The belief that white ministry would redeem the fallen black man was evident in other wartime accounts. John Luce Ramson was convinced his prayers had saved the soul of Herbert Morris before he was executed in Belgium a month later.[46] Abraham's standpoint was partly facilitated by Hubert Clarke's relative powerlessness within these judicial circumstances, such that Abraham successfully dissuaded Clarke from an intended final act of defiance – facing the firing squad unblind-folded. Furthermore, Abraham attempted to assert authority through terms suggestive of feminised and animal qualities in the condemned man. Nevertheless, his account still strikes home as a moving condemnation of an unjust sentence, all the more so for its reverence of the human form. Applying strips of plaster to mark the prisoner's heart for the firing squad, he continued:

> I looked up at the man. His eyes were gazing at me *soft as a gazelle's.*
>
> Finally I stepped back and someone produced a handkerchief to blindfold him.
>
> 'May I die with my eyes open?' he said in the educated tones so surprising to those who do not know the West Indian negro.
>
> 'Better not,' I said quietly.
>
> 'All right, Doctor,' he answered *submissively;* and they slipped it over.
>
> A few seconds later the quick wording of command rang out; then came the volley; and then the great beautiful body crumpled and suddenly fell.[47]

It was not until Abraham and his companions encountered a scene on the return journey that restored the racial hierarchy of Empire, that he was jolted from his reverie. 'No one spoke until we passed a gang of coolies putting up wire fencing. That broke the spell.'[48]

While black soldiers were claimed as subjects for homoerotic contempla-
tion, more commonly they were reduced to objects of entertainment, portrayed
as playthings or at play to reflect their childlike status within discourses of race
and Empire. When the BWIR marched in London, one newspaper reported
that the men's 'eyes roll[ed] with pleasure at the reception given them'.[49] A
photograph in one colonial newspaper, bore the caption 'Happy Darkies at the
Front: No Bad Teeth in That Lot!'[50] The *Liverpool Courier* pictured black soldiers
forming a human pyramid and declared "Happy West Indians' ... enjoying a
trial of strength'.[51]

A more subtle approach conceded black West Indians a degree of cultural
sophistication, to both convey a common struggle and to further dehumanise
the German foe. 'Their civilisation is on a much higher plane than that of the
Kaiser and his hordes ... they are soldiers of sterling quality and speak English
fluently', reported the *War Budget*.[52] Speaking the tongue of the white man
could be the affront *par excellence* to white notions of racial superiority.[53]
However, this article was illustrated with pictures of black soldiers sparring and
'dancing the rag', possibly an attempt to reassure the reader that black men
would not usually attain the height of white cultural achievement.

Language that assumed an air of familiarity and social nexus towards the
black soldier blunted more threatening black masculine images. Claude McKay
remembered a rather well-meaning white woman, Mrs Newcombe, who ran a
club for black soldiers in London, whom she referred to as 'my coloured boys'.[54]
Alfred Horner frequently used the term *le soldat noir aimable* (the friendly black
soldier) to describe his men and reported that the British Tommy found the black
soldier-performer most endearing: 'If a canteen full of Tommies can only get our
boys singing or dancing they are contented, and many a time and oft the role of
society entertainer has fallen upon BWI boys'.[55] Even in the sick bay the black
soldier was expected to perform. Horner insisted that on the hospital ward the
black soldier 'if he [was] at all civil and obliging, ... [became] the pet and play-
thing of both inmates and staff'.[56] Susie Joy, a white Jamaican nursing members
of the BWIR on the wards of a military hospital in Alexandria, recalled the men
were 'such nice boys, quite black of course, so intelligent, and full of fun'.[57]

The reassurance of racial superiority provided by these benevolent and self-
satisfied imaginings was limited. The black showman also represented authen-
ticity, symbolising the traces of humanity that had survived the upheavals and
horrors of war. Black soldier-entertainers were popular because they had the
capacity to become an emotional repository for white combatants inhibited by
the straightjacket of military masculinity. The West Indian was regarded as
having 'a considerably larger emotional capacity than the English race generally possesses'.[58]

The stereotype of *le soldat noir aimable* can also be compared to the 'Quashie' figure of plantation slavery. 'Quashie' confounded the planter or overseer by feigning stupidity and clumsiness in 'a form of devious protest'[59] that was also appropriate under the rigours of military discipline. If assigned as a batman (soldier-servant) a man might polish only one of his officer's boots, leave them out in the rain or crease uniform trousers down the side. But he could do this:

> with such a naive simplicity, coupled with a wondrous self-satisfaction that he is absolutely doing it all in a friendly spirit that, when the explosion of disapprobation has subsided, the officer will have a good hearty laugh at it all.[60]

Some white observers were keen to suggest a sense of familiarity with the black soldier to authenticate their imaginings and to maintain an air of paternal authority. Others insisted on applying exotic qualities to non-white soldiers to emphasise racial and cultural differences that could perpetuate the hierarchies of Empire. The war artist, Massia Bibikoff, who sketched the Indian Expeditionary Force in France described how her 'imagination turned eagerly' towards the 'Native troops', whose 'child-like enthusiasm crossed with a fighting instinct', 'disciplined and tempered by British civilisation' produced 'warrior-like dripping tigers'.[61]

The emergence of a distinctive uniform for the West India Regiments illustrates the process of exoticisation. Despite a proud tradition of service, the regiment was increasingly regarded as an object of curiosity. Until 1868, the men had worn uniforms similar to those of the other line regiments of the British army. During the Crimean War, the uniforms of French Zouave troops caught the eye of many observers, partly due to the heroism, ferocity and élan associated with these crack regiments. The Zouaves were originally drawn from the hill tribes of Algeria and Morocco recruited by the French colonial army from the 1830s. Shortly before the Crimean War, the French army was restructured and the Zouave regiments were henceforth composed of native Frenchmen. Algerian and Moroccan recruits, whose traditional attire influenced the Zouave uniform, were redesignated *Turcos* or *Tirailleurs Algériens*. In 1868, proposals were made to dress 'native' regiments in uniforms more suitable to the climates they served in. At the suggestion of Queen Victoria, who had 'an eye for the exotic' and who had seen the French Zouaves on parade, the adoption of a Zouave-style uniform for the WIR was agreed.[62]

Rather than associating the WIR with the Zouave military tradition, the new uniforms increasingly marked out the regiment's 'native' status and its transition from a key component of the colonial armed forces, to an ceremonial symbol of Empire subjecthood to be paraded at events such as Queen Victoria's

Jubilee in 1897. It is significant that the regiment's white officers remained kitted in more traditional military attire.

Although standard tropical issue replaced the Zouave uniform for active service in the First World War, the image of the exotic black West Indian soldier persisted. When men from the first BWIR contingent paraded in London, in late 1915, one newspaper observed: 'All the civilised warriors of the world seemed to be represented here ... when the West Indians appeared – all huge and mighty men of valour, black as night, with their white teeth flashing, the picture reminded one somewhat of a scene from "Salammbo"'.[63] This reference to Flaubert's novel, set in Hamilcar's Carthage, implied that the black soldiers were part of a benighted race that lacked the finer qualities of European civilisation. One critic, writing in 1931, said of *Salammbo* 'there is no joy, only a savage laughter. Its characters have no sensibility. All Flaubert's creatures ... are violent and passionate ... the hero, Matho, is childlike and credulous'.[64]

The ability of many black servicemen and war workers to appropriate white cultural mores muted the process of exoticisation. White observers had their racial preconceptions disrupted when they realised that the West Indian contingents spoke English and had a knowledge of metropolitan history and culture. But the educated black soldier could then be portrayed as an aberration that in itself insisted on an exotic quality. A particular fascination was reserved for fundamental markers of racial status such as dress and hygiene. A British nurse based in Mesopotamia, where a contingent of the BWIR was posted, remarked that '[s]ome ... were cultured, educated men, more fastidious than many a British soldier with their array of toilet articles on their lockers – tooth brushes, sponges, talcum powder, etc.'.[65] This contrasted markedly with her description of African troops who were described as 'wild savages from the Gold Coast or Nigeria'.[66] As Anne McClintock has observed, 'Victorian cleaning rituals were peddled globally as the God-given sign of Britain's evolutionary superiority, and soap was invested with magical, fetish powers ... Both the cult of domesticity and the new imperialism found in soap an exemplary mediating form.'[67]

But the insinuation was that the West Indian volunteer or war worker applied himself rather too enthusiastically to what were ultimately feminine diversions, rather than directing his full energy into the more purposeful activity for the war effort. The dandy, white or black, was regarded as something of a shirker or draft-dodger. A correspondent to a local newspaper in East London described himself as a 'reformed dandy' who joined the French Red Cross as an ambulance driver when rejected by the army because of a withered arm. 'I made a determined resolution to cast off my tight waist overcoat, patent leather shoes and plush hat in exchange for a more up-to-date style and at last succeeded in getting a whole new suit of clothes more creditable than any I have worn.'[68]

The populist weekly, the *Empire News*, having supported attacks against the Chinese seafaring community instigated by the National Sailors' and Firemen's Union, became increasingly hostile towards the entire non-white population in the metropole. The paper endeavoured to stir up particular resentment towards relationships between black men and white women. In September 1917, a feature article reported:

> The black dandy is a familiar figure in our city streets these days. Sambo or Rastus, in the stetson hat, his coat cut squarely at the shoulders as though hanging from a clothes-horse, and wearing bull-nosed boots that reflect Broadway, is gone. To-day the high-price tailor has the patronage of the black men in our midst. The forty-shilling suit (so some of our leading tailors informed an Empire News man) is an outrage on the coloured man's taste. Mention a fine, light-grey tweed, a fashionably tinted blue at about ninety shillings, and there is a chance of business. These men are as fastidious as a woman over the cut of clothes, the shape and colour of boots and the mode in hats. The outfitters have to quicken their wits to provide the 'real stuff' in underwear and ties, whilst the rubber collar merchants are boycotted. No wonder the feminine eye is charmed. Ask the girl you have seen coquetting with a black dandy what she means by it. You will promptly be told he looks like a gentleman, generous, and no commoner. He must be a student of something or other and his father a landed man who grows most of the world's needs. [69]

For the black population in the Caribbean, well-chosen attire was a means of placing distance between the menial drudgery of plantation labour and of ensuring visible expression for hard-earned pay. Pre-war, white observers were quick to mock the appearance of a fashionable black man who 'walk[ed] with a curious strut – for all the world like a half-lame peacock'.[70] But now, images of well dressed black men stood in marked contrast to wartime frugality and the battle-weary British Tommy. The anxieties of wartime white masculinity were mapped onto non-white men of all shades, resulting in increased hostility towards black men employed as seafarers and war workers in London, Manchester, Liverpool and Birmingham.

From Autumn 1916, the trade union movement voiced concern over the proposed introduction of black labour in munitions factories and unskilled reserved occupations, to free white manpower for the front line. Enmity extended towards men from the West Indies and West Africa already attracted to Britain by wartime employment opportunities.[71] The Triple Alliance of mine, rail and transport workers passed a resolution that demanded a halt to 'the sinister movement to import coloured labour into this country'.[72] The Alliance expressed 'irrevocable opposition to any and every effort in this direction' and urged organised labour to take appropriate action.

Pro-war elements in the labour movement were not just concerned about the potential competition from cheap imported labour. Rather, the presence of black labour brought the manhood and honour of the nation into question. Addressing parliament in November 1916, Will Thorne, leader of the munici-pal workers and MP for West Ham South, suggested that '[i]f all whites did their duty there would be no need for blacks'.[73] But many men in Thorne's own constituency, that included the docks of Canning Town, were simply not fit to 'do their duty' – they had been invalided from the forces already or were in poor health. Mansfield House, a university settlement in the area, reported a steady stream of discharged soldiers. Some had been rejected at the training stage; others had been wounded or had suffered serious disease. If they were fit to work at all, most were only capable of light work.[74] Relatively fit black men seek-ing heavy work in the munitions factories or attempting to enlist, could not have provided a starker contrast, and fuelled the anxiety of those preoccupied by economic and sexual competition.

As fear shifted from German occupation to 'this coloured invasion', a correspondent in the *Umpire* expressed astonishment that black men could be found 'mixing with whites, and enjoying the full privileges of the people of England'.[75] He demanded: '[I]n the interests of all concerned, our governing authorities should at once take the necessary steps for the proper control of these men'.[76] The correspondent, who had apparently spent time in South Africa, called for the appointment of a 'Commissioner for Native Affairs', to combat the 'increasing disorderliness among blacks in different parts of the country',[77] through segregated public transport, exclusion from public pave-ments and the prohibition of alcohol.

Black men observed 'knocking about English streets with their tool bags, suggesting that they are employed as artisans' were not regarded as part of the war effort. Rather, they were 'loitering ... in search of the opposite sex',[78] threatening the very social fabric of metropolitan society. An article in the *Empire News* that suggested that the presence of black labour was a necessary evil, did so in terms that underlined the association of black skin with physi-cal prowess, unwittingly alluding to the potential attraction black manhood posed in relation to the battle-fatigued Tommy. The writer, who had recently encountered 'a finely-built, coal-black Hercules, accompanied by his small white wife',[79] cautioned his readers, 'We want every hand we can get, every ounce of muscle, every effort, and we cannot afford to quibble about the colour of the skin ... when we get down to the bed-rock of things it is only by the strength of men – actual muscular effort and the sweat of the brow – that we can win this war'.[80]

At the root of these concerns were fears women might disregard the obligations of national service, that stipulated control and public-spirited self-sacrifice, and even more importantly, that the sexual boundaries of Empire would be breached.[81] 'Where we formerly saw one white woman married to a black, or living with him, we now see scores', complained the *Empire News*. To police these threats to national and Imperial order the writer urged the provision of separate black districts, out of bounds to local white women, and providing black war workers with 'rational amusements' to stop them 'loung[ing] at corners outside public-houses'. Any reward that accrued to the black war worker should be enjoyed 'beneath the sunshine of his native skies'.[82] Working-class women were regarded as 'easily tempted by free-handed Negroes earning good money',[83] who were portrayed living in squalor and alcoholic excess. Women who took up with black men were to be discouraged from forming permanent relationships that might result in 'treason to their ... gift of motherhood'.[84] Offspring from such relationships raised the spectre of racial degeneration and miscegenation in a society already sensitised by the alleged dysgenics of war and the differential birth rate.

By the summer of 1917 reaction to the black presence was more hostile. The Manchester-based *Daily Dispatch* carried a series of articles, reprinted in the Jamaican press, complaining of 'The Black Peril', in particular alleging the 'pronounced weakness' of black men 'for associating with white women'.[85] Parents of young women were said to be 'crying out ... that conditions should be returned to normal',[86] a sentiment that underscored a desire for the apparent peacetime certainty. An 'Anxious Mother', articulated the widely held belief that women should not engage in behaviour that transgressed the boundaries of race, class and gender while their men risked death or injury at the front.[87]

> It makes me feel sick to see so many of our white girls walking about with black men. These girls appear to have lost all sense of shame and self-respect. If they have not the sense for themselves then the Government should step in and remove a temptation which is daily becoming more hideous.[88]

The Salvation Army commissioned an investigation 'into the danger attendant upon this coloured invasion'[89] in Manchester, waging war on 'sin' that encompassed black men, alcohol, dancing and the 'selling of bodies'. A female Army social officer bemoaned that in a 'public-house named the –, in – street, –, a number of young girls, from 16 years upwards, are night after night consorting with and listening to the persuasions of coloured men. No notice is taken by anyone. Can no one save them? It is heartbreaking .'[90] The insinuation was clear – while white men served the nation, the hordes of Empire had swept in to beguile their unprotected and unpoliced wives and daughters.

As white women were condemned for ignoring the sexual boundaries of Empire, the spectre of black men taking white women by force was resurrected. The 'Dusky Lady-killer' in khaki was now literally viewed as such. Women ignored the vitriol of the press and middle-class anxieties when they formed relationships with black soldiers, seamen and war workers. But women could also be drawn into anti-black violence and this may have been linked to representations of black men as violent and sexually predatory. The *Umpire* suggested that in South Africa, '90 per cent of the cases of rape, and other indecent assaults on white women, are committed by the Kaffir', adding '[t]here is generally a gang to way-lay its victim'.[91] The case of a servant girl in Edinburgh, apparently abducted by two black men and driven for several miles around the city in a taxicab, before escaping was also reported.[92] Such stories implied an absence of white male guardianship and were given added potency against the backdrop of white male ineffectiveness represented by the mental and physical consequences of the war.

In July 1917, disturbances occurred in London's Canning Town, which had become home to a significant black and Asian population linked to maritime trade, including Jamaicans.[93] Several black seamen were attacked in their lodgings or on the street. Two male and three female assailants were subsequently found guilty of assault and damage to property. A black seaman was fined for discharging an unlicensed firearm in an attempt to disperse the mob.[94] Local newspapers reported the case under the headline 'Baiting Black Men: Girls Infatuation Leads to Trouble: In consequence of the infatuation of white girls for black men in the district some of the inhabitants are greatly incensed against the blacks.'[95] But the black seamen and their white female companions were viewed as the primary transgressors as is evident in the following courtroom exchange: 'In reply to the Magistrate, Inspr. Ashton said the feeling in the neighbourhood was that the blacks were getting a little too big.

The Magistrate: On account of the stupid conduct of the girls in going about with them? – Yes, sir.'[96]

Images of unrestrained black sexuality also served to restore the racial hierarchies of Empire, by presenting black men as lacking in self-control and rationality. In February 1919, Ernest Nembhard, a black Jamaican recruited to the 3 King's Own Yorkshire Light Infantry by the British military mission in New York, was accused of indecently assaulting a woman after he wandered onto a farm at Burstwick, in the East Riding of Yorkshire. Under the headline, 'Mad Negro',[97] the local newspaper reported the accused was unfit to plead.

The incident encapsulated the racial anxieties that had taken hold during the war years. A black man was held to have violated the private and symbolic property of the white man when he strayed onto the farm and struggled with the farmer's wife, Elizabeth Hawley, when she challenged him. Nembhard was apprehended by Farmer Hawley, assisted by several of his labourers, and driven in a cart to the local police station, from where he was incarcerated in Rampton asylum. In the struggle, Elizabeth Hawley had 'felt his hand above one of [her] knees' and according to the husband, 'one of the prisoner's trouser buttons ... was unfastened'.[98] Nembhard for his part, complained that he had nearly been choked by a rope fastened around his neck by the arresting men.

A report from Rampton described Private Nembhard as 'dangerous, noisy, destructive and irrational',[99] characteristics routinely applied to the subject races, particularly when they threatened the status quo. Although the report conceded that Nembhard had 'since written coherent letters, is now quiet, well-balanced and apparently rational',[100] he was still deemed too dangerous to be freed.[101] Ordered to be detained 'during His Majesty's pleasure', Nembhard was, however, returned to Jamaica in late 1919.

Racial attacks blighted black communities in nine seaport towns and cities throughout most of 1919. Between May and September in London's East End black seafarers were routinely assaulted. In July, a black Jamaican, John Martin, on leave from the Navy, was cleared of wounding and discharging a firearm, following unrest in Limehouse.[102] The worst violence occurred in Cardiff and Liverpool during May and June when there were several fatalities. In both cities, former soldiers of the BWIR were attacked, as were Yemeni, Somali and Chinese seamen. Racialised sexual jealousy was an essential element in these outbreaks of violence, as had been the case in Canning Town during 1917. The local and national press, which inflamed the situation by routinely linking black men to pimping and other nefarious trades, reiterated the view that the association of black men with white women, 'who have no self-respect', generated the violence. Black seamen in Hull, some of whom were attacked in a night of violence on 19 June 1920, were said to be 'liberal with money towards women, who prefer to go and live with them'[103] causing much local resentment. But this was not solely a middle-class moral panic. The seamen's union chose to complain of 'the attention paid by coloured men to the waitresses at some ... cafes',[104] rather than economic competition which has often been viewed as the chief cause of the riots.[105]

A chief cause of this racialised sexual anxiety was the relative potency ascribed to black masculinity. Indeed this was recognised by a black letter-writer responding to the racial hostility of the Manchester press. 'People speak of us being young and of fine physique, and fit for military service. In our coloured race ... [t]here are no conscientious objectors. Every coloured man who is a British subject is a soldier or munitions worker.'[106] The post-war spectre of unemployment and poverty only served to underline the poor outlook for white manhood exposed during the war.

Judgements delivered by magistrates after further disturbances in Canning Town during August 1919, reflected this temporary disruption to the racial hierarchy. Black seamen with war service were viewed in a more favourable light than white casual labour – the 'residuum' – who were described in terms that would have more often been applied to the subject races. Thomas Pell, a Jamaican who had been attacked in the Canning Town unrest of 1917, suffered a further assault on the lodging house that he owned. A white man, William Grantham, was sentenced to two months' hard labour for assault and criminal damage. His wife, Florence, was bound over for striking a black man on his doorstep in a neighbouring street. Three Jamaican seamen were accused of discharging firearms over the heads of an angry white crowd; one was found guilty and fined twenty shillings.

Grantham, who had led the attack on Pell's lodging house, was said to have been 'behaving like a raving lunatic' after stirring up racial antagonism in the area for several weeks. The solicitor representing the black defendants related to the court how a number of local butchers had emerged from their premises 'brandishing choppers and other implements of their trade and threaten[ing] to kill the accused [Jamaican seamen]'[107] who fired in the air in self-defence. The stipendiary magistrate described the attacks as unprovoked and stated that the Jamaicans were British subjects 'and entitled to protection as much as any other of His Majesty's subjects. After the gallantry of our subject races during the war it was a very shabby thing for loafers in the docks to turn upon them.'[108] But it remained to be seen whether black veterans would have these ideals of subjecthood and wartime endeavour invoked in their favour when they encountered the military establishment, or the colonial regime when they returned to the West Indies.

Notes

1 Horner, *From the Islands of the Sea*, pp. 7–8.
2 *Daily Telegraph* 4 November 1889, p. 4.
3 Richard Dyer, *Heavenly Bodies: Film Stars and Society* (Basingstoke: Macmillan, 1986).
4 Rhonda Cobham, 'Jekyll and Claude: The Erotics of Patronage', in Cindy Patton and Benigno Sanchez-Eppler (eds.), *Queer Diasporas* (Durham: Duke University Press, 2000), pp. 124–5.
5 Robert H. MacDonald, *Sons of the Empire: The Frontier and the Boy Scout Movement, 1890–1918* (Toronto: University of Toronto Press, 1993), pp. 8–13.

6 Ibid., p. 86.

7 Ronald Hyam, *Empire and Sexuality: The British Experience* (Manchester: Manchester University Press, 1990), pp. 1–2, 127–33.

8 Kobena Mercer and Isaac Julien, 'Race, Sexual Politics and Black Masculinity: A dossier', in Rowena Chapman, and Jonathan Rutherford (eds.), *Male Order: Unwrapping Masculinity* (London: Lawrence and Wishart, 1988), pp. 107–8.

9 Dyer, *Heavenly Bodies*, p. 139.

10 Vera Brittain, *Testament of Youth* (London: Fontana, 1979 [1933]), pp. 420–1.

11 Ibid., 423.

12 Horner, *From the Islands of the Sea*, p. 12.

13 Ibid., p. 33.

14 Sharon Ouditt, *Fighting Forces, Writing Women: Identity and Ideology in the First World War* (London: Routledge, 1994), pp. 38–9.

15 J. A. Mangan, *The Games Ethic and Imperialism: Aspects of the Diffusion of an Ideal* (London: Viking, 1986), pp. 169–72.

16 Stephen A. Hill (ed.), *Who's Who in Jamaica, 1919–1920* (Kingston: Gleaner Co., 1920), p. 247.

17 Fussell, *Great War and Modern Memory*, pp. 275–81.

18 Ibid., 22–3.

19 Extract from poem probably by Horatio Forbes Brown quoted in Timothy d'Arch Smith, *Love in Earnest* (London: Routledge and Kegan Paul, 1970), p. 108.

20 Kenan Malik, *The Meaning of Race: Race, History and Culture in Western Society* (London: Macmillan, 1996), pp. 91–100.

21 BWIR Album, cutting poss. *WICC*, n.d.

22 *Daily News* cited in *The Times History of the War*, Vol. XIX, p. 86.

23 See PRO CO318/344/55651 General Headquarters (hereafter GHQ), British Armies in France to Secretary, WO 8 November 1917 Services of the Battalions of the BWIR; WO95/5318 WD 2WIR entry for 3 July 1918; WO95/4732 WD 2WIR entry for 24 December 1918.

24 *Newhaven Chronicle*, 14 October 1915.

25 Winter, *Great War* p. 32.

26 *Daily Sketch*, 10 January 1917, BWIR Album.

27 Ouditt, *Fighting Forces*, p. 18.

28 Angela Woollacott, '"Khaki Fever" and its control: Gender, Class, Age and Sexual Morality on the British Homefront in the First World War', *Journal of Contemporary History*, 29:2, 1994, 325–47; Glenford D. Howe, 'Military–Civilian Intercourse, Prostitution and Venereal Disease Among Black West Indian Soldiers During World War 1', *Journal of Caribbean History*, 31:1/2, 1997, 91.

29 James Walvin, 'Symbols of Moral Superiority: Slavery, Sport and the Changing World Order, 1800–1950', in J. A. Mangan and James Walvin (eds.), *Manliness and Morality: Middle-Class Masculinity in Britain and America, 1800–1940* (Manchester: Manchester University Press, 1987), pp. 242–50.

30 Jeffrey Green, *Black Edwardians: Black People in Britain, 1901–1914* (London: Frank Cass, 1998), pp. 172–8.

31 *The Times*, 19 September 1911, p. 5.

32 Ibid., 2 May 1914, p. 10.

33 Ibid., 25 May 1914, p. 40.

34 For an overview of black boxers in Britain from the late eighteenth century see Peter Fryer, *Staying Power: The History of Black People in Britain* (London: Pluto, 1984), pp. 227–8, 445–54.

35 *The Times*, 16 March 1914, p. 14; 17 March 1914, p. 14; 31 March 1914, p. 16; 11 April 1914, p. 13.

36 Ibid., 31 March 1914, p. 16.

37 *Zouave* June 1914, p. 88.

38 Cipriani, *Twenty Years After*, pp. 69–70; *Egyptian Gazette*, April–Sept. 1917.

39 C. M. Ogilvie, *A Diary of the Great War* (Kingston: Jamaica Times Printery, 1919), pp. 41–8, 51–2.

40 Phil Vasili, 'Walter Tull, 1888–1918: Soldier, Footballer, Black', *Race and Class*, 38:2, 1996, 60.'

41 James Johnston Abraham (1876–1963) was a Lieutenant Colonel in the Royal Army Medical Corps (RAMC). He served as a surgical specialist in Egypt and as Assistant Director of Medical Services for Lines of Communication troops in the EEF between 1917 and 1919. He published medical, autobiographical and fictional works under his own name and the pseudonym James Harpole.

42 J. Johnston Abraham, *Surgeon's Journey* (London: Heinemann, 1957), p. 186.

43 Ibid.

44 Quoted in d'Arch Smith, *Love in Earnest*, pp. 138–9.

45 Abraham, ibid. There are some striking similarities between Abraham's observations and Henry Bleby's recollections of Sam Sharpe during the 1831 Jamaican slave rebellion: Henry Bleby, *Death Struggles of Slavery* (London: Hamilton, Adams and Co., 1853), pp. 115–18.

46 Ramson 'Carry On', pp. 18–20.

47 Abraham, *Surgeon's Journey*, p. 187 (my italics).

48 Ibid.

49 BWIR Album, cutting poss. *WICC*, n.d.

50 Ibid., *Natal Witness*, 25 January 1916.

51 Ibid., *Liverpool Courier*, 20 November 1915.

52 Ibid., *War Budget*, 28 October 1915.

53 Glenford Howe, 'West Indians and World War One', in Howe, *Race, War and Nationalism*, pp. 89–90.

54 Claude McKay, *A Long Way From Home* (London: Pluto, 1985), p. 67; *Negro World* (magazine section) 13 March 1920.

55 Horner, *From the Islands of the Sea*, p. 50.

56 Ibid., p. 51.

57 *DG* 10 May 1916, p. 11.

58 Horner, *From the Islands of the Sea*, p. 67.

59 Edward Brathwaite, *The Development of Creole Society in Jamaica 1770–1820* (Oxford: Oxford University Press, 1971), pp. 200–1. For further analysis of the 'Quashie' stereotype and perspectives on other forms of passive slave resistance see Michael Craton, *Testing the Chains: Resistance to Slavery in the British West Indies* (Ithaca, NY: Cornell University Press, 1982), pp. 52–7; Orlando Patterson, *The Sociology of Slavery* (London: MacGibbon and Kee, 1967), pp. 174–81.

60 Horner, *From the Islands of the Sea*, pp. 47–8.

61 Quoted in Philippa Levine, 'Battle Colors: Race, Sex, and Colonial Soldiery in World War I', *Journal of Women's History*, 8:4, 1998, 106.

62 Dyde, *Empty Sleeve*, pp. 148–50.

63 BWIR Album, cutting poss. *WICC*, n.d.

64 F. C. Green 'Introduction' to Gustave Flaubert, *Salammbo* (trans. J. C. Chartres) (London: J. M. Dent and Sons, 1931).

65 IWM 85/39/1 Mrs M. A. A Thomas unpublished tss, p. 20. Thomas was born in India and volunteered for nursing service in April 1916 aged 22. She was based at Basra No. 3 British General Hospital, Mesopotamia. She spent an extended period in West Africa after the war.

66 Ibid.

67 Anne McClintock, *Imperial Leather: Race, Gender and Sexuality in the Colonial Context* (London: Routledge, 1995), pp. 207–8.

68 *Stratford Express*, 12 May 1915, p. 1.

69 *Empire News*, 2 September 1917, p. 4.

70 Henderson, *Jamaica*, p. 91.

71 Jacqueline Jenkinson, 'The 1919 Riots', in Panikos Panayi (ed.), *Racial Violence in Britain in the Nineteenth and Twentieth Centuries* (Leicester: Leicester University Press, 1996), p. 96; *The Times*, 23 November 1916, p. 5; 22 December 1916, p. 5; *Umpire*, 17 September 1916, pp. 4, 6.

72 *The Times*, 22 December 1916, p. 5.

73 Ibid., 3 November 1916, p. 12.

74 *Mansfield House Magazine*, XXIV, 7/8, July/Aug. 1917, 80–1.

75 *Umpire* 17 September 1916, p. 6.

76 Ibid.

77 Ibid.

78 *Umpire*, 17 September 1916, p. 6.

79 *Empire News*, 12 August 1917, p. 2.

80 Ibid.

81 Levine, 'Battle Colors', 106, 109; Sonya O. Rose, 'Sex, Citizenship, and the Nation in World War II Britain', *American Historical Review*, 103:4, 1998, 1148–9, 1164–9.

82 *Empire News*, 12 August 1917, p. 2.

83 Ibid.

84 Ibid.

85 *Daily Dispatch*, 8 August 1917, p. 3.

86 Ibid.

87 Fears that white women would be seduced by black men while their husbands were at the front was perhaps more evident in France where large numbers of Senegalese troops were stationed: Melzer, 'Spectacles and Sexualities', pp. 225–9. Colonial migrant workers introduced by the French to maintain wartime production were also a source of racialised sexual anxiety. Often forcibly recruited in their own countries and kept in segregated quarters, migrants from the Far East, North and West Africa were subject to frequent attacks from Spring 1917: Tyler Stovall, 'The Color Line Behind the Lines: Racial Violence in France During the Great War', *American Historical Review*, 103:3, 737–69.

88 *Daily Dispatch*, 8 August 1917, p. 3.

89 Ibid.

90 Ibid.
91 *Umpire*, 17 September 1916, p. 6.
92 *Umpire*, 21 January 1917, p. 1.
93 *Annual Report of the Queen Victoria Seamen's Rest*, 1922, pp. 14–17; For more background to the black community in East London see Rozina Visram, 'Kamal A. Chunchie of the Coloured Men's Institute: The Man and the Legend', *Immigrants and Minorities*, 18:1, 1999, 29–48.
94 *Stratford Express*, 7 July 1917, p. 6 and 14 July 1917, p. 7.
95 *Stratford Express*, 7 July 1917, p. 6.
96 Ibid.
97 *Hull Daily News*, 9 April 1919, p. 5.
98 East Riding of Yorkshire Record Office, Easter Quarter Sessions, Rex v. Ernest Archibald Nembhard, witness depositions 7 March 1919.
99 PRO CO137/735 copy of Rampton report enclosed in HO to WO 28 November 1919.
100 Ibid.
101 PRO CO137/735 WO to USS, CO 24 September 1919.
102 *East End News* 9 May 1919, p. 3; 30 May 1919, p. 5; 3 June 1919, p. 3; 6 June 1919, p. 5; 10 June 1919, p. 3; 20 June 1919, p. 5; 12 August 1919, p. 3; 25 August 1919, p. 4; 2 September 1919, p. 3; 9 September 1919, p. 3; *The Times*, 1 July 1919, p. 4.
103 Hull Times, 26 June 1920, p. 7.
104 *Seaman*, 11 April 1919, p. 2.
105 Fryer, *Staying Power*, pp. 297–311. For further background to the riots see Roy May and Robin Cohen, 'The Interaction Between Race and Colonialism: A Case Study of the Liverpool Race Riots of 1919', *Race and Class*, 14:2, 1974, 111–26; Jacqueline Jenkinson, 'The Glasgow Race Disturbances of 1919' in Kenneth Lunn (ed.), *Race and Labour in Twentieth-Century Britain* (London: Frank Cass, 1985); Neil Evans, 'The South Wales Riots of 1919', *Llafur*, 3:1, 1980, 1–24.
106 Daily Dispatch, 9 August 1917, p. 6.
107 *Stratford Express*, 16 August 1919, p. 6.
108 Ibid.

6 Discrimination and mutiny

As the proximate black male form threatened to destabilise the conventions of racial superiority, West Indian volunteers were treated by the military hierarchy in ways that attempted to restore ideas of the black man as inferior in character, intelligence and morality. The refusal to deploy black West Indian volunteers in the firing line was compounded by official blunders, poor medical treatment and outright racial discrimination.

At Seaford Camp, where the first contingents arrived from Autumn 1915, the British West Indies Regiment was accommodated in damp huts and provided with insufficient sanitary facilities, resulting in high levels of sickness and infirmity. Local hospitals were filled with men suffering from pneumonia. These circumstances did not improve for the duration of the war and set the tone for the regiment's subsequent treatment in other areas. Disease took a far higher toll on the BWIR than enemy action. Some 178 men were killed or died of wounds; 697 were wounded and 1,071 died of disease.[1]

BWIR soldiers stationed in France were routinely excluded from facilities enjoyed by other British soldiers. *Estaminets* – simple cafés run by French civilians that provided the Tommy with some relief from the indigestible army diet – had been ruled out of bounds to men in the Chinese and South African labour battalions by the Estaminet Order. The Chinese and South African battalions were kept in highly segregated conditions more akin to prisoner-of-war camps, despite the essential role they played in maintaining supplies to the front line. The military and Imperial authorities wished to prevent contact between non-white soldiers and white women. Mixed relationships had the potential to destabilise hierarchies of race and class and to undermine ideals of family and nation central to the encouragement of military service in the metropole. With these concerns in mind, the provisions of the Estaminet Order were informally extended to the BWIR, even though the regiment was officially classed as a British infantry unit.[2]

In January 1918, Ernest Price, the head of the Baptist Theological College in Kingston, complained to Governor Manning about the poor treatment experienced by sick and wounded West Indian soldiers in France. An army chaplain had informed him the hospitals were unheated and the food was poor, while German prisoners were kept in comparative luxury.[3] Throughout the war, the men were regularly treated in the substandard 'native hospitals' provided for the labourers recruited from South Africa, China, Fiji and Egypt. This was in defiance of instructions issued by the Director-General of Medical Services for the Lines of Communication troops in France.[4]

In response to Ernest Price's complaints, Governor Manning urged the Secretary of State for the Colonies to investigate medical facilities provided to the BWIR. However, Manning was keen that any investigation should exonerate the military and suggested, like many colonial and military officials, the change in climate was responsible for the high death rate from disease. Any complaints he regarded as unsoldierly: 'I have seen not a few cases which upon investigation have been proved to be unfounded and the work of men who are not always good soldiers. Hardship there must be, but the good soldier takes such uncomplainingly'.[5]

On 2 August 1918 nineteen men of the BWIR protested at their continued detention as 'lunatics' in the Mental Compound of the Marseilles Stationary Hospital. Some of the men had rounded on a medical officer the previous month and Lieutenant Colonel Wilson RAMC, the director of the hospital, ordered the men be kept handcuffed to their beds. The prisoners managed to release themselves and escaped from the compound, obtaining knives and razors to defend themselves from an unguarded store. When the men were eventually subdued twelve were imprisoned in the Fort St Nicholas, Marseilles as they were regarded as 'a danger to the neighbourhood'.[6]

The Director of Medical Services (DMS) ordered a court of inquiry into the episode and it became apparent the diagnoses of mental illness had been used by the authorities at Marseilles as a means of detaining men regarded as a threat to military order. The DMS himself demanded to know why the men had continued to be classified as mentally ill when they adopted a plan of joint action and suggested the riot would not have broken out if they had been handled with more tact. Captain Henry Yellowlees, an RAMC mental specialist who was to achieve post-war eminence, examined the men at the end of August. He reported that 'with few exceptions all the histories and symptoms show a remarkable similarity. The exceptions are clear cases of well-defined mental diseases. Most of the remainder are not truly insane ... but are cases of severe hysteria of a type unfamiliar amongst white men.'[7] While conceding that the majority of the black soldiers were not mentally ill, Yellowlees was nevertheless at pains to dismiss the men's protests as a sign of irrationality and loss of self-control, rather than a considered response to inhumane treatment.

Although Yellowlees recommended the BWIR patients be repatriated to the West Indies, most continued to be detained at Marseilles until well after the Armistice. In early 1919 the men made further protests against their continued detention. An anonymous letter from one of the men reached the War Office and arrangements were made to bring about early demobilisation. In the meantime, extra sugar, soap and toothpowder were issued as a concession. Intermittent disturbances continued and Lieutenant Colonel A. J. Scott, who had replaced Wilson as hospital director, gave instructions the protests were to be suppressed with bayonets and then live ammunition if necessary.[8] Protests by the BWIR patients reached a peak on 20 February when they were allowed to attend a concert at the YMCA. The men deliberately took up front seats reserved for officers and were ordered back to their wards. In the ensuing mêlée, several senior officers were attacked before the men were subdued and returned to their compound. Privates Cameron and Kirby, who were singled out as ringleaders, were confined to the military prison where once again medical examiners came to the conclusion they were not insane and were therefore fit to stand trial before a courts martial.[9]

The poor medical treatment provided to the BWIR and other non-white troops occurred elsewhere during the demobilisation period. The first, second and fifth battalions of the BWIR, who had seen active service in Palestine, were transferred to Italy and placed under the command of a South African, Brigadier-General Carey Bernard, while they awaited transports back to the Caribbean. Bernard insisted on describing the BWIR in all official orders as 'coloured natives', despite the offence it caused in the regimental orderly rooms. The men were denied access to the YMCA and cinema, and when sick were treated in the inferior 'native' hospitals. They were also barred from visiting the local town except on certain days between 4 and 8 p.m. and with the proviso that they had been vaccinated within the last twelve months. Rather than being seen as comrades-in-arms, the men of the BWIR were regarded as potential sources of contagion and a threat to the British military operation.[10]

Poor camp conditions and frequent sickness impacted on training and efficiency. The lack of training meant that the first and second battalions of the BWIR lost an early opportunity to be deployed on active service in the Western Desert. After pressure from Lt Col. Wood Hill, the commanding officer, it was henceforth decided that later contingents should be dispatched directly to Alexandria in Egypt which was deemed a more suitable climate.[11]

Climatic explanations were central to representations of racial difference. Tropical regions were marked out as adverse environments for human endeavour and progress, while colder, Northern climes were associated with industry and cultural advance.[12] Somewhat paradoxically, colder conditions were believed to further impair the poorly regarded military efficiency of black soldiers. This served to legitimise their deployment as labourers, away from exposed trench conditions in France hence avoiding the more vexed questions that could arise if they were deployed in force against white adversaries. Deployment in the Middle East, deemed a more suitable climate for black soldiers, meant that the opposing forces were non-white Turks. The second battalion of the WIR and the detachment of the BWIR sent to East Africa were deployed against the native *askaris* that comprised the majority of the German forces.

These climatic associations reinforced the designation 'native' troops and served to remove the BWIR from the pay increase granted to other British regiments by Army Order 1 of 1918. The Order increased the pay of a private soldier by 50 per cent, from one shilling to one and sixpence per day. In April 1918 the War Office ruled the BWIR was not eligible by choosing to regard the regiment a 'native' unit. Officers of the BWIR immediately wrote to the War Office appealing against the decision, reminding the department that the BWIR had been specifically granted the same pay as other British Army infantry units shortly after its inception by the provisions of Army Order 5 of 1916.[13] The matter was also taken up by the West Indian Contingent Committee (WIC Ctte), an organisation set up under the auspices of the West India Committee to act as advocates for and to cater for the welfare of the BWIR regiment. The War Office tried to evade the issue by stating that the pay increase applied only to units with a depot in the United Kingdom. The BWIR depot had, of course, been relocated to Egypt for 'climatic' reasons. However, the West Indian Contingents Committee pointed out that this had not prevented the pay award being extended to white South African troops.[14]

Even some Colonial Office administrators were taken aback by the decision. Reporting on the matter, H. T. Allen, a Confidential Clerk, conceded lower separation allowances and pensions paid to men in the West Indies were perhaps fair, given the lower rates of wages and standards of living pertaining there. But, he argued, '[t]he economic argument has ... no substance as regards the pay of a soldier on active service. His monetary reward ... is purely nominal, having regard to the value of his services and the dangers and discomforts of his occupation'.[15] Allen pointed out the £500,000 cost of equalising the pay of all non-white colonial troops constituted around two hours of war expenditure. Allen argued that military sacrifice for the Mother Country should be recognised regardless of race and refuted the suggestion that men in labour units should be paid at a lesser rate, pointing out there was no pay difference between white labour battalions and front-line troops. More significantly he feared resentment, leading to unrest, would result, particularly in Jamaica. The BWIR and WIR did not at first receive the War Bonus granted by Army Order 17 of 1919, even though the provisions of the order expressly included the two regiments. It was not until April 1919 after continued appeals to the War Office and considerable unrest that the pay increases and bonus authorised in Army Order 1 of 1918 and Army Order 17 of 1919 were awarded to the BWIR.[16] The War Bonus was also eventually granted to the West India Regiment, but its historic 'native' designation meant only NCOs were awarded the general pay increase of 1917.[17]

Fifteen Jamaicans, including Sergeant M. Halliburton, who had recently won the Military Medal, were among forty-one signatories to a petition of BWIR NCOs serving in Palestine. The petition demanded army pay increases be accorded to the BWIR, their loyal wartime service be fully recognised and the consequent slight cast upon the West Indies be lifted.

> The majority of the men of the British West Indies Regiment are taxpayers ... and loyal subjects of His Majesty, and we feel that this discrimination is not only an insult to us who have volunteered to fight for the Empire but also an insult to the West Indies ... We would like it to be understood that the motive of this memorandum is not so much to get the pecuniary benefits from which we have been denied, as to bring before his Excellency that we are alive to the fact that as West Indians we have been unfairly discriminated against.[18]

Many members of the regiment still felt a personal loyalty to the King despite their ill-treatment. Such a stance was understandable given the involvement of George V in the establishment of the regiment and the reception of his 'Appeal' of October 1915. Anger was directed at local commanders who were suspected of obstructing the sovereign's intentions as epitomised in a 'soldiers' yarn' bemoaning the parlous state of the meat ration: 'Look Yah Sah ... King George send a half a cow teday fe de battalion and dis is all dem gie me fe meat rachine.'[19]

The discrimination in pay and conditions and access to army social facilities was compounded by a harsh disciplinary regime. Many of BWIR officers were members of the West Indian planter class. The most senior commanders were professional soldiers seconded from the WIR, usually nearing retirement and hardened by their years in a regiment characterised by racial hierarchy. Other officers were assigned from other British Army regiments or posted from the least capable applicants for temporary commissions in the New Army.[20] Shortly after the war, George Elliot, a former black NCO with the WIR, remarked that sending raw officers from England was 'not a help to British prestige; for it takes many Europeans more than a year to read a "Black man", and fully three or four years to understand his "pigeon" English'.[21]

White West Indian officers offered a complex mixture of extreme discipline and paternalism. Etienne Dupuch remembered Captain George Dawson of the 4th British West Indies Regiment as the epitome of the Jamaican planter class. Dawson ordered the men to collect material to make him a dugout while they lived in tents exposed to shellfire.[22] Another white Jamaican officer, Colonel Willis of the 9BWIR had a reputation for extreme brutality. In one incident, Willis stamped on a soldier's frost-bitten leg after he had refused to get to his feet, telling a sergeant, 'I'm turning Jesus Christ out here. I'm making the lame walk'.[23] Colonel Wood Hill, commander of the 1BWIR, who had consistently advocated the deployment of the regiment in the front line and frequently intervened to prevent acts of racial discrimination, was not averse to using excessive force. Captain Andrew Cipriani, future leader of the Trinidad Labour Party who regularly defended members of the BWIR in courts martial, wrote a damning indictment of Wood Hill, in his memoir of the war. He described Wood Hill, nicknamed 'Conky Bill', as:

> an autocrat of the first water ... out to get his own way at any cost ... In many cases his viewpoint was so extreme and ridiculous as to almost verge on the maniacal. He was insolent, overbearing and offensive to his officers, senior as well as junior, and in most cases unjust and absurdly despotic to his men'.[24]

In one incident, Wood Hill came close to being cashiered for striking a sergeant under his command. Flogging had been outlawed for men on active service in 1881 and in military prisons in 1907. Many officers, however, continued to regard it as an appropriate form of discipline for 'native' troops. The *Daily Gleaner* reported the case of Lieutenant Eric Larnder of the WIR who was reprimanded for striking a private soldier, James Riley, with a stick. Larnder had been challenged by Riley when the private was on guard duty. The lieutenant countered by accusing Riley of sitting down at his post. A sergeant was ordered to administer six strokes. Larnder himself administered two further blows complaining the sergeant had not used sufficient force. In administering this humiliating treatment, Larnder claimed to be upholding a perverse code of masculine honour. He claimed at the military tribunal he had been trying to preserve the soldier's dignity by carrying out the punishment himself, rather than reporting Riley to a superior officer.[25] This reflected a culture within white Jamaican society, present since slavery, that blacks were answerable to the personal and paternalistic authority of a white man, rather than the rule of law.

That both Larnder and even a senior officer of Wood Hill's standing could be brought to book indicates that black soldiers did enjoy limited protection from physical abuse. The army still retained, however, another routine punishment capable of resurrecting the collective memory of slavery. Field Punishment Number One, commonly known as 'crucifixion', gained a notoriety throughout the British Army during the war, and several campaigns sought to abolish it. A memo from Lloyd George to the French War Ministry detailed the harshness of the punishment while ironically trying to provide assurance sufficient safeguards were in place to protect the soldier. 'FP No. 1' as it usually appears in battalion and disciplinary records, could be applied for up to 90 days. Lloyd George's memo illustrates why the continued use of the punishment may have provoked particularly strong feelings among black soldiers, who had enlisted in a war regularly portrayed in the West Indies as a struggle against slavery. A soldier could

> be kept in irons, i.e. fetters or handcuffs, or both fetters and handcuffs; and may be secured so as to prevent his escape ... When in irons he may be attached for a period or periods not exceeding two hours in any one day to a fixed object, but he must not be so attached during more than three out of any four consecutive days, nor during more than twenty-one days in all ... Stumps or ropes may be used for the purpose of these rules in lieu of irons ... He may be subjected to the like labour, employment and restraint and dealt with in like manner as if he were under a sentence of imprisonment with hard labour.[26]

What Lloyd George neglected to inform the French War Ministry was the 'fixed object' was often the wheel of a gun carriage, across which the offender was spread-eagled, sometimes within range of enemy guns. In the military prisoners' compound at Taranto, Dupuch saw men sentenced to 'FP No. 1' being beaten with sticks, in breach of official guidelines. Dupuch was able to intervene in some cases to get the sentence reduced to 'FP No. 2' – loss of pay, daily fatigue duty and a water and biscuit diet.[27]

The refusal to buckle to white authority resulted in the harshest treatment. Private Hubert Clarke was sentenced to death in August 1917 for lightly wounding a military policeman as he was arrested for jeering a cavalry officer passing the field punishment compound at Kantara, Egypt where he was incarcerated. Clarke, clearly a man with little time for military routine had been sentenced to one year's imprisonment with hard labour the previous month for 'persistently marching improperly.'[28] Clarke and several fellow BWIR detainees adopted the tactic of repeatedly banging their mess tins to protest at their imprisonment. Recommending a death sentence, the local commander, Colonel Lloyd stated

> A severe lesson is needed with regard to the repeated instances of insubordination committed by prisoners of the BWI Regiment ... [who] have repeatedly committed acts of insubordination, the punishment for which has been unduly light, and in some instances, offences beyond the powers of a commanding officer have been dealt with summarily. No disciplinary lesson has been taught to insubordinate soldiers in the case of earlier offences – and the result appears to be total disregard for authority.[29]

Prior to embarkation it was clear members of the Jamaican war contingent men would not suffer insult or injustice lightly. The contingent men with a regular, if small, income and an aggressive confidence, generated some resentment from the civilian population resulting in several outbreaks of unrest. In June 1916 civilians and members of the fourth JWC contingent clashed at Kingston racecourse. When two men appeared in court charged with throwing sticks at the contingent, chair of the bench, S. C. Burke, acknowledged that the soldiers had provoked the incident but stated 'They want to show what they can do and they attack civilians'.[30] Fearful the men's desire to prove themselves might lead to confrontations with civil authority, the contingent was confined to barracks guarded by the West India Regiment.[31]

Up to 200 men of the 5 JWC were involved in a more serious disturbance in January 1917. Shop windows were smashed and civilians attacked in Orange Street, Kingston. A local gang 'the big tree band' retaliated in force, armed with sticks and bricks.[32] The rioting soldiers released a comrade from custody and attacked premises where overwhelmed constables had taken shelter. A military Commission of Enquiry found ridicule by the civilian population, encouraged by the police, had led to the unrest. The relative affluence of the contingent men, particularly landowners from the country districts, was resented, especially when it drew the attentions of the townswomen.[33] Civilians regaled volunteers with cries of 'Him foot not used to boots' or 'Him get a clean suit of clothes',[34] directed at both the rural recruits and the poor quality of locally issued uniforms.

Some recruits held themselves to be above the civil law and expected privileges and respect in recognition of their voluntary enlistment. The Tramway Company, the focus of demonstrations over fares increases in 1912, complained some members of the contingent helped themselves to free rides without official sanction. The Enquiry suggested a number of habitual criminals had found their way into the ranks. These men, it was alleged, sought revenge on the police or used the King's uniform as a front for criminal activity. Such allegations only inflamed military–civilian relationships and did not enhance local regard for the contingent, not only among the urban poor, but by whites who viewed Jamaica, with its voluntary enlistment, as a safe backwater to sit out the war, as the Enquiry bemoaned:

> It is common knowledge ... there are men 'who prefer their job out here' whose sense of patriotism is dulled by their sense of personal comfort and safety, and who to find an excuse for not joining the contingent, take directly and indirectly every opportunity to run down and discredit it.[35]

The colonial authorities remained anxious about future unrest in the contingents. Shortly after the Orange Street riot General Blackden, General Officer

Commanding (GOC) Jamaica, argued in a report concerning the prevention of venereal infection among recruits that confinement to barracks was the only foolproof solution. However, he held the resentment and disciplinary problems likely to arise precluded such a policy as 'confinement would have to be enforced with the whole West India Regiment with butt and bayonet, judging by previous experiences'.[36]

Once overseas, as discrimination and ill-treatment mounted and as the heroic engagements imagined in recruiting campaigns failed to materialise, frustration among West Indian volunteers in France and Italy mounted, morale and motivation slumped. The British command in Italy became so concerned about low output and poor quality of work by the BWIR labour battalions that a conference was called to discuss the issue in December 1917. The camp commandant at Taranto reported the BWIR men 'show[ed] a strong disinclination to work, and [did] not seem to pay much attention to their officers or NCOs'.[37] Additional BWIR battalions and Italian soldiers and 7,500 civilians were requisitioned to make good shortcomings at the ordinance depots and engineering workshops at Taranto. When some BWIR units were transferred to France in the wake of the German offensive in Spring 1918, the British increasingly relied on Italian, Sardinian and Maltese labour.[38] Egyptian labourers stationed at Taranto went on strike during Ramadan in 1917 when it came to light they would be paid only from the date of embarkation from Egypt, rather than the date of enlistment.[39] Between September and November 1918 Italian civilian labour became disgruntled over pay and conditions. Fearing strikes the British conceded improved bonuses and overtime payments to Italian and Maltese labour, including women in the ordinance workshops. Clothing allowances and improvements in night and meat rations were also granted. Italian workers also received full pay when labour shortages elsewhere caused temporary idleness.

Spurred on by the improvements granted to local civilian labour, men of the British West Indies Regiment struck in force. Nearly four weeks after the Armistice, on 6 December 1918, Lieutenant-Colonel Willis, commander of the ninth battalion whose cruel methods have been noted, ordered his men to clean latrines used by Italian labourers. A number of men surrounded his tent, slashing it with bayonets. They dispersed quietly, but the following day, the ninth and tenth battalions refused to work. The men were disarmed, but not before unrest had spread to other battalions. Samuel Pinnock, a Jamaican from Clarendon was shot and killed by his sergeant, Robert Richards, who was subsequently found guilty of 'negligently discharging his rifle' and sentenced to four months' imprisonment with hard labour.[40]

Major-General Henry Thullier, wartime head of the Army Chemical Warfare Department, was sent to take control of the situation. Local Italian units were put

10 British West Indies Regiment officers, Egypt, 1917. Colonel R. E. Willis, whose particularly brutal methods contributed to the Taranto mutiny, is pictured in the front row, fifth from left

on standby and a battalion of the Worcestershire regiment, with half a company of machine-gunners attached, was hastily despatched to Taranto. A further battalion with a field gun was held in reserve. The men of the ninth battalion were immediately dispersed among the other BWIR battalions in an effort to separate the ringleaders. Plans were made for the swift demobilisation of at least four battalions and the dispersal of the rest to Egypt, Malta, Salonika or France, in the hope that overwhelming numbers of white troops would serve as a deterrent. The mutiny was swiftly brought to an end – within days the Worcestershire battalion was continuing with its education programme and demobilisation plans. But the British Italian command was unnerved and delivered harsh retribution. Forty-nine men were found guilty of mutiny and sentenced to between three and five years' imprisonment with hard labour – one man received fourteen years and a Private Sanches, apparently the ringleader, received a death sentence, commuted to twenty years' imprisonment. Thirteen men were further charged with escaping confinement, indicating the determined mood among the BWIR.

Another fifteen men received sentences for disobedience or striking an officer.[41] White labour battalions were sent to Taranto to replace the BWIR and to provide cover in the event of strikes by Italian dock labourers. Italian labour was also ordered to undertake the disputed sanitary duties. However, Etienne Dupuch, who arrived with the fifth Battalion shortly after the mutiny, claimed that the BWIR was still routinely deployed on this task.[42]

The act of mutiny took on added significance when it involved black soldiers. Not only military authority, but the racial hierarchy of Empire was challenged, rekindling fears that Britain was losing its grip on the subject races and revisiting Imperial nightmares such as the Indian Mutiny and the Morant Bay rebellion. Most significantly it threatened what the military and colonial authorities had tried to suppress for the duration of the war – black men outperforming white servicemen. Even in leg irons the black mutineer was perceived as a threat. Fifty prisoners from the Taranto mutiny were transferred to Marseilles by train, each was accompanied by an armed British soldier. But the worst fears of the authorities were almost realised when some of these prisoners were involved in a further mutiny in September 1919. The transport ship *Orca* carried several hundred demobilised veterans, including around 270 Jamaicans, back to the West Indies. Around 200 black seamen and civilians, repatriated in the wake of that summer's race riots were also on board. Military prisoners formed part of the BWIR contingent, including five described as 'desperate' mutineers, guarded by fifty white soldiers. The prisoners' mood had been inflamed when promises they would be released from custody once on board ship were broken. They attempted to free themselves assisted by seamen and civilians, themselves angered by their treatment at the hands of white mobs in the metropole. Some BWIR veterans – one of whom, Private Lashley, a Barbadian was shot dead by military police – also endeavoured to free the prisoners. On arrival at Barbados, the prisoners, now in irons, were transferred to HMS *Yarmouth*; the captain of the *Orca* refused to sail further.[43]

Major Hemsley, commanding officer of the military escort, suggested white soldiers were ineffectual compared to their black counterparts:

> Both NCOs and men were extremely young and totally inexperienced in the handling of convicts. Physically they are quite incapable of dealing with coloured men. In the event of any trouble I should have had to order the escort to open fire at once, which would have caused numerous deaths, as in a hand-to-hand conflict the escort would have been overpowered at once.[44]

Order on the *Orca* was only restored through the efforts of BWIR military police and two 'trusties' who exerted a moderating influence on the military prisoners.[45] By the end of the war, not only had images of white male stoicism been dented by the epidemic of 'male hysteria', but eugenicist fears of a metropole denuded of its breeding stock by four years of attrition were not wholly unfounded. The Australian war historian C. E. W. Bean remarked on the extreme youth of many conscripts in the last year of the war, 'companies of children ... pink faced, round cheeked ... flushed under the weight of their unaccustomed packs, with their steel helmets on the back of their heads and the strap hanging loosely on their round baby chins'.[46]

In the wake of the Taranto mutiny, members of the BWIR formed a short-lived organisation, the Caribbean League, a landmark in Anglophone Caribbean nationalism. The chief aim of the League, 'the Promotion of all matters conducive to the General Welfare of the islands constituting the British West Indies and the British Territories adjacent thereto',[47] did not initially unsettle the military authorities, who received a report of the inaugural meeting from an informer. At a subsequent gathering of sergeants from the 3BWIR, one speaker stated to loud applause, that 'the black man should have freedom to govern himself in the West Indies and that force must be used, and if necessary bloodshed, to attain that object'.[48] It was also agreed that a General Strike should be organised after demobilisation to secure higher wages in the region.

The League was composed predominately of sergeants (the highest rank attainable by non-whites) who claimed political leadership on the basis of their relatively high status in the military hierarchy. In contrast, apart from one man on a temporary promotion, all the Taranto mutineers were private soldiers. Despite its radical agenda, the Caribbean League shied away from direct action, indeed, some League members were wary of involving men of lower rank for 'they might not understand the objects and get excited'.[49] Nevertheless, NCOs took advantage of the mood of the lower ranks to press their agenda. On the first day of the Taranto mutiny, in a precursor to the formation of the League, 180 sergeants of the BWIR signed a petition demanding the pay increase embodied in Army Order 1 of 1918 be granted to the BWIR.[50]

A second facet of the Caribbean League anticipated future difficulties sustaining a pan-West Indian anti-colonial movement. The leadership of the League, comprising sergeants Brown, Collman and Jones, was entirely Jamaican. This had the potential to lead to dissent from men of other West Indian territories. Sergeant Pouchet, who provided British military intelligence with details of the League's activities, argued against the decision taken at the inaugural meeting to base organisations headquarters in Jamaica. This, Pouchet argued, would militate against a stated aim of the League to campaign in all the West Indian territories.[51] The importance of island chauvinism should not be underestimated. Two companies of the BWIR served as a detachment in East

Africa. One comprised men from all the West Indian territories, the other was entirely Jamaican. Although camped only ten yards apart, there was not 'the least sign of fraternising between the two companies'.[52]

Despite the limitations of the Caribbean League, a distinct racial consciousness emerged from the harsh experiences of the British West Indies Regiment during the war and in the demobilisation period, expressed in a poem by Sergeant H. B. Montieth, a former Jamaican teacher, written at the time of the Taranto mutiny:

> Lads of the West, with duty done, soon shall we parted be
> To different land, perhaps no more each other's face to see,
> But still as comrades of the war our efforts we'll unite
> To sweep injustice from our land, its social wrongs to right.
> Then go on conquering – lift your lives above each trivial thing
> To which the meaner breeds of earth so desperately cling;
> And Heaven grant you strength to fight the battle for your race,
> To fight and conquer, making earth for man a happier place.[53]

While the Taranto mutiny was the most dramatic sign of dissatisfaction among the West Indian contingents, even men distinguished by having taken part in front-line action in the Middle East began to react to official discrimination. To prevent further outbreaks of unrest, the demobilisation of the BWIR battalions stationed in Italy was accelerated. But transports to the West Indies were irregular and the disbandment of the Middle Eastern battalions was delayed as a result. Not only had these battalions fought in the front line, they had also enlisted earlier. In April 1919, the Egyptian High Command reported serious discontent had arisen over this delay and warned mutiny would break out if demobilisation was not hastened.[54]

Despite these warnings the Middle Eastern veterans started to arrive at Taranto, en route to the West Indies. They were subjected to the same treatment as the BWIR labour battalions, despite their front-line service. Brigadier-General Carey-Bernard, the South African base commander at Taranto imposed a rigid regime of racial segregation. Having performed with ability and bravery on the battlefield, the Middle Eastern veterans received assurances they would not be deployed on demeaning tasks. Carey-Bernard entirely disregarded this undertaking, declaring

> the men were only niggers and ... no such treatment should ever have been promised to them ... they were better fed and treated than any nigger had a right to expect ... he would order them to do whatever work he pleased, and if they objected he would force them to do it.[55]

Field punishment was imposed for all offences, removing the power of junior officers, who Carey-Bernard believed were too lenient, to punish trivial offences. The men were used as porters for white soldiers in transit and barred from canteens and cinemas; Carey-Bernard declared he 'would not allow British soldiers to sit alongside niggers'. The designation 'native' was re-imposed denying the BWIR access to proper medical facilities. The sick and injured languished in 'native hospitals' with insufficient medicines or blankets.[56] The veterans refused to co-operate with Carey-Bernard's regime, and to minimise the risk of insurrection the Egyptian High Command was asked to ensure the three Middle Eastern battalions did not arrive en masse.[57]

The widespread level of resentment among black soldiers was highlighted when members of the West India Regiment, usually regarded as a bulwark against West Indian insurgency, also mutinied during the demobilisation period. The second battalion was redeployed from East Africa in August 1918 to guard Turkish prisoners and form part of the garrison at Kantara (Qantarah esh Sharqiya) in Egypt, before transferring to Ramleh (Ramla) in Palestine. Unlike the BWIR at Taranto, the WIR was exposed to the widespread discontent gripping the British Army, particularly in the Middle East, during 1919. Resentment centred on the slow rate of demobilisation. Nationalist uprisings in Egypt necessitated the retention of British forces, but the rank and file of the British and Colonial forces held that now the war had been won men should be speedily discharged to their civilian occupations. There was reluctance, particularly among ANZAC units, to police the Empire or to assist the Allied incursion into Soviet Russia.[58]

A Soldiers' Union was mooted in Alexandria, and the men gave notice they would strike from 11 May 1919, six months after the armistice, the date they believed their contractual obligations were over. Throughout April 1919 battalions in the EEF vetoed parades and boycotted duties. The Egyptian High Command reported 3,000 troops refused to be deployed on the railway. Allenby, military governor and GOC, Egypt, expressed great concern that full scale mutiny would ensue if the men's demands were not met. Allenby insisted mobilisation should gather apace, even if the ratio of white troops to Indian units fell. The Indian troops were placated by trips to Mecca.[59]

The subversive mood was evident among many at Kantara, a railhead and communications centre for Egypt, Palestine and Syria. Kantara simultaneously served as a channel of information for the rebellious units. On Easter Monday 1919, men of the Rifle Brigade held a meeting after being ordered as reinforcements while resting at a demobilisation camp. An anonymous letter threatened the men would not undertake their duties unless demobilisation was resumed. Orders were disobeyed and the men paraded under their own elected leaders until they were returned to the demobilisation camp six days later. Military circulars noted dress was poor and saluting almost non-existent and suggested a general breakdown in discipline was immanent.[60] John Patterson, the enthusiastic proponent of Jewish recruitment, was serving in the Kantara district with the Royal Fusiliers. He recalled how

> [a]ll through the early days of May I saw chalked up everywhere – on the Railway Station, signal boxes, workshops, on the engines, trucks, and carriages – the mystic words, 'Remember the 11th of May' I heard it rumoured that there was a conspiracy on foot in the E.E.F. for a general mutiny on that day, and found that men from other units had endeavoured to seduce my battalion from its duty.[61]

For the professional soldiers of the WIR continued pay discrimination, rather than the slow pace of demobilisation, was the chief contention. In April Army Order 331 of 1919 brought BWIR pay, with the exception of separation allowances, into line with other British Army units. But only the officers and NCOs of the WIR were granted the same increase. By this stage the 2WIR had dwindled to around 275 men and an extension of the increase to the private soldier would have cost little to implement. But the War Office was more concerned with perpetuating the 'native' status of the WIR.[62]

Discontent in the West India Regiment had already been evident during Christmas 1918 when officers complained the men were well-presented and physically fit but 'there was rather a tendency to "noise in the ranks"'.[63] Army Order 54 of 1919 had laid down pay rates for soldiers retained in service after 1 February 1919. The measure applied to all units with a depot in the United Kingdom and the South African Overseas Contingent 'and in ... further cases as may be authorised by the Army Council'.[64] Once again the order was sufficiently ambiguous to be the cause of discrimination against the West India Regiment, who in April were transferred to guard the supply depot at Ludd in Palestine, the birthplace of St George.

On 9 May 1919, Major-General Hoskins, the divisional commander, was forced to address the WIR 'regarding the grievances about the pay question'.[65] A white unit in the area, the 1 Devonshire Regiment, was put on standby in case of possible disturbances. The following day, a War Office telegram was read to all units in the sector stating: 'The War does not end at date of armistice, but at signing of Peace Treaty. All men are liable to be retained until April 30th 1920 under Naval, Military, and Air Force Service Act.'[66] This inflammatory and ill-timed declaration precipitated rioting among many British Army units in the Kantara area on the symbolic 11 May. Deciding this was a timely moment to air their grievances over pay, thirty-two West India Regiment privates mutinied the following day. Severe sentences of five or seven years penal servitude were imposed on the mutineers although these were subsequently reduced to one or two years by Hoskins. Significantly, Patterson records that no white soldier was charged at this time. The WIR mutineers were dispatched to the military prison at Gabbari (Gharbiyeh) and arrangements were made to repatriate the rest of the battalion to Jamaica by early July. On 15 May, it was announced the pay regulations embodied in Army Order 54 of 1919 would after all be authorised for the WIR.[67]

Pay continued to be a cause of dissatisfaction in the West India Regiment. In late 1919, when both battalions were stationed in Jamaica, the men got wind of proposals to consolidate daily pay and bonuses, which would significantly reduce earnings. Colonel Carey, the new GOC Jamaica, received anonymous letters threatening mutiny and 'impending storms' and believed 'the fact that these letters have been so numerous indicates at least a considerable discontent exists'. Carey feared indiscipline in the WIR would encourage further industrial action in the climate of protest gripping Jamaica. Some members of the WIR were involved in confrontations with the constabulary and the regiment could no longer be regarded as a bulwark against civil unrest. Indeed, the GOC argued, 'a discontented negro regiment in Jamaica will not only be not worth its cost but may at any time become a positive danger'.[68] As the numbers of officers and men dwindled they were not replaced and the regiment was disbanded, ostensibly on financial grounds, parading for the last time in January 1927.[69]

West Indian soldiers were not only politicised by their direct experiences, but through exposure to pan-Africanist influences and radical black American thought. The Jamaican writer and radical, Claude McKay, arrived in England in 1919 and, visiting a club for black soldiers in London's Drury Lane, saw several black American newspapers circulated among the men. McKay himself distributed radical literature among West Indians at the Repatriation Camp at Winchester where he was invited by a Jamaican soldier. McKay reported on the circumstances facing the black soldiers in London in an article in Garvey's *Negro World*, remarking on the shortage of money and decent food and the racism of the British and American troops. McKay believed the club members, who included black Americans and East Indians among their number, would return to their respective countries and agitate for change. 'We should rejoice that Germany blundered, so that Negroes from all parts of the world were drawn to England to see the Lion, afraid and trembling, hiding in cellars, and the British ruling class revealed to them in all its rottenness and hypocrisy.'[70] The white manageress of the Drury Lane club made McKay a *persona non grata* after the appearance of this article.

The *Crisis*, the paper of the National Association for Colored People, was regularly distributed at the Drury Lane club. The paper covered the contribution of black American soldiers to the war effort, detailing the heroic exploits of black US regiments deployed on the front line.[71] W. E. B. Du Bois, in an article entitled 'The Black Man in the Revolution of 1914-1918', praised the Senegalese troops, who regularly proved to be the backbone of the French army. 'The black soldier saved civilization in 1914-18 ... France not only does not deny this – she is proud to acknowledge the debt.'[72] DuBois reported how Blaise Diagne, the first African deputy in the French parliament who had led recruitment drives in West Africa, had addressed a celebration in Paris to honour the contribution they had made. Since the revolution of 1789, French military service had been inextricably linked to citizenship, recognised by Diagne when he emphasised 'the new obligations incumbent now on the mother country in recognition of the rights of naturalization which native troops have gained on the battle-fields which they share as brothers with their white brothers'.[73]

Crisis regularly took the opportunity to encourage its readers to believe the blood sacrifice of black soldiers would earn emancipation for oppressed peoples the world over. In the 'Soldiers' Number' of June 1918 the poet, James Fenton, represented the war as an instrument of purification which bestowed African-American volunteers with the mantle of past black revolutionaries and warriors.

> Toussaint, old man of the mountains,
> Is tramping through the streets of Port au Prince.
> 'Whither do you go, Graybeard?' challenges the sentry.
> Toussaint's voice is soft and low.
> 'I go to arouse the sleeping men of Ethiopia,
> 'This is the hour that tries the nations and the races'.[74]

The spilling of blood as a purifying and sanctifying act was a recurrent theme in nationalist movements, perhaps exemplified by the Irish republican, Padraic Pearse upon his conversion to armed struggle in 1913 with the words: 'There are many things more horrible than bloodshed; and slavery is one of them'.[75] At the famous 'graveside oration' for another Irish patriot, O'Donovan Rossa, in August 1915, Pearse declared: 'Life springs from death, and from the graves of patriotic men and women spring living nations.'[76] This symbolism was taken up by supporters of black enlistment who believed black self-sacrifice would not go unrewarded. In his 'Sonnet to Negro Soldiers', Joseph Cotter Junior, declared:

> They shall go down unto Life's Borderland,
> Walk unafraid within that Living Hell,

Nor heed the driving rain of shot and shell
That 'round them falls; but with uplifted hand
Be one with mighty hosts, an armed band
Against man's wrong to man – for such full well
They know. And from their trembling lips shall swell
A song of hope the world can understand.
All this to them shall be a glorious sign,
A glimmer of that Resurrection Morn,
When age-long Faith, crowned with a grace benign,
Shall rise and from their blows cast down the thorn
Of Prejudice. E'en though through blood it be,
There breaks this day their dawn of Liberty.[77]

The small detachments of West Indians who arrived at Winchester before their onward journey to the islands were radicalised by exposure to this literature. Some white American battalions, used to the more overt racial segregation of the US Army, were also based at the camp. Antagonism developed between the two groups and on 29 April 1919 fighting broke out and an American soldier was injured. That evening, the black soldiers marched into Winchester, armed with sticks, and harangued passing US servicemen. Resenting this assertive spirit, passing white British soldiers came to assist the Americans and the two sides had to be dispersed by civilian and military police with armed reserves.[78] Believing the West Indians had been slighted by the US troops and anxious to avoid further disturbances, the Mayor of Worcester, Alfred Meades, appealed in the local press for volunteers to come forward and 'stimulate good feeling' by providing motor trips, guided walks, concerts, hospitality in private homes, 'to show our appreciation ... and thanks for the glorious and successful work ... [the black soldiers] have done for the Empire and for us'.[79]

The mutinies at Taranto and Ludd sent shock waves through the colonial establishment, not only in Jamaica, but throughout the British West Indies. In Trinidad, a petition was presented demanding the release of men imprisoned for their involvement in the Taranto mutiny. In July 1919, demobilised veterans, who were among those repatriated from the metropole after the attacks on the black population, were involved in attacks on sailors from HMS Dartmouth. In December, ex-soldiers supported a dock strike in Port-of-Spain in which the employers were forced to concede a 25 per cent pay increase after a plea from the Governor.[80] On 22 July 1919 in British Honduras, which had supplied some 530 men to the war effort, veterans took a leading role in the protests against rising prices and discrimination. Order was only restored after the intervention of a contingent of former soldiers who remained loyal to the crown.[81]

In this climate and despite the rhetoric of collective endeavour, the Jamaican authorities were uneasy at the prospect of receiving thousands of politicised veterans into a society increasingly polarised by wartime hardships. The price of food had risen by around 33 per cent between 1914 and 1918. The Military Service Law of 1917 prevented labourers passed as physically fit from travelling to Cuba and Central America, traditional destinations for those unable to find local employment. Many Jamaicans felt that this clause enabled the employers to take advantage of a larger pool of surplus labour.[82] Fearful of unrest, the Jamaican authorities had discouraged police officers from volunteering for the contingents. Unlike their counterparts in other West Indian territories and Jamaican civil servants, Jamaican constables did not receive the pay of their former occupation while in the army as 'the retention of ... constables for service in the Island was more important than their accession to His Majesty's Forces'. In an attempt to ensure the loyalty of policemen who returned to the constabulary after the war, a sum was eventually set aside to make good shortfalls in pay experienced during the war.[83]

From 1917 restlessness among the workforce had risen. The vulnerability of the colonial apparatus was highlighted when the fire service struck in April 1918. In June, pier labourers loading United Fruit Company ships won a 33 per cent increase, matching wartime inflation. Stevedores coaling visiting ships achieved a similar increase, despite attempts to break the strike with convict labour. Fearful these victories would increase the confidence of other workers, Governor Probyn recommended that strategic groups, such as railway and sanitary workers, be granted equivalent increases.[84] The Governor also established a Conciliation Board at the end of June 1918 to intervene when employees and employers could not agree terms.[85] These concessions only served to increase the determination of the Jamaican workers. Sugar workers at Vere, who had recently achieved wage increases, struck in July to demand more. Probyn blamed a 'criminal element',[86] but the plantation workers were eyeing a share of the profits accumulated during the wartime sugar boom.[87] Three days into the strike, police fired on a crowd of demonstrators, killing three and wounding twelve. The West India Regiment was deployed to contain further unrest that spread to Bog Walk, St. Catherine and Spanish Town.[88] During July, Chinese shops and businesses accused of profiteering were attacked.[89]

Trade union militancy continued into 1919. The longshoremen, organised by Bain Alves, who had led a tobacco workers' strike in 1917, walked out in April 1919 and achieved pay increases. In July, government railway workers struck for a 33 per cent wage increase, paid holidays and sanitary provision in the workplace. The government was forced to concede their demands. In October 1919 the ban on trade union organisation, embodied in the 1839 master and servant legislation, was lifted, although unions were not granted immunity from legal damages. Despite this concession, strikes involving, dockers, tramcar drivers and even the police continued well into 1920 as workers sought to redress the erosion of earnings that had occurred during the war years.[90]

In January 1919, Governor Probyn urged the Colonial Office to ensure war pensions and allowances were swiftly settled to preempt unrest, when the first veterans, expected in May, arrived home. The War Office strengthened the Jamaican garrison with a battalion of British infantry. Lord Milner, Secretary of State for the Colonies, pleaded for a warship to be stationed offshore, ostensibly on manoeuvres, to deter insurrection.[91] Contingency plans were laid to promptly disperse veterans to their homes by special train. In the larger towns the police were put on stand-by, reinforced by the first battalion of the WIR who had not been politicised by service overseas. Constables were instructed not to antagonise the veterans and to provide any advice and assistance that would hasten their journeys homeward. In an effort to assuage official anxiety the Inspector-General of Police wrote 'It must not be assumed that these instructions are issued under any sense of fear or panic. They are mainly precautionary and remindful.'[92] When the first contingent of veterans arrived, Jamaica Military Headquarters adopted a similar tone, issuing a press statement claiming, contrary to rumours, a steam pinnace and a WIR detachment were not intended to overawe the returnees, but to offer protection against over-enthusiastic well-wishers.[93]

Official composure was persistently undermined by rumours that veterans intended to incite a rising of the black population in Jamaica, and with the further intention of carrying anti-colonial agitation throughout the West Indies. Although island parochialism had contributed to the early demise of the Caribbean League, ironically the authorities were now faced with widely dispersed groups of disaffected soldiers who were consequently harder to police. Acting Governor Johnstone received a telegram from Lord Milner, the Secretary of State, circulated to all West Indian governors on 3 July 1919 warning of an imminent uprising involving war veterans. Johnstone, who had recently assumed the governorship on the departure of Leslie Probyn and wishing to convince the Colonial Office he enjoyed total control, quickly provided assurances to the contrary. However, within days, on 18 July, ex-servicemen and discharged seamen were involved in a fracas in Kingston with sailors from HMS *Constance*. Several of the latter and some white civilians were injured. Chanting 'kill the whites', the black veterans wanted to exact revenge for the racist violence and official mishandling they had experienced during the riots in Cardiff, London and Liverpool earlier in the year. The authorities

feared the unrest would mar the Empire-wide Peace Day celebrations scheduled for 19 July and placed British sailors armed with clubs and sections of
the WIR on stand-by.[94]

A Trades and Labour Demonstration formed the centrepiece of the celebrations. Organised by Bain Alves – president of the Longshoremen's Labour
Union, the core of the Jamaican Federation of Labour (JFL) – and W. G.
Hinchcliffe, the demonstration included displays by local trades and benevolent
associations and veterans marching alongside their official war trophy, a
captured German gun. Placed at centre stage with temporary public acknowl-
edgement the veterans mood was tempered. The occasion also celebrated
continued affection toward the monarch, a sentiment capable of diluting
antagonism towards local and metropolitan institutions. 'Fear God and honour
the King' was the motto of the JFL and Alves astutely used the Kingston pageant
to present an open address to Lord Milner for communication to George V.
Urging the monarch to intervene and improve economic and social conditions
for the Jamaican masses, Alves underpinned his plea with strong inferences
that Jamaica's wartime sacrifices should be duly rewarded.

> We His Majesty's Loyal subjects impressed with the fullest sense of the good-
> ness of God and the sterling loyalty of the sons of the Empire, through whom
> victory has been brought to crown His Majesty's arms, beg to tender through
> you to our sovereign Lord ... our unswerving loyalty and allegiance, and ... to
> assure His Majesty that the hearts of the working men of Jamaica will always
> beat true to his sacred person; and we hope, we trust and we pray that our
> Almighty Father may endow you and His Majesty's Ministers with wisdom
> from on High that you may use the powers vested in you to the great moral,
> intellectual and material advancement not only of Jamaica ... but of the Empire
> as a whole.[95]

The peace celebrations did not pass off without incident, however.
Although there were no signs of organised insurrection, ex-servicemen were
involved in disturbances at Morant Bay and Savannah-la-Mar. At Chapelton, a
BWIR veteran was killed in clashes with civilians.[96] The Kingston parade was
disrupted when trams were stormed by local people who refused to pay their
fares. The police stood by, apparently powerless to intervene. Reporting the
latter incident, the *Daily Gleaner* reverted to discourses of respectability to re-
articulate race and class status. Complaining 'only those who are prepared to
rub shoulders with the unwashed can travel on the cars',[97] the *Daily Gleaner*
asserted the black majority was incapable of running its own affairs, despite its
contribution to the war effort. Any ground relinquished by the colonial
machine would spell the end of civil society. What might otherwise have been

regarded as high-spirited exuberance on a festive occasion, indicated irrationality and chaos in the eyes of the white elite. Furthermore, the Kingston masses had audaciously intruded in events of world importance.

> Acts of lawlessness were committed with a degree of impunity which no civilized society can afford to tolerate without running a grave risk of ultimately losing the distinctive mark of civilization ... some persons are apt to allow ... their joy to get the upper hand of reason and commonsense; particularly when these two latter attributes are present in only small quantities ... on a unique occasion, the celebration of one of the most momentous events of history, hooligans interrupt[ed] a peaceful and orderly demonstration of citizens.[98]

Those veterans who remained within the bounds of 'acceptable' behaviour were worthy of the benefits of citizenship. But those who refused to accept their station and became involved in unrest were regarded as 'less creditable'.[99] It was the duty of a true soldier to stand firm in the face of privation as the Jamaica legislature pondered over the meagre provision to be made for ex-servicemen.

Throughout the summer of 1919, the authorities continued to receive rumours of impending rebellion. Anonymous letters to the Governor, GOC and Inspector-General of Police claimed an uprising was planned for Emancipation Day, 1 August 1919; Kingston would be burned and the white population attacked. A concerted assault on the colonial regime did not materialise but demands continued for Jamaica's war contribution to be recognised.[100] For a time these were led by seamen who returned home in the wake of the race riots in the metropole. Having fought back against white mobs, black men, many with wartime naval service, found themselves placed on trumped-up charges or kept under house arrest, while the authorities pressed them to return to the Caribbean or West Africa. Sixty-nine seamen were repatriated in early August 1919 on HMS *Cambrian*. Their frustrations were vented in a brief outbreak of violence against the white sailors of the *Cambrian* on landing in Jamaica.[101] Rather than accept that the returning seamen had legitimate grievances, officials renewed the charge of black combustibility. The Inspector-General of Police described the men as 'unruly' and 'impudent',[102] while the master of the SS *Santille*, who had transported the men for part of their homeward journey, believed the seamen were 'more like wild beasts than human beings'.[103]

After seeking the advice of the radical journalist Alfred Mends, now vice-president of the JFL, over forty seamen signed a petition to the new Acting Governor, Colonel Bryan, asking for the losses they had suffered in the metropole to be made good and for their wartime service to be recognised. Appealing to sentiments of military brotherhood and ideals of British justice, the petitioners believed the future stability and development of the Empire would be assured only if measures were taken to erase class and race discrimination. The seamen called upon Bryan

> to redress our grievances according to the time honoured immemorial customs and usages of the Realm so that the honour and prestige of the Empire may be upheld ... in order that throughout the whole British Empire there may dwell harmony, friendship and peace ... and that varied mixed races ... may fully appreciate and honour the British Constitution to which we forever owe allegiance, and [to] which we demonstrated our unswerving loyalty in the late War ... [W]e would beseechingly appeal to you as Governor as a soldier [and] as a British gentleman that our grievances be fully redressed in the interests of Colonial expansion and that of Empire.[104]

More seamen returned to Jamaica in October 1919 in the wake of the *Orca* mutiny. The Colonial Office had arranged a limited compensation scheme for those repatriated after the race riots. Attacks on white seamen were renewed when the returnees heard rumours they would not receive their entitlement.[105] Discourses of respectability, mental capacity and temperament, blurred class and race distinctions and were redefined to disparage and marginalise Jamaicans not prepared to suffer injustice in silence. Oscar Skyers, identified as the leader of the demonstrators, was said to have 'had a lot of the unwashed [marching] behind him'.[106] Skyers was arrested and sentenced to twelve months' imprisonment. The *Jamaica Times* complained 'respectable citizens' white, black and 'coloured' were also attacked, urged on by 'hooligans' and 'women of the street'. The latter, it was claimed, were especially violent. Rioters who displayed a 'colour animus' were regarded as the 'more ignorant',[107] whereas those who attacked non-whites were 'enemies of their own colour ... the enemy of every good citizen'[108] – beyond the pale of civilised society and unworthy of civic participation. Such attitudes anticipated how war veterans would henceforth be categorised as either deserving or undeserving of public sympathy and assistance.

The experience of volunteers who had returned early from the war was not encouraging. The third war contingent had left on board the *Verdala* in March 1916. The ship was diverted via Nova Scotia to avoid enemy attack. Insufficient clothing and blankets and inadequate accommodation and heating resulted in widespread frostbite. Over 100 men returned to Jamaica suffering amputation of hands or feet. The *Daily Gleaner* argued 'those incapacitated are as surely sufferers on behalf of the Empire as those who have lost life or limb on the battlefields of France and Gallipoli ... We cannot tolerate that those so wounded should be left to charity. Should they be permitted to sit at the corners of our streets begging for a livelihood it will be an eternal shame.'[109]

The paper advocated retraining and land grants for those still able to under-take some work. Ex-soldiers often became embroiled in lengthy struggles to obtain disability pensions. In September 1917, I. J. Livingstone, reported a gloomy outlook for the discharged soldiers in a letter to the *Daily Gleaner*. 'I have heard it said, and it seems to be a fact, that most ... cannot live long in a community on account of their impoverished means; and their doom is always the Alms House or another place'.[110]

However mindful of the events at Taranto, official minds became more focused around provision for the veterans on their return. In the weeks after the Armistice, the Jamaican press heaped praise on the contingents, but simulta-neously expressed fears that the veterans were a potentially verminous and uncivilised rabble who would wreak social dislocation if they were not steered in the direction of purposeful employment.

> Now that the great war is over, we are all looking forward to seeing once more our brave lads who had left these shores to do their bit ... When the fuss is over, what then ... Are these men going to be let loose in the street like rats out of a bag to wander about ... They are sure to want money and good food, and if they can't get these necessities ... well we know what will happen.[111]

U. Theo McKay, the elder brother of the writer and radical, Claude, drew more considered conclusions. The veterans would 'not go back to the pick and shovel' to work for 'one shilling or one and sixpence per day'.[112] McKay believed employment or land should be guaranteed to each serviceman, but recognised this was only possible if the Jamaican economy was revitalised. Addressing the first contingent of demobilised veterans in May 1919, Governor Probyn assured the men they would be welcomed by former employers and outlined a limited programme of public works and land settlement for, in his words, 'no man wants to rest for ever and ever'. Anticipating the future for many of the veterans, Probyn cautioned each man to 'make friends with Thrift'.[113]

Probyn drew on the vocabulary of common purpose adopted during the war which elided the hierarchy of race and class. He conceded Jamaican veter-ans conditional entry to the military fraternity by assuring the men they would be accorded a place within the island's history. The achievements of the contingents reflected prestige back onto Jamaican society as a whole. But the projection of masculine virtue also aimed to encourage in the veterans an acceptance that each individual was the driving force upon which economic status and social standing rested, past military endeavour notwithstanding. Here, Probyn echoed the sentiments expressed by de Lisser that war repre-sented an opportunity for Jamaicans to engage in manful industry, casting off the curse of tropical sloth:

[y]ou know it to be the fact that the War was won chiefly by the good-hearted co-operation on the part of the Allies. This, then, is the nature of the help that you can give your neighbours that progress is obtainable only by means of brotherly co-operation. You can explain your meaning in another way, by saying: I am going to do my duty to my neighbour: my neighbour must also do his duty to me: and, if these things be done, we all shall have good cause for contentment both as regards the body and the spirit.

I want Jamaica to become prosperous; and I want all people, in future, to reckon that this prosperity began to run from the day on which Jamaica's brave sons came back from the War.[114]

The many gatherings organised in the Jamaican parishes to welcome the men reiterated the Governor's theme. The veterans, it was declared, had entered the Jamaican pantheon and having undergone the masculine rigours of war and as brothers-in-arms of the Empire they were entitled to greater civic participation. G. P. Brown, a member of the Montego Bay recruiting committee, restated this view at the town's welcoming ceremony. Once again, the language used offered diverse interpretation according to the race, class and experience of the audience. The veterans, Brown declared,

had played their part with honour to the Empire ... Fighting side by side with the liberators of the race, their names would go down to posterity with honour. They should always maintain that honour, and let it be handed down, not alone to their children, but to their grand children and great grand children. They should let it be said of them as of the Romans who were proud to be Roman citizens 'I am a British soldier'.[115]

To confirm this temporary promotion in the hierarchy of Empire, all veterans, except those discharged for misconduct were granted the vote in the forthcoming elections to the Legislative Council.[116] But the failure to match this token reward with concrete social and economic improvements meant the veterans' wartime experience of discrimination became a central theme in the labour unrest and nationalist agitation that characterised the next twenty years.

Notes

1 *WICC* 539, 29 May 1919, p. 128.
2 Winter, *Death's Men*, pp. 152–3; Gerard Oram, *Worthless Men: Race, Eugenics and the Death Penalty in the British Army During the First World War* (London: Francis Boutle, 1998), pp. 108–9; Levine, 'Battle Colors'; Minutes of the WIC Ctte (General Purposes Ctte.) 18 January 1918, 4 March 1918 and 11 April 1918.
3 PRO CO137/725/10196, Ernest Price to Manning 10 January 1918.

4 Wood Hill, *A Few Notes*, pp. 10–11; PRO WO95/495 WD of 6BWIR entries for February 1918; WO95/3981 WD DMS, Line of Communications (LOC) France entry for 5 August 1918.

5 PRO CO137/725/10196, Manning to Price 15 January 1918.

6 PRO WO95/3981 WD DMS, LOC France entry for 5 August 1919; WO95/4110 WD Stationary Hospital, Marseilles entry for 2 August 1919.

7 PRO WO95/3981 WD DMS, LOC France entries for 16 and 25 August 1919.

8 PRO WO95/4039 WD entries for 18–19 and 31 January 1919.

9 PRO WO95/4039 WD ADMS Marseilles Base entries for 20 February 1919 and 16 May 1919.

10 PRO CO318/353/6843 Cipriani to Colonial Secretary 27 November 1919, Base Routine Orders by Brig. Gen. C. D. V. Carey Barnard, Cmdt. Taranto, 17 July 1919.

11 Wood Hill, *A Few Notes*, p. 2; *Zouave*, February 1916, pp. 18–19.

12 Stepan, *Idea of Race*, pp. 40–3.

13 PRO WO123/60 AO1/1918; WO95/4377 entries for 17 and 22 April 1918; WO123/58 AO5/1916.

14 PRO CO318/347/63228 WICC to Rt Hon. Walter Long, SSCO, 30 December 1918.

15 PRO CO318/348/5991 HTA[llen], CO Memo 'Pay of the British West Indies Regiment' 30 January 1919. Allen was literally correct when he stated that the pay of the British soldier was purely nominal. Compared to Dominion (Canadian) and Australian troops, the Tommy received a pittance. The Canadians were referred to as 'fuckin' five bobbers' as they received five shillings per day compared to the solitary shilling British soldiers received until the implementation of Army Order 1 of 1918. The Australians, whose pay was linked to that of the average worker, did even better at six shillings per day. A simple meal in an *estaminet* cost the equivalent of one shilling: Ferguson, *Pity of War*, p. 343; Grey, *Military History of Australia*, p. 91; Winter, *Death's Men*, p. 153.

16 PRO WO123/61 AO331/1919; WO95/4377 WD DAG, GHQ, EEF entry for 23 April 1919; WO95/4465 WD 5BWIR Alexandria District, EEF entry for 5 March 1919.

17 PRO 123/61 AO 331/1919.

18 PRO CO318/348/16801 Petition of NCOs of 1/2BWIR enclosed with Barbados Govs Dispatch 27 of 13 February 1919 and CO318/348/20991 Copy received by Gov. St Lucia via Hon. W. V. Degazon.

19 *JT* 9 July 1921, p. 2.

20 C. L. R. James, *The Life of Captain Cipriani: An Account of British Government in the West Indies* (Nelson: Coulton and Co., 1932), p. 27.

21 Rhodes House, Oxford, Mss.W.Ind.s.54 CSM George D. Elliott to V. C. Green 24 December 1923 (see also ibid., 4 January 1926).

22 Dupuch, *Salute to Friend and Foe*, pp. 56–8.

23 Ibid., p. 78.

24 Cipriani, *Twenty Years After*, p. 51. For Cipriani's background and subsequent political career see James, *Life of Captain Cipriani*.

25 DG, 9 June 1916, p. 2 and 12 June 1916, p. 6.

26 PRO WO32/5460 Lloyd George to French War Ministry 21 November 1916.

27 Dupuch, *Salute to Friend and Foe*, pp. 78–9; Winter, *Death's Men*, p. 43.

28 PRO WO71/595 Army Form B 122.

29 Col. A. H. O. Lloyd to HQ, Palestine LOC, 7 August 1917.

30 *DG* 7 June 1916, p. 4.

31 *DG* 7 June 1916, p. 13 and 8 June 1916, p. 13.

32 *DG* 28 January 1917, p. 3.

33 *DG* 24 January 1917, p. 1 and 27 January 1917, p. 6.

34 *DG* 2 February 1917, p. 7 and 3 February 1917, p. 6.

35 *DG* 11 July 1917, p. 11.

36 PRO CO137/720 Copy of a Minute by the GOC Jamaica, Enclosure in Jamaica Confidential Dispatch 16 February 1917.

37 PRO WO95/4255 WD Cmdt. Taranto Base entry for 28 December 1917.

38 PRO WO95/4253 WD Asst. Dir. Labour Italy LOC entries for 28 December 1917, 15 January 1918, 28 January 1918, 5 March 1918.

39 PRO WO95/4253 WD WD Asst Dir. Labour Italy LOC entries for 30 April 1918, 12–13 August 1918; WO95/4256 WD Deputy Asst. Dir. Labour LOC Taranto entries for 8, 17 September 1918, 13, 20 November 1918; WO95/4255 WD Cmdt Taranto Base entry for 27 December 1917.

40 PRO WO95/4255 WD Cmdt. Taranto Base entries for 6–8 December 1918; Cipriani, *Twenty Years After*, p. 65; Dupuch, *Salute to Friend and Foe*, p. 78; WO95/4262 WD 7BWIR Italy LOC entry for 9 January 1919.

41 PRO WO33/951 Secret Telegrams 619A Base Cmdt., Taranto to WO 9 December 1918; 620 Ditto, 10 December 1918; 621 Ditto, 10 December 1918; 625 Inspector Gen. of Communications, Italy to WO 11 December 1918; 630 GOC, Italy to WO 13 December 1918; 631 WO to GHQ, Italy 15 December 1918; WO95/4249 WD 1/7 Worcestershire Regiment entries for 9–18 December 1918; WO213/27 Register of Field General Courts Martial and Military Courts to 27 February 1919. Private Albert Denny of the 8 BWIR was executed on 20 January 1919 for a murder offence not related to the mutiny. He was defended by a 'coloured' Jamaican officer, 2nd Lieutenant Hubert Austin-Cooper: WO71/675 Army Form B122; Howe, *Race, War and Nationalism*, p. 155.

42 PRO WO33/951/635 GHQ, Italy to WO 19 December 1918; WO95/4256 WD Deputy Asst. Dir. Labour LOC Taranto entry for 23 December 1918; Dupuch, *Salute to Friend and Foe*, p. 78.

43 PRO CO318/349/59579 Gov. Barbados to Milner, SSC., 25 September 1919, Hemsley to GOC, Jamaica (nd), Hemsley to GOC, Jamaica 29 September 1919 and Maj. H. W. Hemsley 'Memoranda on Voyage of SS *Orca*', 29 September 1919.

44 Ibid.

45 Ibid., Report of Maj. H. W. Hemsley, OC Troops, SS *Orca* (copy encl. in dispatch of 3 October 1919) and Maj. H. W. Hemsley to GOC, Jamaica 29 September 1919.

46 C. E. W. Bean (ed.) *Official History of Australia in the War of 1914–1918* (Sydney: Angus and Robertson, 1921), V, p. 540.

47 PRO CO318/350/2590 Notes of meeting held at Cimino Camp [Taranto], Italy, 17 December 1918.

48 Ibid., Maj. Maxwell Smith to Maj. Gen. Thullier, GOC, Taranto, 27 December 1918.

49 Ibid., Maj. Maxwell Smith (8BWIR) to GOC, Taranto, 3 January 1919.

50 PRO CO28/294/56561 Petition of M. Murphy (3BWIR) and 179 other Sgts. of the BWIR based in Italy, 6 December 1918.

51 PRO CO318/350/2590 Notes of meeting held at Cimino Camp, Italy, 17 December 1918 and Maj. Maxwell Smith (8BWIR) to GOC, Taranto, 3 January 1919.

52 Cipriani, *Twenty Years After*, p. 57.

53 *JT* 28 June 1919, p. 8.

54 PRO WO33/960 Secret Telegrams 10898 GHQ, Egypt to WO 3 April 1919.
55 Cipriani, *Twenty Years After*, p. 62.
56 Ibid., pp. 62–5 (Carey-Bernard quote, p. 65).
57 PRO WO95/4373 WD GHQ EEF General Staff Operations entry for 4 May 1919.
58 Gloden Dallas and Douglas Gill, *The Unknown Army: Mutinies in the British Army in World War I* (London: Verso, 1985), pp. 122–30; Andrew Rothstein, *The Soldiers Strikes of 1919* (London: Journeymen, 1985).
59 PRO WO33/960 Secret Telegrams 11017 GHQ, Egypt to WO 28 April 1919; 10983 GHQ, Egypt to WO 22 April 1919; 11043 GHQ, Egypt to WO 3 May 1919; 11115 GOC, Egypt to WO 16 May 1919; 11121 GHQ, Egypt to WO 17 May 1919; 11218 GHQ, Egypt to WO 14 June 1919; Lawrence James, *Imperial Warrior: The Life and Times of Field-Marshall Viscount Allenby 1861–1936* (London: Weidenfeld and Nicolson), 1993, pp. 179–96; PRO WO33/981 Secret Telegrams May 1919 to April 1920 111045 GHQ, Egypt to Dir. Military Intelligence 3 May 1919; 11115 GOC, Egypt to WO 16 May 1919.
60 PRO WO95/4732 WD 19 Rifle Brigade entries for 29 April 1919 and 16 May 1919; WO95/4696 WD 3rd (Lahore) Div. EEF WD Adjutant and Quarter Master General Routine Orders 30 May 1919.
61 Patterson, *With the Judaeans*, pp. 205.
62 PRO WO123/61 AO331/1919.
63 PRO WO95/4732 WD 2WIR entry for 24 December 1918.
64 PRO WO123/61 AO54/1919.
65 PRO WO95/4732 WD 2WIR entry for 9 May 1919.
66 PRO WO95/4459 WD 1Devon Regt. entries for 9 and 10 May 1919.
67 PRO WO95/4732 WD 2WIR entries for 15 and 18 May 1919; WO95/4373 WD GHQ EEF General Staff Operations entry for 26 May 1919; WO95/4696 WD 3rd (Lahore) Div. EEF General Staff; Patterson, *With the Judaeans*, pp. 205–6.
68 PRO CO318/359/35534 GOC, Jamaica to Sec., WO 28 April 1920.
69 Dyde, *Empty Sleeve*, pp. 262–7.
70 McKay, *A Long Way from Home*, p. 67; *Negro World*, 13 March 1920, magazine section.
71 For an account of the discrimination faced by black American troops see Arthur E. Barbeau and Florette Henri, *The Unknown Soldiers: African American Troops in World War 1* (revised ed.) (New York: Da Capo Press, 1996). Chapter 6 in particular covers the use of black US soldiers as labour battalions.
72 *Crisis*, March 1919, p. 218.
73 *Crisis*, March 1919, p. 218. For further reading on Blaise Diagne see Echenberg, *Colonial Conscripts*, pp. 44–6; Joe Harris Lunn, *Memoirs of the Maelstrom* (Oxford: James Currey, 1999), particularly pp. 59–84.
74 James Fenton, 'War Profiles', *Crisis*, June 1918, p. 65.
75 Padraic Pearse, 'The Coming Revolution' [1913] in Peter Costello, *The Heart Grown Brutal: The Irish Revolution in Literature from Parnell to the Death of Yeats, 1891–1939* (Dublin: Gill and Macmillan, 1977), p. 76.
76 Quoted in R. F. Foster, *Modern Ireland 1600–1972* (Harmondsworth: Penguin, 1988), p. 477.
77 'A Sonnet to Negro Soldiers' by Joseph Cotter, Jr *Crisis*, June 1918, p. 64.
78 *Hampshire Observer*, 3 May 1919, p. 3.
79 Ibid., p. 5.

80 PRO CO295/521 W. M. Gordon, Acting Governor, Trinidad, to Viscount Milner, SSC, 29 July 1919.

81 PRO CO123/ 295 Gov. Hutson to Milner, SSC, 30 July 1919.

82 PRO CO137/722 Blackden to Gov. 10 April 1917; CO137/727/52922, Attorney General to Acting Colonial Secretary, 16 July 1918. The GOC Jamaica, expressed concern that men worried about the possible introduction of conscription would present themselves as emigrants. In the event of being found fit they would take the necessary steps to ensure that they would fail further medical examination if conscription was fully implemented: CO137/722 Brig. Gen. L. S. Blackden, GOC, Jamaica to Gov. Manning 17 May 1917.

83 PRO CO137/719 Pte. L. U. McPherson 2BWIR to WIC Ctte. 26 September 1916, Inspector General of Police, Jamaica to Pte. L. U. McPherson 26 August 1916, Lord Olivier to A. E. Aspinall, WIC Ctte, 13 October 1916 (quote); CO137/720 Manning to Walter Long, SSC 17 December 1917.

84 PRO CO137/726/39474 Probyn to Long, 12 July 1918.

85 PRO CO137/726/42533 Probyn to Long 31 July 1918.

86 PRO CO137/726/40132 Probyn to Long 22 July 1918.

87 Holt, *Problem of Freedom*, pp. 365–8.

88 PRO WO95/5446, WD GOC Jamaica entries for 2–19 July 1918.

89 PRO CO137/726/40132 Probyn to Long 22 July 1918.

90 *DG* 23 July 1919; W. F. Elkins, *Street Preachers, Faith Healers and Herb Doctors in Jamaica 1890–1925* (New York: Revisionist Press, 1977), pp. 65–6; Richard Hart, 'Origin and Development of the Working Class in the English–speaking Caribbean Area 1897–1937', in Malcolm Cross and Gad Heuman (eds.), *Labour in the Caribbean* (London: Macmillan, 1988). For early work on this formative period see G. Eaton, 'Trade Union Development in Jamaica', *Caribbean Quarterly*, 8:1/2, 1962, 42–53 and 69–75; O.W. Phelps 'Rise of the Labour Movement in Jamaica', *Social and Economic Studies*, 9:4, 1969, 417–68. Organised as a local of the American Federation of Labour, the term longshoreman was the preferred term for a dock-worker.

91 PRO CO137/730/4575 Probyn to SSC 21 January 1919; CO137/735 Cubbitt, WO to Milner, SSC 23 January 1919; CO137/735 Milner, SSC to Sec. Admiralty 5 February 1919.

92 Secret Circular Acting Inspector-General of Police 29 January 1919 contained in Clive A. Crosbie Smith, Rhodes House Library, Mss.W.Ind.s. 22.

93 *JT* 17 May 1919, p. 10.

94 PRO CO137/733/50990 Johnstone (acting Gov.) to Milner SSC 14 August 1919; *DG* 21 July 1919, p. 13.

95 *DG* 21 July 1919, p. 13.

96 *JT* 16 August 1919, p. 16; 22 July 1919, p. 1. The failure of the rumoured insurrection to materialise later brought gloating comments from Herbert Thomas, an inspector in the Jamaican constabulary and something of a maverick as far as the Jamaican establishment was concerned. Thomas claimed to have written a minute to the Governor arguing that a revolt would not take place. In his biography, Thomas described how he invited the alleged ringleader into his office to warn him that he faced the gallows 'if half what we had heard about him, was true. He left my office in a properly subdued and humble spirit': Herbert T. Thomas, *The Story of a West Indian Policeman: Or Forty-seven Years of the Jamaican Constabulary* (Kingston: Gleaner Co., 1927), pp. 215–16.

97   22 July 1919, p. 1.

98   *DG* 22 July 1919, p. 8

99   *JT* 16 August 1919, p. 16.

100 PRO CO137/733/50990 Johnstone to Milner SSC 14 August 1919.

101 Ibid.; PRO CO318/349/60449 Petition of J. A. Thompson and 43 other seamen to Col.
     Bryan, Acting Gov. of Jamaica, 29 August 1919 (Enclosure in Govs. dispatch 1 October
     1919).

102 PRO CO137/733/50990 Johnstone to Milner SSC 14 August 1919.

103 PRO CO318/349/60449 W. H. Hinds, SS *Santille* to Messrs Scrutton Sons and Co. 17
     July 1919.

104 Ibid.

105 *JT* 11 October 1919, p. 4. Each man was to receive a £5 lump sum (equivalent to the
     basic war bonus for a private soldier). Once in Jamaica, he became entitled to a daily
     income of 4/-, reduced to 3/- and then 2/- for a limited period before he found work.

106 *JT* 11 October 1919, p. 4.

107 *JT* 11 October 1919, p. 4.

108 *JT* 18 October 1919, p. 6.

109 *DG* 4 May 1916, p. 10.

110 *DG* 11 September 1917, p. 13.

111 *DG* 9 December 18, p. 13.

112 *DG* 20 January 1919, p. 5.

113 PRO CO318/348/38685 'Welcome Given by the Governor on Behalf of All Jamaica, to
     the Men of the British West Indies Regiment on Their Return Home, May 2nd.'

114 Ibid.

115 *DG* 7 May 1919, p. 13.

116 PRO CO318/348/38685 Notice, King's House, 22 May 1919.

7 Military endeavour, nationalism and pan-Africanism

Jamaican veterans returned home radicalised by the ill-treatment and discrimination that culminated in the mutinies at Taranto and Ludd. Nevertheless, many retained an attachment to the ideals of heroic sacrifice, despite the marginalised participation of West Indian volunteers on the front line. The emergent nationalist movement mobilised this mythology, alongside the sense of injustice felt by volunteer and professional soldier alike in the pursuit of social, political and economic reform. Among both veterans and the wider nationalist movement, the status and plight of the ex-serviceman became a key emblem in the development of Jamaican nationhood, aside a reawakened consciousness of earlier struggles against slavery and colonial oppression. During the social upheavals that gripped Jamaica and the rest of the West Indies from the mid-1930s, the issues of employment, welfare, land and the extension of the franchise were regularly linked to the unrewarded contribution of the Jamaican war contingents and the West India Regiment.

Official rhetoric and the faint praise liberally dispensed by welcoming committees eager to stave off insurrection and bask in a little reflected glory, granted transient recognition and status to the returning veterans. However, permanent approval depended on the veterans' willingness to yield to the demands of the decaying plantation economy. Ex-servicemen who believed military service merited something more than a return to irregular employment with 'pick and shovel' were dismissed in time-worn caricatures portraying black men as deficient in industry, self-discipline and intelligence. 'Among the returned soldiers ... there will be found the unreasonable element ... inclined to take the view that having fought for King and Country, they should be provided for without having to work, or with only very light and enjoyable work to do for the rest of their lives',[1] opined a *Jamaica Times* editorial. Raised expectations and skills acquired during military service could only be rewarded within the limitations imposed by the Jamaican economy. This was reiterated within a discourse of white masculine rationality calculated to marginalise the most radical of the veterans:

[T]he majority of the returned soldiers ... do not want to be idlers, loafers, or state pensioners ... their desire is to work hard and well. That is the heritage of every honest and manly man ... What is wanted is for the thoughtful, manly, intelligent and moderate element ... to put forward some definite and constructive proposal of what might be done, and what under the present circumstances of the Island is possible to do.[2]

A fledgling veterans' organisation emerged at the end of May 1919. Wartime rank conferred a degree of authority and status in peacetime and several non-commissioned officers took the lead by publishing a statement of aims and objectives of a 'Proposed Association ... of the British West Indies Regiment'. The programme combined a number of broad political aims with a scheme of mutual provision to members. The Association hoped to promote improvements in housing, health and morality through a network of the veterans, their families and neighbours. Financial support and welfare advice would be offered in case of death or illness and members were to be given assistance in the search for employment.

The Association manifesto emphasised individual effort as the key to social and economic standing, reflecting the influence of both colonial and missionary ideology. But there was also a strong emphasis on co-operation that urged the veterans 'to be more industrious, thereby becoming a more self-supporting community'.[3] The Association hoped to promote literacy through the establishment of public reading rooms in each parish, with intellectual and moral development being encouraged through 'the promotion of games ... and stimulating competitions'.[4] This approach had much in common with the muscular Christianity still permeating non-conformist and reforming projects in the metropolitan slums which promised social advance in exchange for clean living and vigorous endeavour. The Jamaican establishment found much to approve of in the Association's proposals. A leadership drawn from former non-commissioned officers was regarded as a moderating influence on the rest of the men and wartime discipline was held to have encouraged a sense of purpose and industry perceived to be lacking among the Jamaican masses as a whole. Echoing the hopeful words of its editor, H. G. de Lisser, at the outbreak of the war, the *Daily Gleaner* intoned:

in Jamaica the environment and atmosphere are deadening – they take the heart and ambition out of a man ... we are convinced that they [the veterans] have changed permanently; and we are satisfied that if they obtain good leaders, men of energy and ability, and consent to be led by these, they will accomplish a good deal of what they now have in view.[5]

But even when veterans adhered to ideals of masculine industry their efforts were confounded by the limitations of the Jamaican economy. Joseph Francis a former lance-corporal, on approaching an overseer for work was handed a knife on a pole and told he could cut and husk coconuts at the rate of 6d per hundred. This derisory wage, rather than the class of work, caused Francis to decline the offer for 'work does not degrade a man ... we Jamaicans should put our shoulders together to work for the improvement of our island'.[6] 'Ex-Sergeant BWIR', a former teacher who had held a senior post before volunteering, exposed as fiction Governor Probyn's promise that men would be welcomed back to their pre-war occupations. Having made numerous applications for teaching posts to no avail the former NCO complained 'idleness is ... a torment, not an enjoyment. I cannot accept it as a fitting recompense for sacrifice'.[7] In an ironic echo of Thomas Carlyle's injunction 'in Idleness alone is there perpetual despair',[8] these correspondents to the Gleaner contradicted images of a slothful black Jamaica.

Other veterans were more humble and asked for work in terms calculated to appeal to the sense of colonial obligation expressed within the infantilising discourse of the 'white man's burden'. An unnamed correspondent of the 7BWIR, entreated 'Victory has been won. God has spared most of us to return. We are as little children who are looking to their parents ... for their temporal welfare, the Government, the learned and the rich are our parents at this time.'[9] Cast in this role, and faced with the industrial unrest gripping the island since 1917, the Jamaican government introduced limited measures to assist the soldiers. The Central Supplementary Allowances Committee, with offices in each parish, was appointed to assist the men in finding work. The men were encouraged to pool their resources in such projects as bootmaking and hemp farming for rope manufacture.[10] An advice booklet was issued to each man and the Jamaican Times established 'The Returned Soldiers' Friendly Column' to advertise employment and promote government initiatives.[11]

From the government's perspective, the most successful scheme, at least in the short term, was the promotion of migration to the Cuban cane fields, removing significant numbers of potentially discontented veterans. The Jamaican government provided Cuban work permits, normally costing £3, free of charge to 4,036 of the 7,232 demobilised Jamaican soldiers. The government also took control of the travel arrangements normally handled by unscrupulous and profiteering shipping agents.[12]

For the veterans who remained in Jamaica, land acquisition, a symbol of black independence since slavery, became the central demand. Embryonic peasant proprietorship had emerged in Jamaica as slaves acquired provision grounds adjacent to the plantation to cultivate their own produce. The provision ground generated a cash income providing the means to slave manumission and post-emancipation land acquisition. By breaching the boundaries of the master–slave property relationship, the provision ground was also central to slave autonomy and lineage. In the post-emancipation era, as peasant development gathered apace, often to the detriment of the plantation labour supply, peasant holdings were a significant factor in the formation of black Jamaican identity.[13]

Although peasant agriculture was undermined by disproportionate taxation and rationalisation of the plantation economy, land ownership retained its allure. For the small affluent black and brown middle class, land ownership provided access to seats in the legislature through the property qualification. The development of an independent peasantry, which reduced the pool of cheap wage labour was regarded as a 'return to barbarism' by the plantocracy and its supporters in the metropole. However, peasant production received limited encouragement from the Norman Commission of 1897 established to enquire into the crisis in the sugar industry. Sydney (later Lord) Olivier, a member of the commission and who became Jamaican governor between 1907 and 1913, argued the encouragement of peasant initiatives would alleviate the employment crisis threatened by the decline of the sugar industry. The moral condition of the peasantry, Olivier believed, would also be elevated as the benefits of economic endeavour were recognised. However, by this stage, peasant development was under increasing pressure from the growing banana export industry which swallowed most land coming onto the market.[14]

To the returning veteran, land ownership represented a symbolic stake in Jamaican society purchased by military duty. Assisting the veterans to acquire land was also potentially attractive to the colonial authorities. Like Olivier, they anticipated that peasant proprietorship would encourage each cultivator to act as his own taskmaster. After the *Verdala* disaster of March 1916 the press, recognising the emblematic significance of land ownership, backed a proposal to present 'a great track [sic] of land ... of many thousands of acres' to the veterans who would be returning to Jamaica early as a result of the tragedy.[15]

In January 1918, Governor Manning recommended an employment retraining scheme to the Colonial Office to enable disabled veterans to supplement their pensions and bonuses. It was 'desirable' argued the governor, 'some provision should be made, to enable them to add ... *something from their own labour*'.[16] The Jamaican Privy Council anticipated the UK Ministry of Pensions would bear the major cost of the scheme with a contribution of £5 for each volunteer who left Jamaica. The island government would grant a further £1 per head. The Colonial Office was unimpressed and reminded the governor that the Jamaican legislature had agreed to defray the contingents' costs through its own coffers. In December 1918, the Legislative Council met to discuss comprehensive proposals for the settlement and employment of the veterans. Various schemes were advanced for the development of public works employing ex-servicemen, notably the expansion of the railway in Clarendon to assist the sugar industry. However, the most concrete proposal adopted was the payment of a small gratuity to each man and access to credit of up to £25 from the Agricultural Loan Bank to buy land, stock or seed.[17]

But it was not until 1924 that a designated ex-servicemen's settlement reached fruition. The scheme, extended to ex-members of both the West India Regiment and British West Indies Regiment, was drawn up at a conference between the Governor and representatives of the Jamaica Old Comrades Association, later superseded by the Ex-British West Indies Regiment Association. A free allotment of five acres was made available to veterans with savings of at least £10 and a means of support while the first crop was growing. Additional acreage could be purchased with loans repayable over twelve years. The Government also allocated £20,000 for road building and bridges on the three Crown estates earmarked for settlement.[18] However, the scheme collapsed amid bitter recriminations still evident in submissions by veterans to the Moyne Commission, twenty years after the end of the war.

The main settlement in the Rio Grande Valley of Portland remained isolated. Most plots were between three and eleven miles from the nearest main roads. Poor communications were compounded during the five-month rainy season as two local rivers became impassable. Government funds promised to overcome these shortcomings did not materialise as they were incorporated into other budgetary legislation overruled by the Secretary of State for the Colonies. The veterans' organisations protested that the settlement administration did not employ ex-servicemen and claimed many land applications were lost or held up for several years. Of the seventy-two veterans who eventually settled in the Rio Grande the veterans' leaders claimed just three endured the requisite five years to earn full title to the land (the Jamaican government claimed thirteen men had title). Peasant subsistence proved most arduous for veterans drawn from urban areas who lacked agricultural skills and were not used to relative social isolation. Although land retained symbolic significance, the veterans' preoccupation with agricultural settlement did not disrupt the imbalance in land ownership in Jamaica. Instead the veterans' experiences reflected the broader pattern in Jamaican society which witnessed increasing urban migration as plantation employment and peasant self-sufficiency declined and the emerging multinational fruit industry monopolised cultivable land.[19]

In 1933 a new land settlement scheme for ex-servicemen was established. By this stage many veterans had returned from Cuba. Between 1917 and 1921 Cuba absorbed around 65,000 migrant workers from Jamaica. However, faced with the post-war regeneration of European beet production and world economic depression Cuba began to repatriate surplus West Indian cane workers. By 1937 the Cuban government had repatriated nearly 13,500 Jamaicans and a similar number had returned voluntarily. The poor outlook for potential migrants became even bleaker when the other traditional destinations of Panama and Costa Rica prohibited immigration in 1933.[20]

Throughout 1932 and 1933, the Ex-British West Indies Regiment Association had lobbied the Jamaican government and visiting metropolitan politicians and officials on a variety of issues, including unpaid wartime pay and pensions and for renewed investment in land settlement schemes. In July 1933, the Association met with Sir Ian Macpherson MP, a former Minister of Pensions who was touring Jamaica, and requested that new lands be made available with a fund to assist the establishment of cultivation. The delegation suggested the Jamaica War Contribution, under which £60,000 was paid annually to the metropolitan government, should be suspended for five years and the funds diverted to benefit ex-servicemen. The Jamaican government had become more sympathetic to peasant proprietorship which was regarded as a solution to the increasing flow of labour to the urban areas. Law 22 of 1935 set aside £100,000 for loans to participants in government land settlement schemes.[21]

Governor Edward Denham, who served from 1934 until his death in June 1938, was positively effusive about the merits of land settlement. He firmly opposed any alternatives to land ownership such as tenancies or *metayage*, a form of sharecropping. 'Don't suggest any changes to land tenure' he pleaded in a personal note to Sir Cosmo Parkinson, Permanent Under-Secretary at the Colonial Office.

> The saving grace in Jamaica is the Jamaican's passion for the land and to own a bit of it, and the provision of land Settlement is the best bond between Government and governed. To suggest leaseholds would rouse a storm of opposition, and it would not be understood. Don't be afraid that the lands will not be cultivated to the best advantage. These people are keen good agriculturists and we have an excellent Agricultural Dept. which is in high repute and can influence and guide the settler.[22]

Under the terms of the 1933 land settlement scheme, 3,406 ex-servicemen were chosen to receive free plots of five acres and a loan of £5, advanced in thirty shilling instalments. In a model settlement at Coolshade, Saint Catherine 400 ex-soldiers received an additional loan of £4. Once more, however, the scheme was beset by poor land quality and insufficient water supplies and access. By 1938 only 2,506 men were still in possession of their lands; 1800 were actively cultivating produce and only around 400 were actually in residence.[23]

The veterans' struggles to gain recognition for their wartime sacrifices took place against a backdrop of increasing nationalist activity and a heightened consciousness of Jamaican identity, reflected in the higher profile of the Jamaica League.[24] Increasing industrial militancy, although not primarily nationalist in motivation, nevertheless highlighted the limitations for economic and social development within the existing colonial framework. The Jamaica League, influenced by the growing turmoil in Jamaican society, showed an increasing concern with the social and economic strands of its programme, placing less emphasis on the cultural preoccupations evident at its launch in 1914. Although the League did not envisage an end to the Imperial relationship, it was influenced by the agitation for self-determination in other European colonies and an increasing recognition of the rights of smaller nations. Opening the League's annual convention in July 1919, the president, T. Gordon Somers, referring to recent Empire-wide peace festivities, observed

> On the 19th July, all the British world celebrated peace and started to usher in a new era of readjustment, consolidation and progress. It is devoutly hoped that the striking lessons of the war will be learnt by all nations ... that the great watch-words of democratic peoples, liberty, equality and fraternity, will find their illustration in national and international life, and none the less than in our own island Jamaica.[25]

Somers' reflections also signalled the endeavours of the Jamaican contingents would henceforth underpin the nationalist agenda. 'In what tangible and abiding form has Jamaica decided to pay its debt of gratitude? Our men did not fail us at the front, have we failed them at the base?'[26] The League was not immune to the colonial and military opinion that upheld the war as a potentially invigorating influence on the black population. But the League insisted sloth was not ingrained in the black character nor a consequence of the tropical climate. Rather, colonial policy had encouraged a culture of inactivity and resignation as the island lurched from crisis to crisis. This view was eloquently expressed by the war veteran and teacher activist, H. B. Montieth, who at the time of the Taranto mutiny had urged his comrades 'to fight the battle for your race'. In a letter supporting the Jamaica League published in the *Daily Gleaner*, Montieth continuing to deploy the rhetoric of military endeavour, proclaimed

> Our country has been lulled to slumber on the edge of a dangerous precipice ... and many of her assumed guardians ... have been watching her from a distance and singing 'Sleep on Beloved, sleep and take your rest!' ... Jamaicans for years ... we have been slumbering, undisturbed, except by dreams. The time for actions has now come! Let us therefore unite, let us co-operate, let us present one undivided front, and with determination let us march forward to conquer the future.[27]

At the launch of a new League branch in Saint Ann's Bay in May 1919, the League's assistant secretary, Ethelred Brown, outlined the new emphasis on economic and social policy. The League advocated Jamaican development through the promotion of 'patriotic sentiment and mutual interest'.[28] The League encouraged a sense of pride in things Jamaican, chiefly though the consumption of local products. Brown encouraged Jamaicans to buy from their black neighbours, rather than Chinese or Syrian traders, who it was alleged, undercut their African Jamaican counterparts, pronouncing 'We could love the Syrian or the Chinaman if we liked; but the folly of loving them to such an extent that we put our own out of existence ... could be easily seen'.[29]

Here Brown represented a Jamaican identity resting largely on the cultural heritage of the majority African Jamaican population. This strand of racial exclusiveness had the potential to increase antagonism towards Jamaica's non-white minorities – the Chinese, Lebanese Syrians, and to a lesser extent East Indians. The anti-Chinese riots of 1918 highlighted the potential for economic protests to degenerate into racial confrontation.[30] Attitudes towards the white population were expressed in softer tones, the League arguing that when a Jamaican and an Englishmen were equally qualified for a post it should go to the former.[31]

By encouraging neighbourly commerce the League hoped to reduce Jamaica's dependence on costly imports and to break the domination of plantation monoculture. To this end, the League advocated the expansion of peasant cultivation and argued that land made available by the post-war fall in sugar production should be purchased by government for subdivision and resale to peasant farmers, to counter the growth of the fruit monopolies.[32] Henceforth the League's rallying cry would be 'Jamaica's Welfare First'.[33]

The Jamaica League most closely reflected the aspirations of the black and brown middle class, whom it regarded as the 'strength of ... this island',[34] who would serve as the guiding hand of the black masses. Policies, such as compulsory schooling at public expense for young people over fourteen years of age, were demanded in the hope the masses would learn 'some useful industry that will fit them for life'.[35] The alternative was a descent into criminality and moral abandon. The League's support for higher wages was finely balanced between curing social ills, such as predial larceny, and a desire not too alienate the prosperous black and brown landowner who benefited from the depressed labour market. Ethelred Brown argued 'the labourer should receive a fair proportion of the money that he had been instrumental in making', but '[h]e was not foolish enough to tell people that every man should get a dollar a day'.[36] However, the League was forced to respond to the rising tide of industrial action gathering momentum throughout 1918 and 1919. The encouragement of co-operation that underpinned the League's approach in other policy areas was re-emphasised to urge consensus and moderation from both workers and employers. President T. Gordon Somers stressed '[t]he demands of labour should be reasonable, the attitude of capital sympathetic, there should always be a readiness to meet each other half-way ... both capital and labour are badly in need of instruction as to their relative importance and their mutual obligations'.[37]

Co-operation and mutuality was the strongest common ground the League shared with the veterans' movement. In May 1919, the proposed BWIR Association had advocated the establishment of communal centres where the 'necessities of life' could be purchased at low prices. Any profits would be used for the development of welfare schemes.[38] The Jamaica League also regularly advanced proposals for a network of co-operative stores in the island. In October 1919, C. A. Wilson,[39] the honorary secretary, shared a vision of co-operative stores throughout Jamaica, based on the British model. Wilson envisaged Jamaicans would take out shares to 'turn the tide of profits into the pockets of the men and women who toil and suffer'.[40] Until now, Wilson argued, '[I]ndividualism ... ha[d] been the bane of effort'.[41] Like other aspects of the League's programme, co-operation could be limited by simultaneous appeals to racial exclusivity. Wilson reiterated that African Jamaicans should show the same loyalty to their race as he claimed was exhibited by the Chinese and Syrian traders often portrayed as profiteering from the black working class. 'The foreigner in our midst with less education than we possess is amassing wealth. He is driven by force of circumstances to unite with his countrymen and by co-operation achieves success.'[42]

F. E. M. Hercules, the Trinidadian-born leader of the Society of Peoples of African Origin and editor of the *African Telegraph*, arrived in Jamaica in July 1919 on a four-month tour, after campaigning against the wave of racial attacks in the metropole.[43] He shared platforms with leading members of the Jamaica League and Ethelred Brown was subsequently appointed the Society's Jamaican representative. Hercules insisted racial unity, pride and consciousness were essential to underpin any campaign for social, political and economic advancement. In so doing he drew on the racial consciousness of the BWIR veterans expressed by the Caribbean League at the time of the Taranto mutiny. Hercules' arrival was viewed with trepidation by the colonial regime as the unrest among repatriated seamen continued. Although the acting governor, Robert Johnstone, rejected calls for Hercules' deportation, he instructed the Jamaican press to give his views minimal coverage.[44]

Hercules undertook a comprehensive study of social and economic conditions in Jamaica and at a public meeting at the end of July outlined the case for reform that he embodied in a memorial to Viscount Milner, Secretary of State for the Colonies. Hercules advocated, like the Jamaica League, the establishment of industrial schools to endow young Jamaicans with marketable skills. He demanded the reform of the tax system which raised the bulk of government revenue from items of general consumption, falling most heavily on the peasantry and working class. But Hercules was more forthright than the League in his support for working-class struggles underway in Jamaica, particularly the campaign of government railway workers, who were taking action for a substantial pay increase, improvements in working conditions, paid holidays and an end to the employment of private contractors. Hercules called on the Jamaican government to set an example to other employers on the island by raising the appalling levels paid to public works' employees. Women breaking stones for roadbuilding were paid just 6d per day, while the average worker barely subsisted on between 1s and 1s 6d per day. Hercules highlighted the high levels of emigration among ex-servicemen, unable to find employment 'after years of faithful service in which they faced death on an equality with the best of the Allied troops because they thought they were making the world safe for democracy'.[45]

Hercules also called for an extension of the franchise, stating, 'it is hardly to the credit of the Mother Country that the Jamaicans are not yet regarded as sufficiently capable of returning to the Legislative Council representatives good enough worthily to express the views of their constituents'.[46] This demand was framed within a continued allegiance to Empire. Hercules argued the franchise should at first be widened to encompass black and 'coloured' men of 'liberal education' and professional or respectable status only. A further transition towards self-government could not come, he believed, until the majority of Jamaicans had achieved similar status.[47] Like many of his contemporaries, Hercules believed stewardship by the educated minority was necessary to guide a subject people towards greater personal and political freedom; wartime service alone did not merit greater civic participation.

Another radical, the veteran trade unionist Alfred Mends, also waged a campaign for representative government. Born in 1871, Mends became leader of the Artisans Union in 1898. An advocate of the co-operative movement, Mends edited several short-lived newspapers, the *Jamaican*, the *Jamaica Penny Weekly*, the *Sentinel* and *Public Opinion*, between 1914 and 1916. He was prominent in the unrest of 1919, when he assisted repatriated Jamaican seamen in their efforts to gain compensation for losses of money and possessions in the race riots in the metropole.[48]

In 1917, Mends prepared a petition demanding a return to the constitution in place prior to the establishment of Crown Colony government after the Morant

Bay Rebellion of 1865. In effect, Mends was calling for the reintroduction of a fully elected house of assembly.[49] To Mends, this represented a significant expansion of democracy, limiting the power of the unelected members who dominated the legislature under the Crown Colony system. Prior to Morant Bay a number of measures, including a poll tax introduced in 1859, had reduced the electorate for the House of Assembly allowing the white plantocracy to retain its hold on the reigns of government. However, it was evident that significant numbers of black and 'coloured' landowners would eventually qualify to stand as members within the terms of the property qualification. Between 1861 and 1865, black and 'coloured' members held twelve of the forty-five seats in the Assembly.[50] Fear of a black and 'coloured' majority greatly influenced the decision by white members of the Assembly to acquiesce to the metropolitan imposition of the Crown Colony system. More stringent property qualifications implemented for the elected portion of the Legislature at the outset of Crown Colony rule stalled the advance of black representation. During a period when the 'industrious' and 'respectable' working class in the metropole was feeling the benefit of franchise reform, 'excitable' and allegedly slothful black Jamaicans were increasingly denied the rights of citizenship.[51]

Mends's proposal to reinstate an elected House of Assembly would have resulted in a franchise and representative system based on property and hence 'respectability'. However, his demands were radical when set against other proposals for changes in Jamaica's legislative status at this time. Some members of the Jamaican establishment supported calls for confederation with Canada to develop Jamaica's industry and access to markets within the Empire, and to counter further incorporation into the economic orbit of the USA. Jamaica would become a junior partner to a white Dominion with a record of responsible government. Anything approaching self-determination, on the other hand, 'would be another name for anarchy and chaos'.[52] The Jamaican masses were seen as unfit for any involvement in the machinery of government. In a leading article in support of Canadian confederation, the *Jamaica Times* argued that the Jamaican masses lacked 'the standard of education, ... informed intelligence and ... sobered sense of civic responsibility ... to justify the extension of our present modicum of Representative Government'.[53]

In 1923 Mends reiterated his demand for a reconstituted House of Assembly in a pamphlet, *Can There Still be Hope for the Reformation in Jamaica?* He described Jamaica as

[a]n Island shouting, wailing, weeping across the broad blue waters of the Atlantic to the peoples of England – the British parliament and our Sovereign Lord the king, amidst seas of misunderstandings, mismanagements,

maladministrations and lamentations – shouting the truth in its political enslavement for a change of her present political Constitution, for a restoration of the status quo ante, 1865 – plaintively shouting the Truth for Full Extended Representation, commensurate with the much vaunted boast 'Civis Britanicus sum' (I am a British citizen).[54]

Mends was deeply committed to the enfranchisement of the returned veterans. Alongside the slogan 'I am a British soldier', which the veterans had been encouraged to adopt on returning to Jamaica, 'Civis Britanicus sum' powerfully underpinned demands for citizenship in recognition for military service. Such a link was frequently made by black veterans and seamen when they demanded protection from white mobs in the metropole. In so doing they attempted to appeal to the ideals of freedom, justice and equality they had been led to believe were the watchwords of the 'motherland' to whose protection they were entitled as subjects of the Crown.[55] Mends' like-minded emphasis on British subjecthood also underscored the limitations of his programme; the extension of legislative freedom and the franchise must come within the existing framework of Empire. Mends did not envisage at this stage full self-determination for Jamaica. While implying that wartime service should be recognised, he took care not to deploy the rhetoric of military sacrifice to advocate action that went beyond the norms of liberal democracy.

> Men and women of Jamaica! Stand up for your rights! ... Agitate! Agitate! Agitate!!! Hammer at the door of the British parliament until we gain admittance. We must show our discontent, in downright British fashion; we must not raise a gun or lift a sword; but fight to restore our political rights and privileges in a legal constitutional and loyal manner.[56]

Granted the vote for the first election after the war only, the veterans resumed their disenfranchised subject status. But the image of the citizen-volunteer continued to be held up as an ideal in Jamaican society. When the flag of the eleventh battalion of the British West Indies Regiment was deposited at the Kingston Parish Church, in 1921, the bishop entreated, 'May it constantly remind those who worship here of the self-sacrifice and devotion to duty displayed by the men of this island'.[57] The Chaplain reminded the congregation that '[t]he good Christian must be a good citizen, recognising the responsibility in political privileges'. Statements such as these from the spokesmen of colonial authority, helped to keep the ideals of military sacrifice alive in the minds of Jamaican veterans. Mends deployed the image of a collective Allied and Empire effort in his campaigns for greater social and economic justice in Jamaica, simultaneously drawing on the experiences and demands of black US veterans to add weight to his demands.

In the late Great War, Jamaicans fought heroically side by side ... with Englishmen, Irishmen, Scotchmen, Canadians, Italians, Frenchmen, and Americans against Austro-Hungarian, Turkish, Germanic artillery and shells as hot as hell. Many gave up their lives, others permanently disabled, to uphold the glory of the British Empire, to keep floating proudly in the breeze, the Royal Standard, the Union Jack ... Can there be anything as dear as life? Where is the reward? The Negroes of America said to President Johnson through Frederick Douglas their spokesman and orator: 'Your noble and humane predecessor placed in our hands the sword to assist in saving the nation, and we hope that you, his able successor, will favourably regard the placing in our hands the ballot with which to save ourselves'.[58]

But it was Marcus Garvey who most effectively appropriated the language of military sacrifice. Disabused of the belief, held at the outset of the war, that black military endeavour would be duly rewarded by the Imperial power, Garvey commandeered its ideals to serve the pan-African cause, transcending the boundaries of Empire in the process. Referring equally to the wartime contribution of black soldiers in the service of the British and French Empires and the USA, his message made a great impact upon the diasporic West Indian communities in North and Central America and the non-Anglophone Caribbean. The 4,000 or so Jamaican veterans, whose dispersal to Cuba and

11 Dedication of the Jamaica war memorial, Kingston, 11 November 1922, taken from Church Street

elsewhere had been enthusiastically encouraged by the Jamaican authorities, were exposed to an interpretation of their experiences that went beyond the struggle for the rights of citizenship in Jamaica alone.

During the war black leaders in both Jamaica and the USA believed a blood sacrifice on behalf of the Allied cause would earn rights and freedoms in post-war society. Now Garvey called directly for that blood sacrifice to be made by Africans for the redemption of an African homeland. In January 1919, addressing a mass meeting at the John Wesley Methodist Episcopalian Church in Brooklyn, Garvey told his audience

> The real fight of the Negro is to come ... Our sacrifices, as made in the cause of other people, are many. I think it is time that we should prepare to sacrifice now for ourselves ... Africa will be a bloody battlefield in the years to come ... We cannot tell who the foeman will be ... but there is one thing we are determined on that we are going to fight him to a finish. That finish must mean victory for the negro standard ... I am now resolved to try the game of dying for myself ... I feel sure that my blood shall have paid that remission for which future generations of the Negro race shall be declared free.[59]

Directing himself more specifically to the West Indian elements of his audience, Garvey called on the administrators of Empire to prove the war really was fought for the principals of democracy and freedom by granting full democratic rights, and ending minority white rule in the West Indian territories.[60] In March 1921, Garvey arrived in Jamaica on a short tour en route from Cuba where he had addressed thousands of Jamaican migrant labourers. Appealing to his Jamaican audiences as a 'citizen of Africa' not 'a British born subject', Garvey demanded the sacrifices of two million black men and women who had served the Allied cause in the war should be recognised alongside those of other subject nations who now claimed sovereignty. The Universal Negro Improvement Association now claimed a membership of four million from the few thousand members that had formed the basis of the Association in 1917. Black independence, argued Garvey, could only be achieved through the establishment of a 'dominion of Negroes' in Africa. In the meantime black Jamaicans who showed no fear in France and Flanders should do likewise by pressing their claim for constitutional rights in their island home as a first step toward African liberation.[61]

In the early 1920s, Garvey's message also found an echo among Jamaican migrants in Cuba, whose numbers now included many ex-servicemen. In August 1921 a WIR veteran, Corporal Samuel Richards, petitioned the King to establish land settlement schemes in Africa for ex-servicemen who now faced pressure to leave Cuba and Panama due to the worsening economic situation.

On 10 October 1921, BWIR veterans who had joined UNIA branches in Cuba paraded in military regalia with the UNIA African Legion during celebrations to mark Cuban independence day.[62]

But it was the next decade that provided a concrete opportunity for Jamaicans and other West Indians to heed Garvey's call for sacrifice in the name of pan-Africanism, when Mussolini's Italian forces invaded Ethiopia in 1935. This marked a further shift from military allegiance to Empire as Jamaican ex-servicemen demanded the right to fight in defence of their symbolic mother-land, Ethiopia.[63] In December 1933, a little over a year before the Italian invasion, Leonard Howell, one of the founding fathers of the Rastafarian move-ment, symbolically signalled this realignment. Howell had been recruited to the British West Indies Regiment in Panama and went thence to Up Park Camp, Jamaica, but arrived after the final Jamaican draft embarked in October 1917. The coronation of Ras Tafari as Haile Selassie, Emperor of Ethiopia in November 1930 renewed the perception of Africa as a spiritual homeland for the black diaspora. Howell told his followers at a meeting in Seaforth Town that they were not British subjects – 'the British Government was only protecting them until their King came' – and encouraged them to sing the British national anthem, 'God Save the King', to signify allegiance to Ras Tafari. Howell was subsequently convicted of sedition for this alleged disloyalty to the British crown and was jailed for two years.[64]

The 1870 Foreign Enlistment Act forbade any British subject from taking up arms against a state that was not formally at war with Britain. But convinced that appeasement would not bring about an Italian withdrawal, the Universal Negro Improvement Association presented a petition to George V calling for the legislation to be suspended. The petitioners 'jealous of the preservation of any part of Africa which is free of foreign domination', demanded they be allowed to 'fight to preserve the glories of our ancient and beloved Empire ... we have every right to have free parts of our country at our disposal whenever it is our desire to go there'.[65] Referring to the contribution of Jamaica to the war effort, another petition of nearly one thousand signatures was collected by Garveyites, Leonard Waison and St. William Grant. The petitioners implored '[t]hat in the same way as we helped to safe guard the integrity of other races, we are asking that our race be protected at this crucial moment'.[66] In a letter to *Plain Talk*, a weekly paper edited by Alfred Mends, another ex-soldier was more vehement: 'if I had the fighting spirit to defend the whiteman against the whiteman then why could I not defend the Abyssinians my mother against those heartless uncivilized Italians?'[67] In the same edition, another veteran, A. H. Brown, called on all trained men to enlist in the fight against the Italians. Brown argued correctly that Mussolini's ambitions would not stop with Ethiopia and believed that the Italians were 'out to take hold of our Motherland Africa where God did provide for us all'.[68] *Plain Talk* also reported that one Jamaican, Allan Parker, was on his way to join the Ethiopian army.[69]

Other Jamaicans waited in the hope that Britain would take a lead in opposing the invasion. Ex-members of the West India Regiment, which in the past had proved a reliable ally of the Jamaican colonial regime, were more reticent in taking the initiative. However, there was still a clear articulation of the wish to endure masculine acts of sacrifice in the name of the greater African nation. A resolution passed by veterans of the now disbanded WIR, approved of British efforts to avert war with Italy and pledged support for peace.[70] George Elliott, a former Company Sergeant major in the WIR, was employed as a sanitary inspector in Kingston. In correspondence with a former officer he stated:

> This Abyssinian war is going to wreck the equilibrium of the world and put back civilization to about 1,000 years ago ... The coloured people of the world ... are watching and taking the deepest interest in this scrap, and if England could only say the words the West Indian element – about 60,000 men – could easily drive the Italian hordes out of Abyssinia ... let England find the fighting planes and she would not have to sacrifice one European, the blacks would do the skirmishing.[71]

The Italian invasion of Ethiopia shifted the association of military sacrifice from Empire to a future African homeland. Nevertheless, Jamaican veterans continued to campaign for their past endeavours to be adequately rewarded during the unrest that gripped the West Indies from the mid-1930s. Although sugar had been supplanted by banana, the two crops between them still accounted for around 90 per cent of Jamaican export earnings. But the dependence on the export market meant that the island economy was severely hit by the Depression of the 1920s and 1930s. The sugar price plummeted, dragging down wages and employment conditions. Workers turned off the land, drifted towards the urban areas in search of work alongside the droves of migrants returning from the USA, Central America and Cuba.

Former soldiers were involved in the hunger marches that became a regular feature of Jamaican life from the early 1930s. These demonstrations were often ruthlessly broken up by the constabulary. The mood of dissatisfaction among the veterans was increasingly inseparable from the increasing militancy of the Jamaican workers and peasants. In May 1935 banana workers and stevedores struck in an attempt to halt the further casualisation of employment and to replace task work with hourly pay. In 1936, Allan George St Clavier Combs, who had served in the West India Regiment before its demise, and Hugh Clifford Buchanan, who had come into contact with Marxist ideas while working in

Cuba, reformed the Jamaica Workers' and Tradesmen's Union which forged links with the Ex-British West Indies Regiment Association.[72]

On 13 August 1937 a delegation of the Ex-British West Indies Regiment Association placed a series of demands before Governor Denham. While seeking preferential treatment for ex-soldiers in the granting of contracts and employment on public works projects, the veterans also addressed the problems facing the working population as a whole. The delegation impressed upon the Governor 'the urgent need for immediate and continuous ... employment ... the need for better wages and shorter hours of labour' and drew particular attention to low pay level among Public Works Department labourers in the country districts.[73]

The delegation appeared to have been satisfied with Governor Denham's assurances that he would investigate their concerns and report back with his findings later in the month. The veterans informed Denham they were not in a position to cancel a demonstration on Kingston Race Course planned to bolster their demands the following day. Up to one thousand veterans and unemployed gathered on the race course on the morning of the 14 August where they were addressed by the governor's representative, Acting Colonial Secretary Brown, who restated the Governor's assurances. The crowd was not impressed and determined to march through the city, despite remonstrations from the veterans' leaders. Several lorryloads of police eventually dispersed the gathering, arresting twenty-three of the demonstrators.[74]

From 1935, and commencing in St. Kitts, the British West Indies was beset by a wave of demonstrations and strikes whose root cause lay in the failure of the plantation monoculture to provide an adequate livelihood to the majority of the population. In Jamaica, between May and June 1938 the island was gripped by a labour revolt as dockworkers, tramdrivers, public service, sugar and banana workers took to the streets. A government announcement to the effect that £500,000 would be invested in a new land settlement scheme – a Jamaican *New Deal* – served to defuse the unrest.[75] In the wake of the these events, the Moyne Commission was established to enquire into the economic and social circumstances throughout the West Indies.[76]

Veterans and their organisations were among those who submitted evidence to the Commission when it visited Jamaica. Before enlistment, most veterans believed that not only would their military achievements bring about improved social status, but the acquisition of land, which they regarded as part of their reward, would improve their standing also. The Moyne Commission presented the opportunity to once again reiterate the associations between military service, citizenship, historical destiny, nationhood and racial pride. One veteran, Sergeant Charles Johnson, epitomised the hopes of the ex-servicemen when he stated 'we would be looked upon as great men of Jamaica our home'.[77] In a simple memorandum, drafted on rough paper, Johnson also expressed the continuing ambivalence with which Jamaican veterans viewed, not only their war service, but their links with Empire and the Mother Country. Although complaining bitterly about the conditions faced by the veterans, Johnson underlined the commitment felt towards the monarch through the military brotherhood of 'the King's men'. Simultaneously, Johnson pinpointed what lay at the root of the continued failure to recognise the achievements of black men in wartime; the anxiety that black soldiers would outperform their white counterparts on the battlefield, thereby disrupting the race and gender hierarchies of Empire.

> Surfdom and dirt are our class Sir so we are begging this Commission to call a stop to this dissatisfaction among ex soldiers and Government, once an for all … So as to encourage that peace and concord and love towards our Great King George VI and that God shall call us blessed. For all the people of the middle class and the upper class stay at home … we the lower class … do their share in the war for they would not go they afraid to die.[78]

Notes

1 *JT* 5 July 1919, p. 17.
2 Ibid.
3 *DG* 29 May 1919, p. 3.
4 Ibid.
5 Ibid., p. 8.
6 *DG* 30 June 1919, p. 13.
7 *DG* 28 July 1919, p. 10.
8 Cited in Catherine Hall, *Civilising Subjects*, p. 348.
9 *JT* 13 September 1919, p. 12.
10 *JT* 28 June 1919, p. 13.
11 *JT* 28 June 1919, p. 14.
12 PRO CO9 50/93 J33 26th Session BWIR Ass. Witnesses; CO9 50/944 Written Evidence, Serial No. 169 Memorandum on Unemployment and Rates of Wages; *JT* 28 June 1919, p. 14.
13 On the early formation of the black peasantry in Jamaica see Sidney Mintz, *Caribbean Transformations* (New York: Columbia University Press, 1989), pp. 146–56; Hugh Paget, 'The Free Village System in Jamaica', *Caribbean Quarterly*, 1:4, 1954, 7–19.
14 *Report of the Royal West India Commission* (The Norman Cm.) (C 8655) (London: HMSO, 1897), pp. 59, 65; Holt, *Problem of Freedom*, pp. 347–55.
15 *DG* 17 May 1916, p. 8.
16 PRO CO137/725/10155 Manning to Long, SSC 25 January 1918 (my emphasis).
17 *DG* 12 December 1918, p. 6; PRO CO137/728/1983 Probyn to Long 17 December 1918.

18 *The Times* 16 June 1924, p. 11; PRO CO137/799/10 A. S. Jelf to William Bennett, C. H. Eastwood and others, 15 February 1933; *Ex-Service Man*, nd, p. 5 in PRO CO950/93 British West Indies Regt. Association Memorandum to Moyne Cm.

19 PRO CO137/799/10 A. S. Jelf to William Bennett, C. H. Eastwood and others, 15 February 1933; CO950/93 British West Indies Regt. Association Memorandum, Sgt. W, Johnson to Royal Cm. (n.d.) and J33 26th Session BWIR Association Witnesses.

20 PRO CO950/944 Serial No. 169 'Memorandum on unemployment and rates of wages', pp. 5, 7. For further discussion of Jamaican migrants in Cuba see Jorge L. Giovannetti, 'Black British Subjects in Cuba: Race, Ethnicity, Nation and Identity in the Migratory Experience, 1898–1938' (University of North London: unpublished PhD thesis, 2001).

21 *DG* 15 July 1933, 7; PRO CO137/799/10 William Bennett and others to Gov. R. E. Stubbs, 19 October 1932, C. H. Eastwood and others to Gov. Sir Ransford Slater, 7 December 1932; CO137/818/3 Gov. Denham to Ormsby Gore, SSC 4 January 1938.

22 Ibid. Gov. Denham to Sir Cosmo Parkinson, CO 30 July 1937.

23 PRO CO137/828/5 Minute by Surveyor-General 10 January 1938.

24 The Jamaica League, initially a cultural nationalist body composed of black, brown and white intellectuals, held its inaugural conference on 3 August 1914 under the initiative of Astley Clerk, a white poet and music shop proprietor. Although Clerk laid out some of the early proposals for the League, it was the black Jamaican, C. A. Wilson, who took the leading role at the conference. The League stood for the 'promotion of patriotic sentiment and mutual interest and the encouragement of individual and co-operative efforts for the intellectual, social and economic improvement of Jamaicans'. Somewhat portentously, the organisers believed that 'Great changes are looming and the hour of co-operative effort has struck' and asked Jamaicans, 'Will you not help us to usher in the brighter day?': *JT* 1 August 1914, pp. 11, 18, 8 August 1914, p. 9, 17 October 1914, p. 15; *DC* 25 August 1914, p. 6.

25 *DG* 6 August 1919, p. 13.

26 Ibid.

27 *JT* 5 July 1919, p. 5.

28 *DG* 7 May 1919, p. 4.

29 Ibid.

30 Howard Johnson, 'The Anti-Chinese Riots of 1918 in Jamaica', *Caribbean Quarterly*, 28:3, 1982, 19–32.

31 *DG* 7 May 1919, p. 4

32 *DG* 6 August 1919, p. 13.

33 *DG* 6 August 1919, p. 13.

34 *DG* 7 May 1919, p. 4.

35 *DG* 6 August 1919, p. 13.

36 Ibid.

37 *DG* 6 August 1919, p. 13.

38 *DG* 29 May 1919, p. 3.

39 Wilson published *Men With Backbone* (Kingston: Educational Supply Co., 1905), which underlined the importance of individual industry to achieve improved status for the black population. He simultaneously advocated equality for women while demanding a strong female presence in the home. Wilson also wrote *Men With Vision* (Kingston: Gleaner Co., 1929), which included biographical portraits of DuBois, Garvey and Booker T. Washington.

40 *DG* 11 May 1919, p. 5.

41 Ibid.

42 Ibid.

43 PRO CO318/351 Director of Intelligence to USSCO 6 August 1919. For further information on Hercules's activities during the 1919 race riots see Fryer, *Staying Power*, pp. 311–16.

44 PRO CO137/733/50990 Johnstone (acting Gov.) to Milner SSC 14 August 1919.

45 *DG* 18 July 1919, p. 3 and 2 August 1919, pp. 21–2.

46 Ibid., pp. 21–2.

47 Ibid.; PRO CO318/351 Director of Intelligence to USSCO 6 August 1919.

48 Elkins, *Street Preachers*, pp. 65–6.

49 Ibid., p. 66.

50 Holt, *Problem of Freedom*, pp. 226–7, 256–8. Black representation had fallen from eighteen in 1860 due to the effects of the 1859 Franchise Act, which reduced the registration of peasant freeholders by around 85 per cent.

51 Catherine Hall, 'Rethinking Imperial Histories: The Reform Act of 1867', *New Left Review*, 208, 1994, 17–21. Franchise reform in the 1880s increased the black electorate significantly – they outnumbered the whites by three to one. However, high property qualifications for office meant that the elected portion of the Legislative Council continued to be dominated by the white elite: Holt, *Problem of Freedom*, pp. 340–1.

52 *JT* 17 May 1919, p. 6. See also *JT* editorial 24 May 1919, p. 6 and supplement of 11 October 1919 'The Question of BWI Union With Canada'.

53 *JT* 11 October 1919, p. 6.

54 Alfred Alexander Mends, *Can There Still be Hope for the Reformation in Jamaica?* (Kingston: Temple of Fashion Printery, 1923).

55 See for example PRO CO318/349/60449 Petition of J. A. Thompson and forty-three other seamen to Col. Bryan, Acting Gov. of Jamaica, 29 August 1919.

56 Mends, *Can There Still be Hope*, 9–10.

57 *JT* 5 February 1921, p. 13.

58 Mends, *Can There Still be Hope*, pp. 11–12.

59 *West Indian* (Grenada), 28 February 1919.

60 *West Indian* 28 March 1919.

61 *DG* 25 March 1921, 11; 26 March 1921, 6; 29 March 1921, 10.

62 PRO FO371/5565; *Negro World* 5 November 1921.

63 See Robert G. Weisbord, 'British West Indian Reaction to the Italian–Ethiopian War: An Episode in Pan-Africanism', *Caribbean Studies*, 10:1, 1970, 34–41; Kelvin A. Yelvington, 'The War in Ethiopia and Trinidad 1935–1936', in Bridget Brereton and Kelvin A. Yelvington, *The Colonial Caribbean in Transition: Essays on Postemancipation Social and Cultural History* (Gainesville: University Press of Florida, 1999).

64 *DG* 14 March 1934, p. 21 and 17 March 1934, p. 6.

65 PRO CO318/418/4/71062 UNIA petition presented to George V (Oct./Nov. 1935).

66 PRO CO318/418/4/71062 Copy Petition to SSC 5 October 1935 signed by L. P. Waison, St William Grant. See also resolution by Spanish Town Division of UNIA to SSC 9 October 1935 which took a similar line.

67 *Plain Talk* 2 November 1935, p. 3.

68 Ibid., p. 10.

69 Ibid., p. 11.

70 PRO CO318/418/4/71062 Resolution passed by Ex-Servicemen of WIR Sept. 1935.

71 CSM George D. Elliott to V. C. Green 24 February 1936.

72 Post, *Arise Ye Starvlings*, pp. 240–3; PRO CO950/93 Sgt. W. Johnson to Royal Cm. (n.d.).

73 PRO CO137/820/13 Gov. Denham to Ormsby-Gore, SSC, 20 September 1937.

74 Ibid. and Report of Inspector General Owen Wright, 14 September 1937.

75 Post, *Arise Ye Starvelings*, pp. 276–84.

76 The commission's findings were not published until the end of the Second World War. See *West India Royal Commission Report* (Cmd. 6607), London, 1945. Lord Moyne did not live to see the publication of the Commission's report. On 6 November 1944 he was assassinated by Zionists in Cairo.

77 PRO CO950/93 Sgt. C. W. Johnson to Royal Commission (n.d.).

78 Ibid. All spelling and punctuation as original.

Index

LaVergne, TN USA
24 February 2010
174017LV00002B/61/P